DARK MOUNTAIN

DARK MOUNTAIN

ISSUE 2 · SUMMER 2011

Published by the Dark Mountain Project 2011

www.dark-mountain.net

ISBN 978-0-9564960-1-0

Cover artwork by Rima Staines

Proofreading by Iona Hine

Set in Linotype Granjon
Typesetting by Christian Brett at Bracketpress

Printed by the MPG Books Group, Bodmin and King's Lynn

DARK MOUNTAIN

ISSUE 2 · SUMMER 2011

Contents

EDITIORIAL

Control, and Other Illusions

What if there was more than one story?

What if there was more than one story about you: about your life, about who you are, and what you do and where you came from? What if you told one story to your parents, say, and one to your boyfriend, and another to your children? What if you told one story to your employer, and one to your secret lover, and one to your neighbour, and one to the doctor, and another to the postman? What if there was a story you told at parties and another you told at job interviews?

And what if all of these stories were true, but all were partial – all were designed to display a certain, favoured aspect of your self to a certain audience? And what if this selective communication was not conscious, not planned, not manipulative or cunning, but was just what seemed to happen when you opened your mouth?

And what if everyone was doing it?

This is what we all do, every minute of every day, whether we know it or not. And what is true of our selves is also true of the culture we come from and have been raised within.

Which story do you tell about civilisation? Do you tell the one about humankind's long, slow, steady evolution from idiocy to enlightenment, or the one about the collapse of indigenous knowledge in the face of the onslaught of modernity? Do you tell the one about the wonders of modern dentistry or the one about soaring rates of clinical depression? Do you tell the one about the Clean Air Act or the one about climate change? Do you tell the one about the death of the peasantry and the theft of common land, or the one about the unbeatable yields of genetically modified crops?

What do you like talking about? Poverty or poverty relief? Over-consumption or consumer choice? Literacy or language loss? Earth Day or ecocide? Democracy or corporate power? Twitter revolutions or children enslaved by Facebook? Do you tell different stories to different people? Do you tell different stories to yourself? What if all these stories are true – all of them, all at once? What then?

Civilisation is a story. It is a story about where we have come from and where we are going. There are many ways to tell that story, but one version has been very much the dominant one in the West for the past couple of centuries. We know this story: It's the one about modern, urban industrial culture's ineffable superiority over all others; the one about human evolution leading inevitably to this point. It's the one about winning the war against nature, being the only species which thinks and loves and dreams; it's the one about machines and circuitry and ingenuity and progress. And it's true, in some ways, at least as far as it goes. But it may not be going much further.

We are clearly, now, living in a time of transition. Our stories are crumbling before our eyes, but we don't have new ones which we are yet prepared to believe in, and the old counter-narratives seem musty, old-fashioned, drawn from a different age. We can see what the industrial economy is doing to the Earth, but not many of us think it can be replaced by peaceful agrarianism or a return to hunter-gathering. We can see the path our machine-addiction is leading us down, but we can also see the time and effort our machines save us. We can see how divisive and disastrous capitalism is, but we can also see the goodies it gives us, here in the bubble, and we are not likely to fight for work-ers' control of the means of production again any time soon. We can see humanity's utter degradation of the rest of nature, but we don't know how to stop doing it – or, rather, we know exactly how to stop doing it but we are not prepared to even contemplate making the changes necessary, because they would break our stories open and leave them exposed to the wind.

Times like this are hard to live through. People may respond in a panic by trying to write instant, comprehensive new stories, but often they don't have purchase because they have no depth and no connection to peoples' reality; they have not had the time to bed in. Or they cling resolutely to old stories – to both the dominant narrative and to counter-narratives that made sense once but don't seem to now, however hard they try to fit them around a rapidly-unfolding reality. They – we – do this because everyone needs a story, and an old, worn-out story seems better than no story at all.

In this issue of *Dark Mountain,* we touch on many of these contradictions and difficulties. John Rember takes a look at our civilisation's meta-narratives, with the help of R. D. Laing, while David Abram examines the human relationship with the rest of nature, and the problems of language itself. Matt Szabo, Catherine Lupton and Rob Lewis all focus on the use and misuse of words, while Vinay Gupta and Glyn Hughes both come to similar conclusions about the need to face the reality of death, openly and honestly, with stoicism and even grace. Luanne Armstrong and Melanie Challenger engage directly with place and nature in an attempt to understand loss, change and disconnection – the unholy trinity of the modern experience.

All of this is in the cause of what we called, in our manifesto of the same name, Uncivilisation. We chose this word carefully and used it deliberately, well aware that it would be misconstrued. Uncivilisation is not a place or a goal, an ideal or a political position – it is a process. The process of uncivilising is the process of unlearning the assumptions, the founding narratives of our civilisation. Once we do this we can begin to walk away from stories that are failing and look for new ones. This process is perhaps something like Vinay Gupta's account in this book, of the journey to enlightenment in Hindu meditation schools. It's a lot of practice, discipline and attention, leading up to a realisation, which is quickly followed by another – that emptying the mind of assumptions and distractions was just the start, and maybe even the easy bit.

To uncivilise our minds, then, and our words: Here is the challenge. To shrug off the failing stories, with no guarantee of easy new ones to take their place – no promise of a soft landing. To give up control and the illusion of control, in exchange for seeing your culture as it really is – or at least as you have never seen it before.

Paul Kingsnorth and Dougald Hine, editors
Ulverston and Brussels
April 2011

MELANIE CHALLENGER

The Forgotten Farm

Life sometimes leaves behind beguiling vestiges, places where concrete knowledge dissolves into impressions and guesses. When I began to think about extinction, it was these haunting or arresting signs of mutability in the landscape that first drew my interest. I wanted to know why they aroused such a sense of intrigue. I became convinced that the nostalgic feeling people experienced for things both disappearing and eternally lost might prove essential to fostering a more favourable approach to nature.

I was then living about four miles from Penzance, working in a cabin on Ding Dong Moor, a small stride of tumbledown farms, mining cottages and Neolithic ruins. The cabin was at the bottom of an unbroken strip of ground, the once clipped order of an old garden still detectable through its wildness. By the roadside stood the striking remains of a tower-like building, its glass-less windows framing the distant and fitful sea. Feuding elements of wind and rain had rendered the stone to havoc and slime. A signpost in the lay-by identified the structure as the ruins of Ding Dong mine, one of the oldest tin mines in Cornwall. Years had obscured the origins of the mine's name. Through the long winter months, gales leased the seawaters from their confinement, demolishing any sense of ocean and sky. Mists steeped each day, hushing up the earth. This old building and its history were becoming naturalised to the soils. In time, there would be nothing left but the eye's uncluttered view of the moors and a nonsensical name on a map.

> Ding-dong! Merry, merry, go the bells, ding-dong! Ding-dong!
> Over the heath, over the moor...

Inside the cabin, there was a makeshift kitchen, a faded floral sofabed and a desk. Rainwater had soaked through the window frames and crept down the panes, spreading into little deltas on the wooden sill. On the far side of the desk, I balanced a mound of books to read during my stay, including two claret-coloured leather volumes of English Poetry. My view from the desk was of the defeated garden, the moorland snarled by bracken and gripping

4

mists, the faint unrest of the sea. For the first few weeks, the weather was relentlessly grim. The rain, dense and sooty from its struggle up from the sea, struck down the view, sealing me inside the cabin and my thoughts. During this confinement, I broke the hours in which I tried to concentrate on my page by staring, absent-mindedly, at the landscape before me. If ever thoughts assembled into wakefulness, they were usually concerned with what I'd been reading moments before. The ancient granites that propped up the moorland, the tough thrust of Cornwall in which the minerals of the region's former prosperity had lain. Three hundred million years ago, these rocks boiled up to domicile in this landscape. *Three hundred million years ago!* A world in which early forms of insects still dreamt of flight and the boomerang skull of the newt-like *Diplocaulus salamandroides* was not yet a ghost in the grit.

Time bound meshes of natural history into the thickness of these ancient rocks. Curiosity or enterprise incited people to rupture them, unsealing ancient realities that shook up their minds. These rocks had thundered through the border of the Permian and Triassic eras, when the unstoppable progress of mass extinction eradicated nearly all of the era's species, disappearances that then made concession to the erratic inventiveness of living cells. Their ceaseless innovation led to new forms – the outward dissimilarities of entities, those strange anatomical conclusions of nature that captivate children's imaginations. The small amphibian *Diplocaulus salamandroides*, whose pronged skull seemed to want to split into two minds, faintly echoed in the hammerhead shark, a beast that fascinated me so thoroughly as a child that I implored my mother to draw it over and over again, as if each trace of its silhouette might vindicate its freakish proportions.

After a few weeks of confinement, jitteriness got the better of me. I abandoned the task at hand and stepped outside, ignoring the blustery weather. Bundled in waterproofs, I left the cabin and took the path across the heath that bordered the ruined engine house. The wrecked mine would soon become the primary source of my first ideas about extinction. Its presence exhibited both the forces involved in our shattering effect on nature and the echoes of loss within us that inspired regret. But before these ideas progressed, I simply paid attention to the landscape before me. It was an early morning in March. Mists swung between the hedgerows, homesick for the seas. The wintering birds sang through a dawn still struggling free of the cold months. The tiny shadow of a solitary buff-brown bumblebee fled across a bed of nettles. The moor wheezed and snapped with haphazard actions of survival and a recent fall of rain weighing on the tangle of plants and undergrowth.

I was acutely aware of being a stranger to the moorland. I had no words for the sounds that I heard. In my ignorance, each birdsong entered my consciousness as a sweet but secret music. All clues and peculiarities as to the type of bird were beaten into the background. Each bee was just a bee, small and sombre, directionless. I wished I could muster the words for the things I saw and heard in an hour or so's brief ramble – the beasts that showed themselves and the telltale signs of others shier of my footfall. The plants that flowered and thorned, the tiny green promises of the coming season. But I couldn't, without falsifying the memory. I was bereft of speech for this landscape.

For years now, I had been emerging from an outlandish sleep to discover the world and I detached from one another's realities. This was not the private sleep that nightfall and temperament determine but a kind of generational amnesia from which thousands of us were waking to find that what we'd taken for reality was the stunned edges of stupor. There was so much we didn't know about the natural world around us. What were the tiny birds that pinged out of the bracken as if my step triggered them against their will? Did these little chirring creatures live inside the moor's prickly clutch all year long? Or was their indignant flight a harbinger of spring? I could see acres of nameless, incoherent greenery, the significance of its colour quite beyond my ken. When would the pluckiest wildflowers appear in defiance of late frosts? And what seasonal eruptions of colour would alter the complexion of the moors throughout the year? My perception confined me to the present.

I recognised gorse and bracken but in the careless, almost indifferent way that I could put a name to daisies or buttercups. I didn't know their influence on the other species or the plants most likely to flower beside them. Nor did I have the faintest idea how to behave towards this squabble of roots and branches. Why should I? Somewhere in my childhood and without due heed, I'd picked up on a determination hammered into the very structures of my environment that the natural world and human nature somehow warranted separation and that each existed, perhaps even existed to advantage, without the other. But the more it struck me just how little I knew about this landscape, the less my ignorance seemed obligatory or reasonable.

Extinctions were visible across the moor, the shabby outlines of ways of life now long forgotten. If I'd had insight into the landscape, I might have been sensitive to other extinctions that had left no trace: quiet once filled by particular birdsong, the deadened hum of an insect, the stripped earth of a familiar flower. My lack of knowledge prevented me from apprehending any such changes to nature. All I could grasp were fragments of the ended practices of human society. Such signs corresponded to people's vanishing memories and skills. They were hidden and intricate changes, entwined with private, individual histories. Old pathways blurred by mud through which farmers once chivvied their grazing animals, scruffy hedges fouled with rusting wire. There was a stone feeding trough, purloined now by birds, their brown heads bowing to the water like worshippers. A gauze of bushes and moss stretched over ancient field systems, greying into the distance. There, the dark back of the sea slowly heaved. The soft scars of previous generations' farming hinted at losses far greater than I could understand, the discrimination of seasons and tendencies, assessments of the land's potential that sometimes crushed and occasionally assisted the abundance of nature. I paused outside an old ruined farmhouse, the rain knocking futilely on its entrance. Staring at the farm's cracked windows battered into blank holes by the wind, I wondered who had once worked the land here. And how the place would have appeared when still a working farm. Why had the farmers abandoned it? Did anything remain of their knowledge in the lives and experience of their descendants?

Even within my own family, there once existed a greater recognition of the natural landscape. Somehow, it failed to pass through to my generation. Although she never said as much, my grandmother seemed to have an inborn sense of what had been forsaken in the decades between us. For as long as I knew her, she experienced a powerful nostalgia for the rural surroundings of her childhood, the sources of her greater sensitivity to nature. She recorded her feelings in a large, pale green notebook on which she wrote the title *Book of Memories*, softly smudged in blue and red crayon. On the first page, she listed the births of her family members, names of siblings I had heard about but never met, *Dorothy, Marjorie, Evelyn, George*. By each of these was the name of the same village in which they were born. She spoke of Kingsclere as an unspoilt, peaceful place, a rustic landscape no doubt softened of its faults and misfortunes by time.

In his autobiography, John Porter, the most successful horse-trainer of the Victorian age, wrote of the flowers of the region, of harebells, wild hyacinth, wild thyme, and saxifrage. He regarded it to be a 'wonderful county for birds', noting the presence of 'warblers and whistlers and twitterers', and particularly the grey plover as the gentle augur of spring. Porter had his stables at Cannon Heath, Kingsclere, where there was a rookery and he often saw kestrels and heard the cry of curlews, the 'jug-jug' of nightingales. The 'rustic merriment' of an agricultural fair took place twice annually, and there was a market of fresh, local produce every Tuesday. Kingsclere then was an enclave of cottages with wooden dormer-windows and gardens propped by flint walls. The ancient Norman custom of the curfew bell still tolled from the old church. There were wheelwrights' shops and saddlers, and general stores selling everything from flour and bacon fat to starch and powder blue. In those days, a Kingsclere breakfast was a hearty confection of trout, steak and strawberries.

My grandmother's family moved to the village when her father returned from the First World War. Horses were then the only means of transport and she noted in the book that her 'Aunt Ada could drive a four-in-hand easily.' I tried to imagine the gruff breaths of the horses, the seasoned stench of their ordure. Her father owned a grocery and bakery store on Swan Street, one of the chief roads through the village. Fresh produce in the store was supplied by nearby farms that, along with several watermills, blacksmiths, and a tannery on North Street, employed many of the villagers. The farms provided milk and cheese, along with meat and skins from the herds, and timber, which was sawn locally. Butter was churned on the farms and chilled against the dank edges of wells. Specialised workers met the needs of the farmers, such as a Mr Bennet, who lived on Union Lane, and fashioned from hand halters for horses, reins for ploughs, and pig nets. I could remember my grandmother's descriptions of the harvests, when rows of brawny horses pulled binders, hugging together the tow-coloured corn. She mourned the loss of the farming land, much of which disappeared under roads and houses in the years after her infancy. It was not that she didn't recognise that it was a hard life for labourers. Workers often rose long before the first hints of the day to come, the demand for sleep hanging like ballast from their bodies, slowing their gait. Commonly, they walked several miles before dawn to meet the beginning of the working day on the farms. But despite the hardships, she believed that there were things that her generation possessed quite effortlessly that had disappeared from our lives. My grandmother lived half her childhood outside, where she felt safe and confederate somehow. She understood that everything she and her family possessed relied on the dormant fertility of the Earth, the scramble of light, rainfall, birds, insects, worms, flowers.

What she spoke of most were the days spent in Hawkhurst woods, close to the village, and of the wildflowers that grew there.

In her old age, this bucolic early history seemed to seed at her side and grow again, invisible to us but so vibrant for her it was as if the trees and flowers took the place of her shadow. Her mind was almost gone, crumbling through dementia each day into the last fragments of her most stubborn or cherished parts of herself. But I could still picture her, animated and intact, in the dark kitchen of her terraced house, dressed in a blouse, pleated skirt and an apron with a dead pheasant on her lap that she was plucking for dinner. Her fingers worked deftly and swiftly, a soft haze of down besieging the movement. She must have gone to a local butcher to fetch the bird but its appearance and this preparation remained mysterious to me. I had only ever known the skinned meat that we bought from the supermarket. And so I sat on the chair beside the battered, old-fashioned cooker and watched my grandmother intently as she worked. Occasionally, she took hold of the pheasant's limp, cleric's neck and raised its scarlet head to tease me. Mostly, she sang old tunes or chanted common nursery rhymes in her sibilant voice,

> *Little Boy Blue come blow your horn,*
> *the sheep's in the meadow,*
> *the cow's in the corn,*
> *where is that boy who looks after the sheep,*
> *under the haystack fast asleep…*

She did not seem to know or at least she never gave any sign that she recognised the border that separated our experiences.

I grew up in a town a few miles from Kingsclere, a backwater blighted by its closeness to London. Strokes of trade cordoned its regions, from the river that attracted the first farmers thousands of years ago, and the canal, constructed in the eighteenth century for narrowboats transporting coal and goods, to the railway, which opened in 1841, bringing an end to the brief heyday of the canal system. By the time my family moved to the town, when I was a few years old, several motorways and major roads strangled it further. As a consequence, I lived with the feeling that commerce immured me, shutting me away from nature. I felt suffocated by the characterless shopping centres, the modern housing estates, and the constant tattoo of traffic left me with a slight sense of dread. Where I could not wait to escape, my grandmother's memories fixed her there, longing for the way it had once been. Her memories overlay the landscape, haunting it with things I could no longer see or understand.

Many of the changes that occurred through her lifetime subdued or annihilated natural elements, replacing them with vexing, manmade orders and materials. What had it meant to lose the reality of the world in which she was born through the enclosing properties of noise and technology, the walling in of natural disorderliness by the establishments of human society? Perhaps my grandmother's nostalgia was in part an angry rejection of this pervasive presence of human society and a sense of impotence against powers of transformation far greater than her own. I responded to the arresting wistfulness of her portrayals of her past in Berkshire, a rural landscape safe from the detention of traffic and enterprise. Unable to go by the paths she followed and encounter the landscape as it once was, I could only ever rely on the force of her words, her insistence that a more luminous, expressive countryside once existed. But could I trust her vision of the past? Was it somewhere towards which I ought to steer? Or, once there, might I find a world in its own way as stifling and threatening as my own? It seemed to me that my grandmother's nostalgia emanated from a compulsion, a deep-seated need. And like all instincts, its target was blurred and, at times, its effects ill-considered, even nonsensical. She idealised her childhood in Kingsclere; she polished the dawn birdsong, she subdued the wind. Everything was softened, sifted of its jagged or painful elements. The adversities that in large part motivated the changes that progressively destroyed what she held dear were hidden like a cancerous body brushing aside the meed that corrupted it.

I stood for a long time, staring at the Cornish farmhouse in the distance. An atmosphere of abandonment diffused into the weather, mist and cloud burning through the edges of vitality, the clear definitions of objects and horizon. The track leading to the farm was now a path of grass, flourishing from lack of daily possession, splashes of golden buttercups and dandelions across its course. Bracken smothered the walls that marked the path, threatening to feast on its collapse, and ivy had spread across the face of the farmhouse and onto the roof, a slow green wave of interment.

JOHN REMBER

Consensus and Other Realities

I

I've been reading R. D. Laing again, mostly when I wake up at 3am and worry about how long it will be before Social Contract Capitulation. That's when people sliding toward the bottom of the human pyramid give up, cash out their remaining retirement funds, use them to buy an assault rifle and a cook-book and start researching how to field dress their neighbour's Bichon Frise.

Worrying about pyramids also causes me to worry that, if the American Federal Reserve ever loses its ability to prop up the economy, the largest employer in America will not be the Federal Government but Amway Corporation. That might not be all bad if you've correctly timed your entry into the Amway family. Amway can't really lay you off once they've sent you a pallet of household detergent and cosmetics, especially if you've taken the time to hide it all in a safe place.

Unsold Amway products will form the nucleus of a new barter economy, which is how goods and services will be distributed after global capitalism finishes making like oil-eating bacteria. As the oil economy starts winding down, your regional Amway dealer will send you a railcar full of unsold diesel pickups to distribute to your friends and family, one tier down the pyramid. You'll be able to trade them for food just as soon as folks learn how to fash-ion crossbows from leaf-springs.

One of the most valuable things you can have in a world where the Social Contract has broken down is a good place to hide stuff. The Swiss have known this for years. Their best customers reached Social Contract Capitulation long ago. But in a good way.

It's thinking like this that wakes me up when it's dark outside and going to stay dark for another four hours.

2

So I turn on a reading lamp, and pick up R. D. Laing. Laing isn't an economics pundit. He's a British psychiatrist, a dead one, except at 4am on dark winter mornings, when he comes back to life, sheeted and gibbering.

One of Laing's foundational ideas is that we humans create false selves to satisfy the demands of family and culture. But a false self, and the story we tell about it, alienates us not just from our real self but from the natural world and from other people and their real selves.

Laing says that this process of creating a false self makes us alienated to the point of psychosis. Bad craziness begins when we start to think our false self is our real self, and that the story we've made up about it is true. We starve our authentic self to feed the false one. We forgo an authentic world and authentic relationships to live in ones that we've constructed out of wishes and lies and projection.

It happens no matter how smart you are. In fact, a side-effect of being highly intelligent is that your false self and made-up world are better and less subject to breakdown than the false selves and made-up worlds of people less intelligent than you. If you're of genius-level intelligence, your false self is likely to be smarter than any other false self you encounter. In philosophical terms, this is known as winning the booby prize.

You seldom glimpse your false self when you look in the mirror, but you can see it when it happens to other people. For example, Ernest Hemingway spent his life constructing a writer's self and its accompanying story about a wounded guy who never complained. When self and story broke down under the pressures of age and alcohol, there was nothing left to sustain his real self, and no real self left to sustain. His shotgun merely provided punctuation for a sentence already complete.

While R. D. Laing is concerned with individuals driven crazy by their false selves, the current economic and ecological crisis makes it obvious that technological civilisation also has a false self and a false story to back it up. For fifty years now, we have been telling ourselves that we're richer than we are, that we can steal from unborn great-grandchildren, that we stand for the noble cause of human freedom, that our economic system isn't subject to the Second Law of Thermodynamics, that we're mining and consuming inexhaustible resources according to their highest and best use.

Our real story is different, because our real self spends more than it makes. It approves the torture of detainees. It investigates the geology of countries before it invades them, because it has wasted most of its oil. It tolerates the manipulation of markets and tax codes that result in the working poor, who aren't free, and the idle rich, who lack the sort of purpose in their lives that would allow them to do something constructive with their relative freedom. It turns its gaze away from observable phenomena when they contradict projections of economic growth and technological triumph.

Laing would say we're in the process of discovering that we're nuts. Hard facts are beginning to destroy the myths we've lived by. When George W. Bush called the American Constitution just a piece of paper, and America's Supreme Court proved him right, American civilisation took a giant step toward reality. Another giant step came when America's military got away with violating the Geneva Conventions. Another came when American politicians enacted more tax cuts and higher spending, which means we've realised that in an inflationary economy wealth is debt, and debt is wealth.

We've reached Capitulation Level with our cultural story. We've stopped believing in things we cannot touch or see, and a bleak, pragmatic survivalism has taken hold, even in that Font of Narrative called the Oval Office.

It's a good thing, because it's the start of sanity. But sanity is an inhospitable environment for American civilisation. It's an inhospitable environment for any civilisation.

3

One of my best writing students ever was a 7th-grader named Darrel. I forget Darrel's family name, but that doesn't matter, because Darrel is the author of the Frank-And-Dave Stories, and that is accomplishment enough to let him go through life single-named, like Madonna or Cher or Eminem. Frank-and-Dave Stories had titles like *Frank and Dave Go Fishing and Catch a Fish*, or *Frank and Dave Push the Explorer Back onto Its Wheels, Change the Tyre and Get Back on the Road*, or *Frank and Dave Watch the Superbowl and Their Team Wins*.

When a Frank-and-Dave Story fulfilled the promise of its title, it was over. There wasn't a lot of conflict in these stories, but they all got to where they said they would go. Frank and Dave weren't complex and interesting literary characters, but they liked each other and helped each other out when the fish stopped biting, or a tyre blew, or the opposing team was up by two touchdowns at the half. Good things happened in a Frank-and-Dave story, and they happened in short, simple sentences full of concrete nouns and action verbs. One of the lectures I used to give the students in my graduate-level creative writing classes was called *How to Write Like Darrel*.

But Darrel's greatest asset as a writer was not his simple, clear, and effective language. It was his intact world. Darrel's parents had raised him in a disciplined but loving environment. They had seen him through the usual challenges of childhood. They celebrated his successes and when he failed, they reassured him that he would do better next year, and then they analysed his failure and actively prepared him to succeed. They set consistent and age-appropriate rules and when Darrel followed them they lovingly rewarded him and when he disobeyed them they lovingly punished him. If Darrel misbehaved in class I had only to mention that misbehaviour in a parent-teacher conference and it never happened again.

The world that Darrel lived in was defined by the story his parents told themselves about their own lives, which had them living in a world where it was possible to make a lot of money in the stock market and then retire in their forties to a ski resort and raise a child in a rational and loving way. When Darrel sat down to write a Frank-and-Dave Story, he was telling yet another version of his life story, where success was always the punch-line.

Reading a Frank-and-Dave Story did not make me wish for more action or that a really serious bad guy would show up or that the wrong team would lose the big game. Instead, it allowed me to visit a completely safe and grammatical world and to want to get back to that world whenever Darrel finished his next story. I gave Darrel an A in 7th grade English.

If you're wondering when I'm going to tell you that Darrel's parents went through divorce and bankruptcy and addiction and criminal prosecution for duct-taping Darrel to the wall on club nights, or that Darrel ultimately responded to his loving-but-overcontrolled upbringing by mowing down a kindergarten class with an AK-47, that's your worldview making assumptions about my worldview.

As far as I know, Darrel turned out all right, even if he didn't continue as a writer. And his parents lived to a ripe old age with their marriage and story intact. They died believing in their story, which isn't the worst way to go.

4

The stories that define life's parameters are called meta-narratives by people whose false selves look like philosophers. Meta-narratives define the world and the purpose of living and how time works and what wealth is for and where we've been and where we're going, among other things.

The End of Civilisation is a meta-narrative. So are Utopia and Ecotopia, stories in which humans have learned to Live In Peace With Human Nature and With Their Planet. So is Laissez-Faire Capitalism, where The Market Will Make You Free, and Marxism, where History Will Make You Free, and Christianity, where Christ's Passion Has Washed Away Your Sins. Techno-futurists believe that The Singularity Will Make You Free Except That You'll Have To Live In A Hard Drive.

A distinguishing characteristic of meta-narratives is their susceptibility to capitalisation.

Meta-narratives can look a little silly when presented this way, but if yours or mine malfunctions, we're in what is called, in philosophical terms, deep shit. R. D. Laing says schizophrenia occurs when a family's or culture's meta-narrative contains enough contradictions that the individuals embedded in it stop believing in it.

2011 sees us surrounded by meta-narratives that are no longer doing their work of keeping us sane. If I had titled this essay Free Energy From The Peaceful Atom or Get Rich Flipping Houses, or Work Hard And Save Your Money And Prosper, I wouldn't have given much help to your false self in its struggle to maintain the illusion of its existence.

Instead, you would have retreated into a less absurd meta-narrative, which might go something like The Marauding Hordes Won't Make It Through My Minefield and Get My Krugerrands, which preserves your false self in the same way you preserve a bushel of peaches: First you kill all the bacteria, and then you seal yourself away from further contamination.

5

The usual response when a meta-narrative breaks is to go through an uncomfortable period of wondering if you have a self at all and then lie like crazy to get things back to where they were before the break, as when a fundamentalist Christian looks at a fossil and declares it an invention of Satan.

Conservatives who insist that the free market doesn't contain the seeds of its own destruction are doing the same thing, as are liberals who insist that entitlement programmes – including the one that supports the Pentagon – haven't bankrupted America.

My own meta-narrative, which is in need of repair on a number of fronts, is that Brilliant Writers Always Become Rich and Famous.

It's hard to experience the breakdown of your meta-narrative as anything but violence to your false self and your family and your community, and such perceived violence begets more violence, usually in the form of scapegoating. New meta-narratives can be forged out of the scrap of broken ones, and there's always a low-life demagogue out there forging one from the basest, nastiest, ugliest, most fearful and least sane parts of the human psyche. The reason those demagogues prosper is that the story they offer is better than nothing, which is what the false self is in the absence of a good story. For people who have butchered their real selves to feed their false selves, the choice is simple enough: Buy into this cheap-ass fiction or wink into non-existence.

6

R. D. Laing has a wonderful experiment that demonstrates how threatened we can get about the boundary we've erected to preserve our false self from the world. Anybody can perform it:

1] Swallow the saliva in your mouth.
2] Sip water from a glass and swallow it.
3] Spit in the glass, and then sip from the glass and swallow.
4] Sip water from the glass, spit it back into the glass, sip from the glass again and swallow.

Laing points out that we can handle the first two, but that three and four cause great anxiety even though they are only variations on the first two.

Our anxiety stems from confusion about what's inside and what's outside, and the sudden consequent knowledge that the boundary of the false self is both arbitrary and permeable, and always in danger of collapse due to an encounter with the real world. For the false self, authenticity is contamination. So things that cross the false self boundary need to conform to rigorous standards of purity. For these reasons, most of us have hard rules about what we put into or take out of our mouths, nostrils, or any other orifice.

In moments of ecstasy, as when making love or when under the influence of psychotropic drugs – or both – the rigid boundary of self softens, and authentic experience is possible. Governments concern themselves with the sex lives and drug use of their subjects because sex and drugs (and even rock 'n' roll) can create a borderless and storyless self, one that by definition will not be a part of a national or global meta-narrative.

Substitute the borders of a country or a farm or a city lot for the borders of the body and you can see how people can get so upset over illegal immigrants and youth gangs, especially the ones who don't work their fields or serve them Big Macs or keep their houses clean and lawns mowed.

Imagine yourself in a twenty-four hour scenario involving mescaline, marathon sex with illegal immigrants and youth gangs, all set to a tape loop playing the Bee Gees' *Stayin' Alive* at 120 decibels, and then try to imagine your false self waking up the next day and trying to fit back in its old life story.

7

Back when I could read fine print, I spent a winter reading the 1972 edition of *The Columbia History of the World*, authored by the Columbia University history faculty. I slogged through all 1,165 pages of it. It was spring when I finished. I was glad the book hadn't been published in 2072, after a lot more wars, refugee migrations, currency collapses and epidemics.

Not that reading all the way to 2072 wouldn't have been worth my while. I would have invested in Microsoft and Apple and Facebook and Google. I wouldn't have hiked to the base of Mount St. Helens in early May of 1980. I would have written a heartfelt letter to the young George W. Bush, begging him to stop his drinking before it caused irreparable brain damage.

But maybe it's better that history appears to end with this morning's cup of coffee and this edition of the paper. We wouldn't want to know if the weddings we attend are the opening acts of bitter divorces. Knowing where and what the next terrorist attack would be, for example, would start a desperate attempt to stop tragedy, with new tragedy coming out of the effort. A struggle with fate would replace freedom in our lives, and you don't have to be Oedipus to know that's a lousy trade-off.

Of course, the people with starring roles in *The History of the World* saw themselves free of fate, too, when in fact they were trapped within it. It's the way you and I are going to appear to any historian of 2072. We could all be in the position of a Jewish physician with a loving family, a flourishing practice, a fine home – in Prague, in 1933.

8

But history never tells us what's going to happen. It only tells us what *can* happen. That said, knowing what *can* happen usually expands our estimation of what might happen. If you refrain from cherry-picking history to support your peculiar vision of the future, it can help you to understand how unpredictable and even unimaginable the future can be.

9

Margaret Atwood's dystopian novel *Oryx and Crake* shows a near-future where biotechnology underwrites the world economy, where health and truth are sold to the highest bidder, and where as soon as a technology is developed, it is immediately indentured to commerce. But Atwood is no prophet. The time she's writing about is our own, unexaggerated because there's no way to exaggerate what drug companies, life-extension researchers, and bioweaponeers are doing right now. There is no way to exaggerate the commodification of the world, no way to pretend that uncontrolled technology isn't making us its slaves. Watch a kid playing a videogame, and you'll see what I mean.

Atwood writes in the grand tradition of dystopian novelists. George Orwell's *Nineteen Eighty-Four* was about its year of publication, 1948. Aldous Huxley's *Brave New World* incarnated the dreams of 1930s eugenicists. H. G. Wells wrote *The Time Machine* as a satire on the class system in Edwardian England. Hailed as prophets of what would be, these writers just saw the implications of that which was.

10

The *DSM-IV*, the *Diagnostic and Statistical Manual of Mental Disorders*, contains a diagnosis called *Folie à Deux*. It means madness shared by two persons, and it's helpful to point at when you're trying to make a case that consensus reality, dependent as it is on false selves and false narratives, is a form of psychosis. Such craziness does not live in neurotransmitter dysfunction, it lives in the space between two or more people.

The data does not make the reality. If Frank notices that all of Siberia is bubbling methane, Dave says that it's normal climate oscillation. If Frank says that tropical diseases are colonising Canada, Dave blames South American immigrants. If Frank notes that we're in the middle of a mass extinction, Dave demands to see the evidence because he just doesn't see any extinct animals around. If Frank says that the stock market is rising while more people lose their jobs, Dave praises the wisdom of the Free Market. If Frank quits his job, buys weapons and ammunition and a team of horses and moves to a small farmstead in an isolated valley in Alaska where the cabbages grow to the size of pumpkins, Dave sinks his life-savings into the stock market and studies to become a broker.

Fortunately, Frank and Dave are headed for consensus. Eventually Dave will join Frank in Alaska for cabbage-and-bear stew or Frank will move south to join Dave's brokerage as a junior partner. They are bound together in ways they don't consciously understand. In spite of their friendship and good will toward each other, each of their false selves is fighting for its life when they get into an argument. The false self that wins gets to write the story for the false self that loses. That's the nature of Frank and Dave, and unfortunately for their and our real selves, that's the nature of humanity. The false selves of the winners get to write the narrative for the false selves of the losers, which is another reason not to place your faith in History. Or even in Frank and Dave stories, set in a world where God is named Darrel.

Where is the real self in all this falsity and fiction? Often enough, to use a philosophical term, it's extinct. But if your real self is still alive, you can nourish it and heal it by carefully listening to and observing the world without preconceptions or paranoia. Buddhists say there's no such thing as a real self, but suggest that reality can be found in chopping wood and carrying water, which is a gnomic way of saying that reality – and the authentic self, if it exists – lives in doing and not in being, in the microcosm and not in the macrocosm, in production rather than distribution, and in witnessing the world rather than shouting it down.

NAOMI KLEIN

On Precaution

I just did something I've never done before. I spent a week at sea on a research vessel. I'm not a scientist but I was accompanying a remarkable scientific team from the University of South Florida that has been tracking BP's oil in the Gulf of Mexico.

The scientists I was with are not studying the effects of the oil and dispersants on the big stuff – birds, turtles, dolphins. They are looking at the really little stuff, which gets eaten by slightly less little stuff, which gets eaten by the big stuff. What they found is that water with even trace amounts of oil and dispersants can be highly toxic to phytoplankton – which is a serious problem because so much life depends on it. So contrary to those reports we heard back in August last year about how 75 per cent of the oil has sort of disappeared, this disaster is still unfolding, still working its way up the food chain.

This shouldn't come as a surprise. Rachel Carson, the godmother of modern environmentalism, warned us about it back in 1962. She pointed out that the 'control men,' as she called them, who carpet-bombed fields and towns with toxic insecticides like DDT, were only trying to kill the insects, not the birds. But they forgot one detail: the fact that birds dine on grubs and robins eats lots of worms – now saturated with DDT. And so robin eggs did not hatch; song birds died en masse. Towns fell silent; thus the title: 'Silent Spring.'

I've been trying to pinpoint what keeps drawing me to back the Gulf of Mexico. I'm Canadian after all. I can claim no ancestral ties. And I think part of the reason is that we still haven't come to terms with the full implications of this disaster. With what it meant to witness a hole ripped in the world. With what it felt like to watch the contents of the Earth gush forth on live TV, 24 hours a day, for months.

After telling ourselves for so long that our tools and technology can control nature, suddenly we were face to face with our weakness, with our lack of control, as the oil burst out of every attempt to contain it: top hats, top kills and, most memorably, the junk shot, the bright idea of firing old tyres and golf balls down that hole in the world.

But even more striking than the ferocious power emanating from the well was the *recklessness* with which that power was unleashed. The carelessness, the lack of planning, that characterised the operation from drilling to cleanup. If there is one thing BP's watery improv act made clear, it is that as a culture, we are far too willing to gamble with things that are irreplaceable and precious to us. And to do so without a back up plan, without an exit strategy.

BP was hardly our first experience of this in recent years. Our leaders barrel into wars telling themselves happy stories about cakewalks and welcome parades. Then it is years of deadly damage control. A Frankenstein of sieges and surges and counter-insurgencies and, once again, no exit strategy.

Our financial wizards routinely fall victim to similar overconfidence, convincing themselves that the latest bubble is a new kind of market, one that will never go down. And when it inevitably does, the best and brightest scramble for the financial equivalent of junk shots – in this case, throwing massive amounts of much needed public money down a different kind of hole. And as with BP, the hole does get plugged, at least temporarily. But not before exacting a tremendous price, paid in homes lost and destroyed livelihoods.

We have to figure out why we keep letting this happen because we are in the midst of our highest stakes gamble of all: deciding what to do – or not to do – about climate change.

As we all know, a great deal of time is spent in the climate debate on the question: 'What if the IPCC scientists are all wrong?' The far more relevant question, as MIT physicist Evelyn Fox Keller puts it, is: 'What if those scientists are right?'

Given the stakes, the climate crisis clearly calls for us to act based on the Precautionary Principle, the theory that holds that when human health and the environment are significantly at risk, and when the potential damage is irreversible, we cannot afford to wait for perfect scientific certainty. Better to err on the side of caution. Moreover, the burden of proving that a practice is safe should not be placed on the public that could be harmed, but rather on the industry that stands to profit.

Yet climate policy in the wealthy world – to the extent that such a thing exists – is not based on precaution but rather on cost-benefit analysis; finding the course of action that economists believe will have the least impact on GDP. So rather than asking, as precaution would demand: 'How can we act as quickly as possible to avert catastrophe,' we ask bizarre questions like: What is the latest possible moment we can wait before we begin seriously lowering emissions? 2020? 2050? Or, how much hotter can we let the planet get and still survive? 2 °C? 3? 4 – what we are heading for right now?

This last question is interesting because the assumption that we can safely control the Earth's awesomely complex climate system as if it had a thermostat – making the planet not too hot and not too cold but *just right*, Goldilocks style – is pure fantasy. And it isn't coming from climate scientists, it's coming from economists imposing their mechanistic thinking on the science. The fact is that we simply don't know when the warming we create will be utterly overwhelmed by feedback loops.

So, once again: Why do we take these reckless risks? A range of explanations probably pop to mind. Like greed. Or perhaps hubris. And greed and hubris are intimately intertwined when it comes to recklessness. Because if you happen to be a 35-year-old banker taking home a hundred times more than a brain surgeon, then you need a narrative, a story that makes that disparity okay, and you don't have a lot of options. Either you're an outrageously good scammer, and you are getting away with it, or you are some kind of boy-genius the likes of which the world has never seen. Both options are going to make you vastly over-confident, and therefore prone to taking riskier gambles in the future.

I think it's somehow significant that Tony Hayward, former CEO of BP, had a plaque on his desk engraved with the following inspirational slogan: 'If you knew you could not fail, what would you try?' A lot of people have that plaque. And there are certainly circumstances in which pushing fear of failure out of your mind can be a very good thing – if you are training for a triathlon, say, or writing experimental fiction. But personally, I think the men with the power to detonate our economy and ravage our ecology would do better having a picture of Icarus hanging on the wall. Because I want them thinking about the possibility of failure all the time.

So we've got greed, and we've got overconfidence/hubris. But let's consider one other factor that could be contributing in some small way to our societal recklessness: Gender.

All kinds of studies have shown that, as investors, women are much less prone to reckless risk-taking, not because of biology but precisely because they tend not to suffer from overconfidence. So it turns out that being paid less and praised less has its upsides – for society at least. The flipside, however, is that being constantly told that you are gifted, chosen and born to rule has distinct societal disadvantages.

This problem – call it the perils of privilege – brings us closer to the real root of our collective recklessness. And none of us in the global north – neither men nor women – are fully exempt. Here's what I mean:

Whether we actively believe them, or consciously reject them, our culture remains in the grip of certain archetypal stories about our supremacy over others and over nature. The narrative of the newly discovered frontier and the conquering pioneer. The narrative of manifest destiny, of apocalypse and salvation.

And just when it seems that these stories are fading into history, they show up, in unlikely places. For instance, I recently stumbled across a Motorola advertisement outside the women's washroom in the Kansas City Airport. It was for the company's new rugged cellphone. As a man gnaws on the phone to prove its ability to withstand the elements, the ad exhorts us to 'Slap Mother Nature in the Face.' And it struck me that, in its own way, the bizarre ad was a crass version of our founding story – we slapped Mother Nature around and won. And we will always win, because dominating nature is our destiny.

But this is not the only fairytale we tell ourselves about nature. There is another one, equally important, about how that very same 'Mother Nature' is so nurturing and so resilient that we can never make a dent in her infinite abundance.

Let's hear from Tony Hayward again. You remember this one: 'The Gulf of Mexico is a very big ocean. The amount of volume of oil and dispersant we are putting into it is tiny in relation to the total water volume.' In other words, the ocean is big. She can take it.

It is only this underlying assumption of limitlessness that makes it possible to take the reckless risks that we do. Because this is our real master narrative: However much we mess up, there will always be more: more water, more land, more untapped resources. A new bubble will replace the old one, a new technology will fix the mess we made with the last one.

That is the story of the settling of the Americas, the supposedly inexhaustible frontier to which Europeans escaped. And it is also the story of modern capitalism because it was the wealth from this land that gave birth to our economic system – one that cannot survive without perpetual growth and an unending supply of new frontiers.

The problem is that the story was always a lie. The Earth always did have limits, they were just beyond our sights – and now we are hitting those limits on multiple fronts. I believe that we know this. And yet we find ourselves trapped in a kind of narrative loop. Not only do we continue to tell and retell the same stories, but we are now doing so with a frenzy and a fury that frankly verges on camp.

How else to explain the cultural space occupied by Sarah Palin? On the one hand exhorting us to Drill Baby Drill because God put those resources in the ground in order for us to exploit them. And on the other, glorying in the wildness of Alaska's untouched beauty on her hit reality TV show. The twin message is as comforting as it is mad: Ignore those creeping fears that we have finally hit the wall. There are still no limits; there will always be another frontier. So stop worrying and keep shopping.

Would that this were just about Sarah Palin. In environmental circles, we often hear complaints that, rather than shifting to renewables, we are continuing with 'business as usual.' That assessment is far too optimistic.

The truth is that we have exhausted so much of the easily accessible fossil fuel that we have already entered a much riskier business era – the era of extreme energy. That means drilling for oil in the deepest water – including in icy Arctic seas, where a cleanup may simply be impossible. It means large-scale hydraulic fracturing ('fracking') for gas and massive strip-mining operations for coal. Most controversially, it means the tar sands.

I am always surprised by how little people outside Canada know about the Alberta tar sands, which this year are projected to become the number one source of imported oil to the United States. It's worth taking a moment to understand this practice because it speaks to recklessness like little else.

The tar sands lie under one of the last magnificent old-growth boreal forests. But the oil underneath those trees is not liquid; you can't just drill a hole and pump it out. Tar sands oil is solid, mixed into the soil. So to get at it, you first have to get rid of the trees. Then you rip off the topsoil and dig up the stuff – a process so disruptive it requires enlisting the biggest dump trucks ever built. It also requires a huge amount of water, which is then pumped into massive toxic tailing ponds. That's very bad news for local indigenous people who are facing unusually high cancer rates.

Tar sands extraction is growing so fast that the project can already be seen from space and could grow to an area roughly the size of England. This is not oil drilling. It is not even mining. It is terrestrial skinning. Vast vivid landscapes are being gutted, left monochromatic grey. I should confess that as far as I'm concerned, this would be an abomination if it emitted not one particle of carbon. But the truth is that on average, turning that gunk into crude oil produces about three times more greenhouse gas pollution per barrel than it does to produce conventional crude oil in Canada.

How else to describe this but as a form of mass insanity? Just when we know we need to be learning to live on the surface of our planet – off the power of sun, wind, and waves – we are frantically digging to get at the dirtiest, highest emitting stuff imaginable. This is where our story about endless growth has taken us: to the tar sands, this black hole at the centre of my country. A place of such planetary pain that, like the BP gusher, one can only bear to look at it for so long. As Jared Diamond and others have shown us, this is how civilisations commit suicide: by slamming their foot on the accelerator at the exact moment they should be putting on the brakes.

The problem is that our master narrative has an answer for this too: At the very last minute, we are going to get saved. Just like in every Hollywood movie; just like in the Rapture. But of course our secular religion is technology.

You may have noticed more and more headlines like 'Geoengineering: A Quick, Clean Fix?' (*Time*) or 'Solar Shield Could Be Quick Fix for Global Warming' (*New Scientist*). The idea behind this form of geoengineering is that, as the planet heats up, we may be able to shoot sulphates or aluminum particles into the stratosphere to reflect some of the sun's rays back to space, thereby cooling the planet. The wackiest plan would put what is essentially a garden hose 18-and-a-half miles into the sky, suspended by balloons, to spew sulphur dioxide. It's the ultimate junk shot.

The serious scientists involved in this research all stress that these techniques are entirely untested. They don't know if they will work, and they have no idea what terrifying side effects they could unleash. Nevertheless, the mere mention of geo-engineering is being greeted in some circles with relief tinged with euphoria: An escape hatch has been located! A new frontier! We don't have to change after all!

The bottom line is that we badly need some new stories. We need stories that have different kinds of heroes – and we need heroes willing to take different kinds of risks. Risks that confront recklessness head-on, and that put the precautionary principle into practice, even if that means direct action.

Like the hundreds of young people getting arrested blocking dirty power plants, or fighting mountain top removal coal mining. Like the indigenous people and ranchers in the US banding together to stop a new pipeline carrying tar sands oil. The organisers call it the 'Cowboys and Indians coalition' – a new twist on an old myth.

Most of all we need stories that replace linear narratives of endless growth with circular ones that remind us that what goes around comes around; that this is our only home. There is no escape hatch. Call it Karma if you like. Call it Physics: action and reaction. Or call it precaution: the principle that reminds us that life is too precious to be risked for any profit.

WILLIAM HAAS

Coal Sarcophagus

A backdraft fed the fire down the coal chute and incinerated two miners. The black air backfilled the mine shafts and clogged the men's sinuses. The survivors hung a nylon tarp to protect their oxygen. They huddled in that hutch, broken-legged and coughing black blood, talk of families frittering away the remaining air. Before the headlamps' batteries died, the walls glared yellow-white, as if behind them shone a bright and everlasting light.

By the time the miners were recovered, the black dust had settled and their bodies appeared to be formed in rock and known by God forever. The sole survivor was an onyx statue. His breath rippled the channels of mucus that cut the soot beneath his nose and dribbled around his mouth. A week-long special on cable news, he was forgotten in recovery. He stopped speaking and no longer paid his electric bill. Near the creek behind his trailer, he dug a hole.

Night falls. He crawls into the grave and dusts himself with dirt. Each finger a taproot, he reaches through the earth past potato bugs, night crawlers and boll weevils. He fractures sandstone and splits shale before alighting on a seam of coal. If time respools over millions of years, the layers lift and the sellable seacoal decompresses into fauna and flora. Cyclads and ferns untip, take root and tower into the air. Mammal, reptile and dinosaur carcasses shiver to life, unsplash from the swamp and forage for food. Water ripples into mosquitoes' wings and across the legs of dead millipedes. Life encroaches on death, and the sun is an engine of combustion not yet stored in flammable stone. The next morning he awakens rooted in the humus. No one remains to dig him out.

NICK HUNT

My Wife Designs Beasts

My wife designs beasts. This is what she does. And every day, I must hunt the beasts through the dark pine forest that surrounds our house, and drag their pelts home through the snow to lay before her fire.

She releases the beasts before dawn, when I am still in bed. She opens the door and sets them loose, the beasts she has designed. Sometimes they are reluctant to go, I hear them rasping and moaning in the cold, and my wife must shoo them away with a broom or pelt them with lumps of coal. And then she brings me hot sugared tea, porridge, thick bread, slabs of butter and cheese, and she makes certain I wolf it all down because she does not want me to stumble, despair or succumb to the freezing wind.

Together we wait for the sky to turn the colour of blood and gold. My wife dresses me for the cold, in my layers of fur and my winter hood and my ropes and my sacks and my snowshoes. She slips leather gauntlets on my hands, and gently wraps my fingers around the slender hunting needle I use to lance the beasts through their tiny hearts and send their bright blood bubbling into the snow.

I set out at a steady pace, following the tracks of the beasts where they leapt, hopped, slithered, crawled, lurched or bounded over the hill, and from there descended into the woods, to merge with the shadows of pines. From their tracks, I make assumptions about the forms their bodies have taken. I note the scrape of a trailing wing, the indentation of a horn, the prints of toes or talons or stumps, the drag-mark of a tongue.

Through the black and threatening firs I plunge, with no thoughts in my head. I must chase the beasts to the end of the earth. That is what I must do. My snowshoes crash through deadwood and crunch deeply in the snow. They slip and slither over frozen streams, and sometimes I trip and go tumbling down, face-first into whiteness. I pick myself off, dust the snow from my clothes, and continue without respite. I do not allow myself to tire. I do not allow myself to pause. There can be no rest until I have the beasts at my needle's point.

It has been this way for a year and a day. Ever since our wedding night, when my wife designed her first set of beasts. Ever since our honeymoon, when she first sent the beasts out into the snow. Ever since she made it clear that she wanted me to deliver their pelts, soft and warm and wet with gore, to where she sits by the fire at night, toasting her feet before the flames.

The tracks run together for the first few miles, and then they split different ways. They diverge along separate paths, weaving complicated knots through the trees, in an attempt to throw me off and force me to turn back. This means the beasts have heard my pursuit, pressed their misshapen heads to the ground to feel my thudding footsteps. I imagine they think I can simply be confused, that I can be made to falter. But the beasts should know I will not be stopped. That the pattern will never be changed.

By noon, I have run the first to ground. Made dizzy and careless with exhaustion, it will have paused to catch its breath, sucking the frosted air through its snout, or its beak or its swollen purple lips. I fall upon it through a mist of powdered snow. The needle slips through matted fur, rainbow scales or casing of bone. I hear the muffled pop of its heart. Steam pours from the tiny hole. Its blood paints a red map on the snow. I gently stroke its head as it fades, wiping away its teardrops of blood, smoothing its crumpled feathers.

Deftly, barely pausing for breath, I remove its pelt with the notched, bone-handled hunting knife that hangs at my side. I loosen the muscle and flesh from the bone, and slip its skin from its skeleton as if I'm tugging a woolly jumper off the body of a sleeping child. I roll the pelt up like a rug and stuff it into one of the sacks that dangle from my shoulders. I clean the needle with a fistful of snow, draw breath, and plunge back into the trees. The others will still be far away. Mindlessly, pointlessly running.

Deeper into the woods I go, where the trees darken and the ground becomes littered with rocks and fallen branches. I stagger uphill, crashing through the thickets of thorns that tangle my path, tearing into my winter furs, whipping across my face. After hours of pursuit, I come upon the second, the third, the fourth, the fifth, the sixth, the seventh, scattered at intervals in the trees, foam-flecked, flanks heaving. Sometimes they have injured themselves in a fall, smashed headfirst into the trunk of a tree, or fallen through a thin patch of ice halfway over a frozen river. Sometimes the joints of their limbs have popped. They might attempt to continue like this, dragging useless extremities behind them, and I will find tattered strips of their skin caught on protruding branches. Sometimes their lungs will have given out. They will be too weak to go on. They are not designed to run too far. My wife sees to this.

I dispatch them cleanly, efficiently. I don't like to shout or make a fuss. By this point I'm as exhausted as them, and I take no pleasure in it. Occasionally they try to fight, flailing, bellowing, kicking up snow, but most of the time they await the needle in silence, even expectantly. Sometimes they seem almost relieved. Sometimes I think they understand why their deaths must happen.

It's dark by the time I get back to the house. My entire body hurts. I see the lights glinting through the trees. I smell the rising wood-smoke. I stamp off snow at the front door, and collapse into the room. My wife unwraps my ropes and sacks, tugs the frozen furs from my body. She drags me over to the fire, rubs my arms and legs with hot towels, and coddles me in blankets. She bathes my wounds. She brings hot spiced wine. She unfreezes the skin of my face with kisses. And then she unrolls the pelts I have brought her, and while I nod off to sleep in my chair she kneels on the wooden floor, examining them meticulously in the flickering orange light.

I see the pleasure on her face. I hear her admiring words. I've been doing this for a year and a day, ever since we married. My wife designs beasts. This is what she does. There can be no rest until I have the beasts at my needle's point.

One day, I am too sick to go out. I moan as my wife pulls away the covers, and cannot swallow the tea she brings, and gag at the sight of porridge. My chest is glistening with sweat. It looks like the belly of a fish. I lie there and stare at my chest as it heaves, and my heartbeats boom inside my head.

Perhaps it was something I caught in the cold. Perhaps one of the beasts showered me in poison. Or perhaps I didn't eat enough thick bread, or drink enough hot sugared tea. When my wife insists I get out of bed, my legs buckle and I fall to the floor. My head feels strange. I don't know up from down. Sweat pools in the backs of my knees.

All morning my wife tries to bring me back to strength, growing ever more impatient as the sun climbs in the sky. She rushes back and forth from the kitchen, trying to spoon things into my mouth. She brews chicken broth, nettle tea, dark medicinal concoctions steeped with forest herbs. She sticks cones of garlic in my ears. She steams my feet in spearmint tea. She presses hot bowls upon my back. It only makes me sicker.

I swim in and out of nightmares while my wife fusses around me. Beyond the wall, I can hear the beasts. They must have gathered around the front door, huffing the air through the crack where the draft blows in. They want to get out, but she will not let them go. As the day goes by, their anxiety grows.

They begin to shriek, pawing at the floorboards. I can hear their nails raking the wood. The next time my wife leans over the bed, adjusting the blankets I have thrown off, I take her shoulders with my clammy hands and tell her I cannot leave the house. I say she must let the beasts go without me, on this one occasion. She presses her fingers to my lips, instructs me to be still.

I cannot move for five days and five nights. It feels like a year. My body feels yellow, then black, then green. My fingers have turned into thumbs. My hands feel bloated, full of dense liquid. I imagine them swollen to the size of hams, but when I drag them before my face they appear completely normal. A heavy stench lies over the bed. My skin is leaking like a muslin cloth. My condensation drips down the walls and windows.

My wife continues designing beasts every night while I am sick. I want to tell her that she must stop, that she must wait until I'm well, or there will be too many.

The beasts are filling up the house. They don't have anywhere to go. They crowd against the windows and doors, desperate for release. The walls shake as they bang into them, the crockery rattles on the shelves. My wife cannot stop. This is what she does. I do not know what will happen.

On the fifth night, my sickness peaks. It plunges me through swirling clouds, clouds of lurid pink and green. The sky is flashing horribly. I am lost in a storm of beasts. I close my eyes to make it dark. Through the darkness, my wife comes. I think it is my wife. A dark shape bending over me, a blackness blacker than the black, devoid of form or features. She watches me through a mist of dreams. She holds me with her eyes. I want to touch her, to speak some words, but I cannot move a muscle.

She watches me through the long, black night. She never makes a sound. Later, I find I can move my hand. My body is starting to function again. I attempt to reach out for my wife, but she is no longer there.

I awake to white light streaming through the window. Its brilliance hurts my eyes. I pull myself up to sitting position and wipe frost off the glass. Everything is white outside. The world is clean and cold. Above the boundary of the pines, the sky is turning the colour of blood and gold.

My feet find their way to the floor. My fingers grip the bed-frame. My legs tremble, but support my weight. I stagger from the room.

There is silence throughout the house. The fireplace is cold. A cloud of ash hangs over the hearth, and the embers are dead grey. I cannot remember this happening before. There is no tea, no porridge, no bread. The furniture is disarranged, and the floorboards deeply scored. My wife is nowhere to be seen. A blue and white china plate lies broken on the floor.

The snow is all churned up outside, and a stampede of many tracks, far too many tracks to count, leads towards the forest. They must have had several hours head start. There is no time to lose. I do not allow myself to tire. I do not allow myself to pause. I am stumbling through the snow, following the tracks of the beasts where they leapt, hopped, slithered, crawled, lurched or bounded over the hill, and from there descended into the woods, to merge with the shadows of pines.

Before I have reached the crest of the hill I am bent almost double, staggering for breath. I have to drag myself up the slope with hands already turning blue. It is at this point I remember something. My hunting needle is back in the house, in its rack on the wall. I turn my head, peering back down the hill. There is wood smoke rising from the chimney. The door is standing open. Something moves in the white field, and it is now that I see the man, in his furs and his winter hood and his ropes and his sacks and his snowshoes, hunting needle in gauntleted hands, lift his head from the tracks at his feet and begin to run, in long easy strides, towards me, up the hill.

VENKATESH RAO

The Return of the Barbarian

Our cartoon view of history goes straight from the Flintstones to the Jetsons without developmental stages of any consequence in between. Hunter-gatherers and settled modern civilisations loom large, as bookends, in our study of history. The more I study history though, the more I realise that hunter-gatherer lifestyles are mostly of importance in evolutionary prehistory, not in history proper. If you think about history proper, a different lifestyle, pastoral nomadism, starts to loom large, and its influence on the course of human history is grossly underestimated. This is partly because civilisations and pastoral nomad cultures have a figure-ground relationship. You need to understand both, to understand the gestalt of world history.

Modern hunter-gatherer lifestyles are cul-de-sacs in terms of cultural evolution. They stopped mattering by around 4000 BCE, and haven't significantly affected world events since. Pastoral nomads, though, played a crucial role until at least the First World War. Until about 1405 (the year Timur died), they actually played the starring role. And, in reconstructed form, the lifestyle may again start to dominate world affairs within the next few decades. Their eclipse over the last 500 or so years, I am going to argue, was an accident of history that is finally being corrected.

The barbarians are about to return to their proper place at the helm of the world's affairs, and the story revolves around this picture:

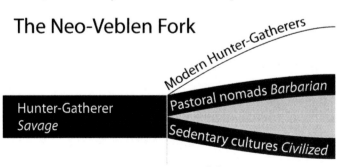

The Neo-Veblen Fork

Modern Hunter-Gatherers

Hunter-Gatherer
Savage

Pastoral nomads *Barbarian*

Sedentary cultures *Civilized*

~15,000-10,000 BC

Illustration by Edmund Harriss

I am about to zoom from about 15 000 BCE to 2011 CE in less than ten pages, so you may want to fasten your seat belts and grab a few pinches of salt.

Savagery, Barbarism and Civilisation

From hunter-gatherers to early pastoral nomads, you get a gradual evolution, and at some point (the Neolithic revolution, probably between 15000 to 10000 BCE) you get a fork in the road. One path leads to settled civilisations and the other leads to increasingly sophisticated modes of pastoralism. Pre-Columbian Plains Indians could be viewed as being right at the fork: They didn't quite herd domesticated beasts so much as follow buffalo around on their normal migratory routes. There were also other tribes that were more sedentary, but didn't develop into full-blown settled civilisations like their cousins further south in Central and Latin America.

On the pastoral nomad branch of the fork, you get, in reverse chronological order of influence on world history, Turks, Mongols, Arabs, Northern Europeans and Proto Indo-Europeans.

On the sedentary branch, you get, in no particular order, American, Soviet, British, Continental-European, Persian, Graeco-Roman, Ancient Near Eastern, later-stage Arabic (the Abbassids more than the Ummayads), Sinic and Indian. There aren't actually more of them, though it looks that way. They are merely easier to count off since they stay in one place and give each other names that stick.

I like Thorstein Veblen's labels for hunter gatherers, pastoral nomads and settled peoples (savage, barbarian and civilised respectively, from his 1899 classic, *The Theory of the Leisure Class*[1]) but lest you take offence (and in case it isn't obvious), in this essay, 'barbarian' is a term of approbation, while 'civilised' is an insult. The term for hunter-gatherers, 'savage', is neutral.

My treatment also differs from Veblen's in one crucial way: what he views as a linear progression, I view as a forking path with barbarian and civilised branches evolving interdependently and in parallel. Like other thinkers of the nineteenth century, he also used the metaphor of progression from child-like to adult stages (a sort of 'ontogeny recapitulates phylogeny' idea applied to cultural evolution) to think about the linear model, which I think is fundamentally mistaken (though it persists as a trope in movies and television). So to acknowledge my debt to Veblen, while distinguishing my views from his, I am going to call the anchor picture the Neo-Veblen Fork.

This essay is partly an attempt to reconstruct a portion of Veblen's ideas, but it is intended to stand independently of the original. I strongly recommend the book though; it covers vastly more territory than I do here (though mostly within the context of late nineteenth century Robber-Baron America), and most of it applies without any reconstruction in 2011.

The Idle Savage

Hunter gatherers need and create very little technology. They manage to live in a stable relationship with their environments. To the extent that they follow their main prey species around, they are more like proto-nomads. To the extent that they live around their main plant food sources, they are like proto-sedentary cultures. These are the lifestyles Veblen labelled savage.

The biblical archetype for hunter-gatherers has traditionally been the Garden of Eden. Savages are minimalist predators, and simply live off the bounty of nature, in areas where it is effectively inexhaustible. To the extent that their gathering has evolved into agriculture, it is slash-and-burn agriculture based on immediate consumption and natural renewal rather than accumulation and storage of vast quantities of non-perishable food over long periods of time. You could call their style of farming 'nomadic', since they move from cultivating one cleared patch of forest to the next, rather than staying put and practising crop rotation in a small confined patch of land.

For the record, I think the Garden of Eden story has it right. Savagery is the most pleasurable state of existence, if you can get it (until you annoy the witch doctor or get a toothache). Not in the sense of the noble savage (an idea within what is known as romantic primitivism, currently enjoying a somewhat silly revival thanks to things like the Paleo Diet), but in the sense of what you might call the idle savage state. In some ways, an idle savage is what I am, in private, on weekends.

Though they don't play a big part in this story, don't underestimate what they did when they were centre-stage: fire, spoken language, art and archery are all savage inventions. Wisely, they didn't get addicted to invention and stayed idle.

Idle savagery is basically unsustainable today unless you retreat completely from the mainstream, so though I'd like to be an idle savage, I've settled for the compromise state of being a barbarian. That's where it gets interesting.

The Illegible Barbarian

Pastoral nomads need, and develop, a good deal more technology, and, in areas that matter to them, are usually ahead of settled civilisations. They are not quite as predatory as hunter-gatherers. Unlike hunter-gatherers, they don't just follow prey around. They consciously domesticate and manage their herds. Rather than let the herds move by instinct, they direct their migratory instincts (hence 'herding'). They don't just occasionally slaughter what they need for food and clothing. They develop dairy, husbandry and veterinary practices as well. You could say they cultivate animals (a more demanding task than cultivating plants). The biblical reference point is of course Abel the shepherd, of killed-by-Cain fame. (At one point I was enamoured of Daniel Quinn's reading of the Cain-Abel tale in *Ishmael*, which I now think is a case of confusing hunter-gatherers with pastoral nomads.)

I've argued elsewhere that barbarians were responsible for the development of iron technology.[2] I'd also credit them for the invention of the wheel, chariots, leather craft, rope-making, animal husbandry, falconry and sewing (via sewing of hide tents with gut-string and bone needles, which clearly must have come before cloth woven from plant fibres needed sewing). Basically, if anything looks like it came out of a mobile lifestyle, pastoral nomads probably invented it. At a more abstract level, barbarian cultures create fundamentally predatory technologies: technologies that allow you to do less work to get the same returns, freeing up time for idleness. What Hegel would have called 'Master' technologies. The barbarian works to earn the idleness which the luckier savage gets for free.

Barbarian technologies, like savage technologies, are fundamentally sustainable, since using them tends to fulfil immediate needs rather than causing wealth accumulation. The connection to mobility is central to this characteristic: Nomadic cultures do not accumulate useless things. It is a naturally self-limiting way of life. If it doesn't fit in saddlebags or is too heavy to be carried by pack animals, it isn't useful.

Mobility is also the fundamental reason why barbarian cultures are illegible to civilised ones, in literal and abstract ways.[3] They self-organise in sophisticated ways, but you cannot draw organisation charts (the Romans tried and failed). For most of history, they've owned most of the map of the world, yet you cannot draw boundaries and identify proto-nations, since they are defined by patterns of movement rather than patterns of settlement. They practice the most evolved forms of leadership, but actual leaders change from one situation to the next (a fact which confused the Roman army no end when it fought them).

Pastoral nomads come in two varieties, which Veblen called lower and higher barbarian stages. Lower-barbarian pastoral nomads include groups like the twelfth century Mongols. Higher barbarian stages look like settled civilisations on the surface, but (and this was Veblen's enduring contribution) are characterised by a vigorous ruling class, with roots in pastoral nomadism, that generally maintains at least a metaphoric version of that lifestyle.

Among the more obvious symbols, as late as the nineteenth century, the higher barbarians often maintained herds of unnecessary domestic animals, hunted for sport (rather than for sustenance, unlike the hunter-gatherers) and generally spent their wealth recreating idealised pastoral-nomad landscapes.

When the vigorous leaders of a higher barbarian culture start to settle down like their subjects, you get civilisation.

The Stationary Civilised

Veblen's notion of 'civilised' roughly corresponds to agrarian (or more generally, production-accumulation based) cultures governed by social contracts and non-absolute rulers. By this measure, parts of the Near East became 'civilised' by about 1500 BCE (I regard the Hittites as the first true examples), followed by southern Europe around 800 BCE, and northern Europe around the time of the Magna Carta.

Asian cultures are much harder to track: Veblen considered them all 'higher barbarian,' but depending on how you read the history of Persia, China and India, they've oscillated between 'higher barbarian' and 'civilised' over the centuries (for instance, the 'growth and consolidation' reigns of Ashoka and Akbar were civilised while the entrepreneurial 'startup' reigns of their respective grandfathers, Chandragupta Maurya and Babur, were higher barbarian; I don't know Persian and Chinese history well enough to cite equivalent examples).

The mark of 'civilisation' is the replacement of sustainable predatory patterns of life based on immediate consumption with unsustainable non-predatory ones based on accumulation. Civilised cultures create different types of technology compared to barbarian cultures. What Hegel would have called 'Slave' technologies. Technologies that keep you working harder and harder to accumulate stuff. Civilisation is the opposite of idleness. It is a treadmill of increasing industriousness and productivity.

This isn't irrational: Sedentary lifestyles allow you to store everything from grain to gold in large quantities and lower the risk of future starvation. The carrot and stick of surplus-fuelled hedonism and starvation-avoiding accumulation lock sedentary people into human zoos that become fundamentally harder to break out of over time.

But the effects are inevitable. As you settle down and accumulate stuff, the risks of existence gradually decrease and the surpluses available for hedonism increase. The net effect of both is that less actual thinking, but more work, is required to exist. To peek ahead a bit, settled civilisation is a fundamentally *Gollumizing* force.[iv] It makes you comfortable, stupid and addicted to the security and accumulated fruits of your labour.

Which brings us to the figure-ground interaction pattern that scripts world history.

The Barbarians and the Civilised

The most famous lower and higher barbarians in history are Genghis Khan and his grandson Kublai Khan respectively. They represent the classic historical pattern of interaction between pastoral nomads and civilised peoples.

The pattern is a simple one: A settled civilisation grows old, stupid and tired, and a vigorous barbarian culture swoops in and takes over from the top, and gradually gets civilised and stupid in turn, until it too is ripe for destruction by pastoral nomads on its periphery.

Modern Europeans since the time when Gibbon wrote his *Decline and Fall of the Roman Empire* have managed to rejoice in a rather contradictory view of themselves: They celebrate their dual origins in the vigorous barbarian cultures of the North and the exhausted cultures of antiquity. Over the protests of modern Italians and Greeks, Northern Europeans have successfully managed to appropriate for themselves the role of 'true' stewards of the achievements of Greece and Rome, cultures that their barbarian forebears were instrumental in destroying (if you want to know which origin myth is closer to the hearts of Europeans, look no further than the tattoos of white gangs in prisons: they tend to be drawn from Scandinavian mythologies).

Here's a rather suggestive piece of European history that illustrates the barbarian/civilised dynamic. In the traditional account of the 'civilisation of Europe,' wine played an interesting role. The Gauls (so the story goes, according to Gibbon) became Romanised first, as Roman wine-making techniques spread to what is today modern France. The Goths were interested in many of the luxuries of Rome, but the one that tempted them the most was wine, which they grew to prefer over the cruder spirits they themselves distilled.

I don't want to hang my entire theory of civilisation on this little item, but it is interesting that the barbarians were civilised, in part, through the temptations of an addiction: better booze, the refined product of an agrarian accumulation culture.

Enough examples, let's note the two interesting questions that emerge, that deserve analysis:

First, how is it that apparently 'inferior' cultures have repeatedly swooped in and destroyed and/or taken over 'superior' cultures? Why was Genghis Khan able to take over China, and how did his grandson successfully create the Yuan dynasty? How did Arab armies conquer the vastly more civilised and sophisticated Persian society? How did Turks pretty much take over most of South Asia, the Middle East and North Africa? Going further back, how did the Proto Indo-European (or 'Aryans') take down the entire Bronze Age family of civilisations?

Second, given the astounding win record of the 'barbarians' against the 'civilised', how come history isn't written from the point of view of the pastoral nomads? Why aren't the histories of Egypt, Greece, Rome, Babylon, Persia, India and China sideshows, with pride of place being given to Mongols, Turks, Arabs and Northern Europeans (pre-1000CE)? Isn't history supposed to be written by the winners?

Refinement and Stupidity

Here's the answer to the first question: 'barbarians' are on average, individually smarter, but collectively stupider than a thriving settled civilisation.

One-on-one, a lower barbarian can outthink, outfight, and out-innovate a civilised citizen any day. But a settled civilisation at its peak can blow a lower-barbarian civilisation away. Not least because at the very top, you still have Veblen's 'uncivilised' higher barbarians (or, to use my preferred term, sociopaths). But once it begins its decline, the greater live intelligence of the barbarians begins to take effect.

The explanation for this contradiction is a very simple one: By definition, civilisation is the process of taking intelligence out of human minds and putting it into institutions. And by 'institution', I mean something completely general: any codified organisational form based on writing will do. Writing, as Plato noted in the *Phaedrus*, is the main medium through which intelligence passes from humans to institutions.

> [Writing] will introduce forgetfulness into the soul of those who learn it: they will not practise using their memory because they will put their trust in writing, which is external and depends on signs that belong to others, instead of trying to remember from the inside, completely on their own ... You'd think they [written words] were speaking as if they had some understanding, but if you question anything that has been said because you want to learn more, it continues to signify just that very same thing forever. When it has once been written down, every discourse roams about everywhere, reaching indiscriminately those with understanding no less than those who have no business with it, and it doesn't know to whom it should speak and to whom it should not. And when it is faulted and attacked unfairly, it always needs its father's support; alone, it can neither defend itself nor come to its own support.[5]

In the short term this works brilliantly. The ideas of the smartest people (usually embedded higher barbarians) are externalised and encoded into the design of institutions, which can then make far stupider people vastly more effective than their raw capabilities would allow. (This is the reason why the modern economic notion of 'productivity' is so misleading.)

But in the long term this fails. The smart people die, and their ideas become obsolete and ritualised. Initially, more intelligence is being externalised into institutions than is being taken away through ritualisation, but at some point, you get a peak, and the decline begins. As entropy accumulates, it becomes a simple matter for another wave of lower barbarians on the periphery to take down the civilisation.

The reason this seems like a strange phenomenon is that we confuse refinement with advancement. Finely crafted jewellery is not more advanced than roughly hewn jewellery. A Boeing 747 is about a million times more capable than the Wright Flyer 1, but it does not contain a million times as much intelligence. It is merely more refined (in the sense of cocaine, by the same logic I applied in 'The Gollum Effect').[6] The difference between advancement and refinement is clearest in disruption. A beautifully crafted sword is not more advanced than a crude gun; it is merely more refined. Or to go back to our earlier example, wine isn't more intelligent than a crude country brew. It is merely more refined.

The intelligence manifest in an artefact is simply the amount of human thought that has been externalised into it. Refinement on the other hand, is a measure of the amount of work that has gone into it. In Hegelian terms, intelligence in design is fundamentally a predatory quality put in by barbarian-Masters. Refinement in design is a non-predatory quality put in by civilised-Slaves.

We miss this dynamic because of a curious phenomenon: history is only written by the winners if the winners can actually write. At their apogee, when civilisations have the most surplus wealth, they indulge in the most refined forms of writing: writing histories with autocentric conceit, they focus on the visibly refined glories of their own age, rather than the higher-barbarian sensibilities at the foundations. Genghis Khan is the sole exception in being more famous than his grandson. In the other two examples I've mentioned, Ashoka and Akbar both traditionally get 'the Great' added to their names. Their empire-founding barbarian grandfathers do not. The most famous symbol of the Mughal empire is the Taj Mahal, which was built by Shah Jahan, who bankrupted his empire in the process, hastening the fall that followed his reign. Babur's tomb is a modest little building in Kabul that few would recognise in a photograph.

As a civilisation becomes increasingly refined, and far less intelligent, it becomes easy prey for pastoral nomads on the margins, who swoop in to cleanse the culture of accumulated stupidity, and revitalise it with a fresh infusion of barbarian blood at the top.

You might even say that barbarians operate at a meta-level: They plant and harvest value out of civilisations. They are civilisation farmers, just as they are animal herders.

The Eclipse and Return of the Barbarian

The reign of Timur was the last time a barbarian ruled a significant proportion of the world. Since his death in 1405, the barbarian has been in decline. The process reached its peak during the Cold War. In America, the Organisation Man threatened to squeeze higher barbarians out of the capitalist world, while in Soviet Russia, forced settlement and collectivisation in Siberia and Mongolia threatened to corral the last of the wandering lower barbarians.

It almost seemed like the fountain of barbarian culture, at which humanity drinks to renew itself, was about to be exhausted once and for all.

The moment thankfully passed. The Gervais Principle kicked in to reinvigorate capitalism, and the High Modernist doctrines of the Soviet state collapsed (followed by a remarkably quick return to pastoral nomadism in Mongolia and Siberia).[7]

That was just the opening act. Today as institutions of all sorts crumble and collapse, and the written word becomes a living, dancing, hyperlinked thing that would have made Plato happy, the barbarian is set to return. He may be armed with a laptop and smartphone and fight his battles in the fluid and illegible world of virtual free-agency, while enjoying the idleness of a 4-hour working week, but he will have more in common with Genghis Khan than with his parents or grandparents.[8]

1. Thorstein Veblen, *The Theory of the Leisure Class* (New York: Macmillan, 1899).

2. Venkatesh Rao, 'The Disruption of Bronze', *Ribbonfarm.com* (2 February 2011). [http://ribbonfarm.com/2011/02/02/the-disruption-of-bronze.]

3. For more on this, see Venkatesh Rao, 'A Big Little Idea Called Legibility', *Ribbonfarm.com* (26 July 2010). [http://ribbonfarm.com/2010/07/26/a-big-little-idea-called-legibility.]

4. See Venkatesh Rao, 'The Gollum Effect', *Ribbonfarm.com* (6 January 2011). [http://ribbonfarm.com/2011/01/06/the-gollum-effect.]

5. *Phaedrus* 275d-e

6. See note 4, above.

7. See Venkatesh Rao, 'The Gervais Principle, Or The Office According To "The Office"', *Ribbonfarm.com* (7 October 2009). [http://ribbonfarm.com/2009/10/07/the-gervais-principle-or-the-office-according-to-the-office.]

8. Some of the ideas in this essay were inspired by Seb Paquet's two-part series of blog posts on how social movements happen. See 'How Social Movements Happen, Part II: Hollowing Out, Self-Organisation, New Stories, Renaissance', *Emergent Cities* (March 2011). [http://emergentcities.sebpaquet.net/how-social-movements-happen-part-ii-hollowing.]

   This was also partly motivated by the impending publication of Francis Fukuyama's *The Origins of Political Order*. His first book, *The End of History and the Last Man* (1992) was in many ways my personal introduction to this subject matter. And no, I am not a neocon.

THOMAS KEYES

October Black Isle Pheasant Stew

Ingredients

One pheasant
Hazelnuts
Hogweed stem
Burdock root
Ground elder
Wild chervil
Chantarelles
Brown birch bolete (*Orange would be better, but none to be found on the day.*)
Lycoperdon pyriforme (*A woodland puffball I can find no simple name for; Latin has its uses for classification but in terms of description and association the common or folk names of wild foods are more useful and accessible.*)
Potatoes
Onions
Garlic
Cabbage
Runner Beans
Kale
Cooking apples

The first thing is to do an autopsy of the pheasant; the more recent the kill, the more damage it's reasonable to put up with.

This one was still warm when I found it, so although the guts had been a little mangled – hit from behind, rather than a nice clean knock on the head – it was still fresh. The meat was good and this recipe involves boiling the hell out of it anyway.

It's easier to skin the bird, rather than pluck it, both practically and to dis-assemble the characteristics of life more quickly. Remove the head and wings with the skin, then cut all the good meat and fat from the carcass. The meat is the real prize here, along with the hazelnuts; enough energy to compensate for the effort with plenty to spare. The life that flowed through this meal will soon be the energy running me, interpreting the process of life as a component, not a consumer or viewer. The chain is so direct, it can be seen. No wonder they used to worship the sun.

Next, shell and crush a few handfuls of hazelnuts and put them in a pan with some fat from the pheasant. Warm them on a low heat and then add the onion, chopped finely; there's enough oil in the nuts and fat to fry the onion.

Now is the perfect time to pick hazelnuts. It is the most human of activi-ties, the one primates are made for, a timeless experience no tool can inter-rupt. By Poyntzfield, there are loads in the burn. It's clear under the hazel, except for a few ground ivy and dead nettle blow-ins struggling. They hold back the bracken and brambles, creating a series of interconnected glades run-ning up the banks of the burn; deep spaces with one rising side and a sense of intangible length; water flow subtly adding to this impression. We were there before the fall, getting the first choice of nuts still on the trees, better adapted than any other creature around here to take this harvest. No grey disruption; the mice have to wait.

Last year we shared. It was an exceptional year and they fell early and in synchronicity, such a dry summer that the trees by the bottom of the burn, usually damper than hazel prefer, took advantage and produced ten times what there is today. The mice are more frugal this year; it will be different. We picked for two hours. While the trees still clutch them, we have the advantage, but this will all change next week.

I should have painted here last year, when surplus bought the time and they fell early in good light. It will be too close this time; the light will be gone before I have time to spare. Twice now I've promised myself this, and each time the imagined process of the work is refined. Next year, it will be even better. I started with a woodcut, but this year that model no longer suffices, it's a paint job, a drawn out event that needs its light more than its shapes. Too simple a process to be reduced to a lithograph, it needs raw painterly digestion. As hand and eye pick, they paint.

When the onion looks done, chuck in the pheasant carcass along with the burdock root, hogweed stems, ground elder stems, wild chervil and garlic. This is just the time to dig burdock. A bit late for the rest, though places which have been strimmed or mown tend to have a second flush, hogweed some-times even flowers this late. Ground elder and hogweed tend to get a bad press. The first, introduced by the Romans as animal fodder – an invasive species in all senses of the word – is now a gardener's nightmare. I've earned a few days work unthreading its endless root network. Hogweed is photo-toxic, so will give you a rash in sunlight, but like nettles, once you get around that it's a great staple.

Alter the quantities to taste, but the aim is to get a really earthy, gamey stock. Add enough boiling water to cover and simmer.

While waiting for the stock, take more crushed hazelnuts. Fry an onion with them as before and add in the pheasant meat, chopped into lumps, fat left on. When the stock is ready, add the meat to the pot, along with the potatoes, mushrooms, cabbage and kale.

There's no more enjoyable harvest than potatoes. The schools still have tattie holidays here. There is a real suspense around digging them, since the crop is hidden right until the end. We can only imagine the thrill or terror this crop inspired when life depended on it.

Simmer until the potatoes are softening. Add in 2 diced cooking apples and the runner beans; simmer until they are soft and you're done.

Eating, this is good food, rich, heavy and thick. Beyond that, it has allowed me to tie a series of fortuitous events and harvests into a meal. The apples worked. Too many chantarelles. A few small stones, so the gizzard must have been ruptured. I didn't pick this up during the initial post mortem, but it tells us more about our bird's final moments. Struck from behind, across the back, suggesting an attempt at flight, or a car with very low profile bodywork – after this, it seems she was thrown into the air, before landing head first on the verge. The relatively closed wings, the completely uncontrolled landing say the death happened at the first impact. Hardly dignified, but quick at least.

It's not a moral choice, eating like this. Of course, everything about the recipe is self-reliant, anti-consumerist, anti-globalisation and the rest, but I don't always eat this well. Every now and then, the kids pester me into a Burger King; XL Bacon Double Cheese evaporating any resistance.

This time, the decision was made for me. I live nine miles from the nearest shop, my car died last week, it's Sunday and the heating oil is running out. My day would consist of beans on toast in three jumpers, if the land didn't provide.

I've just chosen the ability to choose. And when that's the way things go, it's a satisfying experience. It would be possible to go further: instead of mains water and the electric oven, boil rainwater on an open fire. Here we are, surrounded by wood on the estate and forestry.

Free men used to be granted estover, the right to collect dead wood. Maybe one in ten of us was free, when this was law. There's always a catch. We're all free now, of course, and can't touch it.

ROBERT KEEGAN WALKER

The Record Keeper's Visit to Spurn Point

Which I was given because
I loved him and we had
Terrible times together.

Lines on Roger Hilton's Watch, W.S. Graham

I

He extracts the pencil from the page
For pause   for thought   for time must be sought
To know her distance from here.
Two forty-five   the clock says
Not long then   time to grab some things and verify
To set his scales to *delicate*
To check his barometer for the atmospheric pressure
Grab an A to Z   the camera   a pad for notings
His hip-flask of whiskey   a first-aid kit   a map of the constellations
And what they mean   a pocket knife
A reminder of the Beaufort Wind Scale
And just in case   a survival guide.
You're so meticulously careful it's painful
She once said   to which he replied
Something his father had told him   about preparing to fail ...
She arrives with a ringing   on cue   this time
Their clause is set   in symmetry   this time
She wears a smile   as her livery   for him.
They hug   brush cheeks

And she eyes the rucksack in the back seat.
They negotiate the streets   and talk of simple things
Like work   and friends
And begin sentences with *how is?*
Plain nothing to match the fast sights of the city
Houses and salons   coffee shops   and charity ones
And suited Jehovah's pestering the young.
They pause at a crossing   and in each window
See some half-reflected self in the passing people
Her sight passes through to a girl labouring with books from uni
And he sees a man   stumble out   of the alcoholic's drown-house
And clunk off down the street shouting out ideas with arms
Some tiny storm.
Fuck me! It's half-three   he says
She makes eye-contact   the light goes green   they go their way…
Through the town centre with its glass building and happy shoppers
Around round-abouts   and through industrial parks
Until they have a clot of water on their right
With a bridge to cross it   they pass it.
On till the city walls fall and fade to fields   where only drops of buildings dwell
Cloud-factories   adding to the sky…
They feel more alone together   away from the crowds
And they settle into the cosy motion of the car   that smells like slept-in clothes.
What's this place called again?   She asks
Spurn Point, there's some notes in the dash
Minutes pass…
One of the best places in the UK to watch the migration of birds?   She asks
A remembered face, where she exaggerates a demand for an explanation
He laughs   moments pass…
He tries now   to start conversations like   *remember the time?*
And she grows quieter.
They pass older things   a weathered sign   an old farmhouse
Drying out to dust
That used to be a home   he tries
Quietly   she replies   *it's all so horrible and beautiful*
All at the same time
Together   they are more alone…
They pass towns with grim, English names   and then break out into countryside

With the grey sky weighing down with solitude   she sees it
The weather looks like its turning   we'll be fine   he replies
And the land slowly cracks away   on either side
Until they seem surrounded by water
On the right the Humber Estuary   and on the left The North Sea.
She reads from his notes:
It's three miles long and in places as little as fifty yards wide.
And they bobble down the road like a kicked stone
Bouncing off the mud and the shrubs   hardly a road.
Are those train tracks?   She points
Yeah, there must have been a railway line down here, once upon a time.
A black and white lighthouse   disused   appears on the skyline
Can we stop for some pictures?   She asks   they do
It's colder than they though outside
Yet she looks for good light   uses the road reaching out in front for framing
Snaps a bunch of pictures   none of him
He's propped on the bonnet scribbling
What are you writing?   *Nothing*
She always mocked his spelling
How's your writing going?   He asks   she shrugs
He always mocked her poems ...
They aren't in the car long   until they need to carry on on-foot
So they explore a beach on the estuary side
Shielded from the wind on the other
They find an underground room built into the land
Must be from the Second World War
Out on the beach   there is a rumble in the atmosphere
Some hawk-thing fighter jet screeches past at a threatening height
Ripping a tear in the air fixing the eyes
Looks like a Tornado   he says
I thought nothing could fly because of that Icelandic volcano?   He shrugs.
Then they potter-off at different timesuntil he sees at the top of a dune
He clothes and hair   swishing about her in the wind
She waves   he joins her
Shall we move on?   He says
Where are we going?   *I'm not really sure; I know it ends out this way ...*
So they walk down the sand on the bearable side
And point out a lifeboat just off shore

And behind it   larger slug-like sentinels   future-orca
Trudging out on the estuary.
Then they near the end of that land   that hangs off the mainland
As a cape in the wind   would flutter off a shoulder
And come to the edge of that beach   to round the tip
And break out   into unsheltered space ...

II

And the air out there   my god   the air
It shatters past   as though ripping up land-bits
Which of course   it is
They have sand on their skin   in their hair   in their eyes
All scent stripped but salt   all raw skin gets pricked
And if they each held a hand   they both retain a soft palm
But they don't.
Yet side by side they stammer on   on as the good do
And walk as though the air were capricious water
Out to the point where the sand ends.
Then sit   as one would when reaching a summit
And move closer   but not too close
And hoist up their shins as wind-breaks.
He dares wipe from her a wind-tear   out on the point   all rushing and waves
And wishes he could save it as a jewel.
A gull above flaps   but does not move   as though this were the centre of gravity
Fighting furiously   yet pinned in flight
Or rather   tacked as a dead thing   on a centrifuge's wall
As the Earth spins and stuns it   into a progress silence
Or, more simply   a "moderate gale"
On his wind-scale   thirty knots will cripple a small thing.
He does   he tries to do words
That will clap into tablets mid-air
But he thinks the wind steals them   for she looks blankly back
She hears them though   she just slows his comprehending
So he looks to one-thirty   towards Grimsby
A town held there as a miniature by distance
And there he imagines people   as though observed on film

Doing daily things before some grand calamity
And he hopes that somewhere there   exists some moments
Like the ones they've shared   and almost utters …
She leans forward now   to near the water line
Draws now in the sand
Delicate hands   do a message   to remain a remnant
A fleeting recall   scrawling some residue of her
Where ignorant armies clash by night   she writes
Then stands   and dusts herself delighted in the wind
What's it from?   He tries
And she raises her eyes   up to a banished sun
A reaction with no reprise   like when failure in a child brings forth a smile
In their innocence   beautified
But rather   a lack   again   of reflection
A compromise of pre-signified   their demise is built on evidence.
There comes foreboding on distance then a flash
And again a flash
Some strikings out on sea somewhere   writhing for its calming
So they clatter back to the car   for it's cold and growing colder
And the sky will collapse and darken the lad   with some build-up outpouring …
They pause for minutes to rub themselves   and let the air warm between them
Old habits say they do a slow kiss   their chapters used to end that way
Some ritual they conjured   wove from the meme-sphere
But that was then.
Then they drive away to be 'dropped off'   and say 'goodbye'
And 'stay in touch'   each back to some unshared place
Where the seconds hang as tears do   upon the lid of an eye
Some Damocles-drop whose value should be measured
In that it hangs at all   and not in its trembling fall …
Back in his room   he drops his things
And he knows that *they* are done
And he thinks of how poor a part he played   and how her face will grow with age
In another's eyes   with each wrinkle and tear layering their love
Entwining like DNA
And he thinks of the things he said   mainly the things he said
That made her go away …
        But his is less than loss   for this day never was

They just waltzed in waves of info'
               And so is but auras with the blanks filled in
And with no thanks or forgiveness left   she becomes to him a dream
So he thinks up a day   as his way to measure its meaning
And it seems fair to him   to place them there
Out at Spurn Point   the end of the earth   or so it seems ...
So he slow moves about his things   and can feel right then in their divide
All that lived   was cracked   shattered   broken up   and died
And with it comes that *din*   the anti-core to an echo
Till he's petrified and shaken
Some Icarus-thing   except it's the sun that falls from the firmament
Trapped as a bird on the wind   trying to fly ...
He imagines pictures he does now own
And thinks of the warm days they lost
Through the fear   the impassable nuisance of some number theory
Until the gained   the established
Drains into some bleary story.
They picked apart a flower   and decided to settle   on a different petal
And so he fears to yearn a scent   he never once really knew
Or hear her breath   or watch her dream
And be as simple as she could be   and how that would be wonderful
And so concedes to her being spent   in even offerings so slight
And feels her now diminish   as a day does   turning in the light.
A church bell chimes to its clock outside
The street feels it   it hums in the mouth of a tulip   but people don't
Their homes are blitzed-up in sound
It says that night is dawning on day
So he sits by his window   to watch the falling shadows grey things
Before the town rushes back into sight
Like a motherboard flicked-on and warming out   casting a shadow of light
And as the last of the bell hum   slips   slowly away
He remembers he is a Record Keeper and that records must be kept
And shocks himself   by saying aloud   *Okay*
So he unpacks his belongings   all the things he though he needed and didn't
The A to Z   the camera   the pad for notings
And writes things like:

                Atmospheric pressure   *tiny storm*
            Adding clouds to the sky   *Tornado*
    Volcano   *ringing*   *once upon a time*
              Grimsby   *Calamity*
                    30 nots will cripple a small thing
        Wind-tear   *diminish*   *dream*
            Spurn Point   *church bell*   *away*
                    Record Keeper   *Okay*

I extract the pencil from the page
We never did get to share a day.

PAUL KINGSNORTH

Upon the Mathematics of the Falling Away

'If you think I am wandering here, hold your tits or your balls or hold somebody else's. Everything fits here.'

I

Control

'What matters most is how you walk through the fire.'

Four years ago, someone very close to me committed suicide. I don't talk about this much, and I still don't know what I feel about it.

This is not a short story.

This is non-fiction.

I know this makes it harder for you, and I'm sorry about that.

When I got the phone call I was picking chamomile flowers in my back garden. That sounds twee and bucolic, but it was a tiny, urban back garden and the flowers were there when we moved in and I didn't want to waste them. I quite like chamomile tea. I don't know why I'm apologising.

One of the thoughts I had not long after hearing the news was how I could eventually write about this; the thing itself, and all the horrors that had led up to the thing. I knew that one day I was going to have to. I then felt guilty about thinking this, not because I thought it was the wrong thing to be thinking but because I knew I ought to think that it was the wrong thing to be thinking. It was selfish and calculating and slightly psychopathic, and these are all things that nobody ought to be at any time, let alone at a time like this. What could I do? It was just what came into my head.

This is not a short story. I'm sorry.

When your world collapses you tell yourself that you couldn't see it coming, but you could see it coming. You wait for it to 'sink in' but it never 'sinks in' because you are not made of quicksand, you are made of glass. It never sinks in at all, it just glances off and then comes a glimmer of light as the sun goes down and then you just feel guilty forever.

Other people tell you things too. Mostly they tell you that it's not your fault, and them telling you this makes no difference to anything. You know, not so far down, not so well hidden, that it is your fault, will always be your fault, you know this as well as you know anything that is true or is not true. But everyone tells you it anyway because they are trying to be kind and they don't know what they're talking about.

I will tell you the secret thing about suicide. The secret thing about suicide is that it is enticing. People who have lived through the suicides of others or who have seen the consequences or suffered them do not like to hear people say this. Suicide is not glamorous, they say. This is true. Dead bodies are not glamorous. But suicide is still enticing. It is enticing because suicide is protest, suicide is willful disobedience. It pisses in the face of progress and all its wan little children, sucking so desperately at the withered teat of immortality. Suicide is good because suicide is one hard, sharp scream at the meaning of what we pretend to think we are. Chatterton, Plath, Curtis, Cobain: pick a card. Trade it in if the meaning is not quite to your liking. Somebody will speak to you in the end.

Suicide is everywhere in this culture, under every stone, and once you come to be a part of that great, unspeaking clan of people who have been touched by it, you see this. Three years ago, my wife and I had a baby daughter. Before she was born I never noticed babies except when they annoyed me in cafes. Now I see babies everywhere. The streets are full of toddlers, they cascade from the doorways and overflow from the drains. Experience changes you. Nothing else changes you.

Birth is worshipped, death is feared, suicide is held under.

We are the Men of the West.

Suicide has often enticed me. Not in the sense that I have thought about doing it to myself, not really, not often. Only in the sense that a forbidden thing will attract damaged and curious souls more surely than anything else. Why would somebody do this? What would they hope to gain? Why would they not leave a note? Not even a note.

Suicide is everywhere and nowhere. We are coming to it, all of us, in our own time. It circles us like the Wild Hunt, howling for the blood of Men, and we crane our necks to see it pass across the face of the harvest moon. Perhaps it will call to us. Perhaps we will be chosen. Do not choose us. Choose us!

Some suicides are a final, defiant act of control. This was my experience. They say: I control my death, I control how my death is seen, I control the consequences. I do this. Me. Not you. Me. I decide.

You tell yourself that you couldn't see it coming, but you could see it coming. I know what I'm talking about on this one. It never sinks in.

This is not a short story.

II

Ash

'I'm for the true human spirit, wherever it is,
wherever it has been hiding.'

Everybody else in the world has already written about this, but I am going to do it anyway. Something is rising to the surface today.

I was due to fly in to New York on an American Airlines flight from Mexico City on 12th September 2001. I had been in Chiapas for six weeks, living with Zapatistas and learning Spanish and feeling radical and young, and I didn't want to go. But I had never been to the USA before, and it is impossible not to want to. Which citizen of a windswept backwater of Empire does not want to see Rome?

I got up on the morning of 11th September and took to the streets of Mexico City, hunting for breakfast. I am self-absorbed at the best of times, but when I am hungry, I am a black hole.

There was a strange atmosphere, which I mostly ignored.

I found a cafe which opened out into the street. A group of men were gathered around a television fixed high on a wall. A building was burning. Some disaster film. I stopped to watch, but couldn't make out what was going on.

A man turned to me. 'New York' he said, indicating the TV with a nod of his head.

'Oh, right', I replied, noncommittally. What was he telling me that for? I went looking for the menu.

It was days before I got it. When the airline told me that afternoon that my flight was cancelled and they didn't know when there would be another, I thought only of myself. No flights! To New York! What was this, World War Three? What a lot of shitting about for nothing. What an over-reaction.

Possibly it was World War Three, it just didn't feel like it at the time.

When I got to America, I quickly realised that I'd been there before. I spent a month or so in the States, and I felt like that all the time. New York was Annie Hall and Ghostbusters. The Nevada Desert was Close Encounters. San Francisco was Easy Rider and Tales of the City and Escape from Alcatraz. The Utah Flats were High Plains Drifter. LA was hell. I drove along Route 66 (Badlands) and stayed in motels (Psycho) and ate pastrami (The Godfather) and all of it was dulled by knowing what came in the next reel. Steam really did come out of vents in the New York streets (Taxi Driver). I felt like I'd come home, which excited me and made me feel lost and worried.

Twenty-First Century Syndrome: knowing a place so well that you're bored by the time you first visit.

What I remember most about New York was the ash. There was ash every-where, literally everywhere. On the streets, on the tops of mailboxes, on cars, on rooftops. I walked down every street running my fingers through the thick, grey ash that had gathered on the sills of the windows. It glinted like iron pyrites; there was something in it that glinted.

The closer you got to where the World Trade Center had been, the thicker the ash got. I went there and gawped like a ghoul through the steel mesh fences, pretending to stand in silent solidarity, hoping to see bodies. The hell-ish heap of rubble was still on fire. The ash was in the air. The city stank, and was very quiet.

Near the mount of burning stone, in every doorway near to that place and leaning up against lamp posts and tied to windows and in the windshields of cabs and cars were hastily erected boards, hand-drawn posters, notes. On each was written the name of somebody missing. Often there were photos. Have you seen my son? His name is Oscar. He may have lost his memory. He may be injured. Please phone. Please phone.

The ash I had seen before, and the tsunami of fire which had canyoned be-tween the tall buildings, and the collapsing skyscrapers. Independence Day. King Kong. But these agonised denials of reality, these horrible screams into the void, this pain and fear and loneliness, the scrawls and the smiles and the dissolving hope that came with them: this was new. This was original. No scriptwriter had thought of this one, not in any film that I'd seen.

Chess

'Strange thoughts are much like hangovers:
you feel better without them.'

I had never seen anything like Jakarta before. The finely-balanced chaos of a great city in what we have now learned to call the 'developing world' (They are well on their way to becoming Us; there is no need to panic) is something impossible to understand unless you have seen it. It is an untuned instrument that somehow plays a cohesive melody. Who is in charge here? No-one is in charge here. This machine runs on its own energy, its own internal logic. This is anarchy in action. The first time you see anarchy in action you are wary, scared, and then later you are thrilled and then you want to throw it all away and join the circus. But you never can because you do not belong here and you never will, and in any case when you face with honesty the dirt and the squalor of this you want, actually, to fly home and take a bath and feel relieved and then begin to arrange your colourful photos in chronological order.

I was 21. It was the first time I had seen the poverty and desperation and colour and creative electricity of the great slum cities of the poor world. I was a tourist. There was a group of us, and we were staying in a hotel down some grubby backpacker alley which to me seemed impossibly exotic. If I had brought a linen suit I could have pretended to be Graham Greene, but I didn't know what linen suits were when I was 21, and come to that I'd not read any Graham Greene either. I didn't know much when I was 21, which was why I thought I knew everything.

I can't remember the guy's name, but he was in our party and he was one of those posers I take an instant dislike to. He might have had dreadlocks. He certainly wore combat trousers and, despite being about the same age as me, was working hard to exhibit a man-of-the-world insouciance that stirred envy and irritation in me at the same time. This Jeremy had already spent a few months trawling around Asia with various Tabithas and Quentins and was full of stories, most of them probably lies, about his daring adventures.

On our first night in the exotically hot and dirty hostel, this guy disappeared for an hour or so, out onto the street. I thought he was stupid and naive, was

probably being knifed or robbed or angrily stripped by a baying mob, and I
was feeling smug and teachery about this when he turned up again. It seemed
that Jeremy had made friends with a couple of locals in the street and had
been playing chess with them. Chess! In Jakarta! On the street! With locals!
Christ.

What was wrong with this? Everything was wrong with this. I didn't know
why, it just seemed wrong that Jeremy should be so confident, so big, while I
was so small. Making friends with Indonesians in the street! Playing chess
with them! I didn't even know how to play chess. I wouldn't have known
how to speak to an Indonesian. Fuck Jeremy. Why wasn't I more like him?

Jakarta was great back then because Jakarta was a tyranny, and tyrannies
are great for tourists. These were the Suharto years, the dog days of the
waning dictator's grip over this great, sprawling country. The general, who
had seized power in a coup thirty years before, had liquidated so many
communists, tribespeople, opponents, rivals and even family members that
his hold on power, for now, seemed assured. His face looked down from the
wall of every rural police station and city school. He had his spies everywhere,
they said.

The chaos I had seen was chaos because it was permitted to be chaos. You
could play chess with locals in the street under Suharto because Suharto,
unseen, up there, was holding this all together. These 17,000 islands, these 700
languages, these 300 ethnicities, this great bright, impossible archipelago
empire: it hung together, it avoided chaos, collapse, disintegration, because of
the strong hand, because of the weapons my government was selling the
strong hand.

A few years later the dictator fell, brought down by feckless markets and
hungry people. That was when the falling away began for Indonesia; the
breaking apart, the dissolving. It is still going on over there, still working its
way out, like the moves in a chess game. Before the chaos, the calm which is
moulded by the will of the strong seems as if it is simply The Way Things
Are. But the strong are not what they used to be.

I've learned, since then, how to play chess. I play it very badly. When I play
chess I can think I am in the running, I can feel like I have things in hand,
I can be planning ahead, feeling a surge of excitement rising within me –
It could actually happen this time! I could actually win! – and then, suddenly,
from nowhere: bang! Checkmate. How did that happen? Where did that
come from? Afterwards, it's as obvious as daylight. But afterwards is too late.
Afterwards is no bloody use to anyone.

IV

Home

*'You begin saving the world by saving one person at a time;
all else is grandiose romanticism or politics.'*

As I get older, my ambition drains away. I like this, although sometimes it worries me too.

When I was in my early twenties I was desperate to be famous and I had no idea why. These days, knowing more about why, the idea increasingly appalls me. These days my role model is not Hemingway, but Salinger. I will hide from them all. I will be photographed by men in hedges on my way back from doing the shopping. I will be Emily Dickinson. Publishing is for the weak. I will write and write and write and stick the lot, all anyhow, in my desk drawers. They can sort it out when I'm dead. Why would I care? I don't write for them anyway.

I used to long to be on *Newsnight* every week, offering up my Very Important Opinions to the world. This was in my twenties, back when I didn't know anything. Only people who don't know anything want to be noticed for offering up their opinions as if they were facts. I don't know why or when I lost my hunger for this, but now it only occasionally bubbles up to the surface, a pale reminder of what I used to be, like a few strands on the head of a bald man, left to waft in the breeze for old time's sake.

Over time, I did enough of this stuff to realise how little I wanted to do it. I wrote columns for the smart newspapers and the clever magazines, I went onto *PM* and *Today* on Radio 4 to argue about God knows what – I can't even remember, it matters so little. I went on TV a bit too; I even, it pains me to say, sat on the sofa with Richard and Judy. This is absolutely true. Jerry Springer was sitting next to me. It was ... strange.

I did the big book stuff as well, and before I was thirty. Got paid big advances, got flown across the world to speak at book festivals, got extracts from my books run big across the centre pages of mass market papers. I shouldn't complain; I don't complain. I just don't want it anymore, not like that. I don't want to be on TV, I don't want to be fêted, I don't want to worry about where my book is on the Amazon charts. I have stopped believing that I am important. I feel small. It feels like a great freedom, a true release.

I sometimes worry that I have given up, caved in, lost my spark, but actually it's not my spark I've lost, just my vanity. Most of it, anyway. I wonder, as I write this, whether that suicide four years ago sucked it out of me, and I think now that if that isn't true it ought to be, and not just for reasons of narrative closure.

Look: here's how it is, how it seems to me right now. Life is a series of collapses, staggered and staggering. If there is a trick – and we seem to think there always ought to be – then maybe it is simply to remember that collapse is not always bad. Death is not always bad. Suicide: maybe even suicide is not always bad. Or if it is, if it is always irretrievably bad, at least maybe it is not always your fault. Lose something, let go of it as it falls away, and you may gain something else. Or you may not, but at least if you have let go, said your goodbyes, accepted your given load – then maybe you can watch it fall with lighter shoulders.

These days my desire, overpowering sometimes, is for some land. An acre or two, some bean rows. A pasture, broadleaved trees, a view of a river. A small house, my kids running about. Solidity, hard ground beneath me, something there to stop me sinking. Clean air, food, meat, water. Family, Earth, mud, all the small wonders and irritations of life rising up to meet me as I come home. Having a home.

Everything falls away in the end, or sooner. Collapse comes every autumn. Sooner or later your vanity will go, too, and then you will discover where you are in the cycle and that the cycle cannot be halted. Then you will have to lower your shoulders, not raise them, as the rain gets up. You will have to attend to your smallness, then.

Everything falls away in the end. It's not your fault. It's just the way it is. It's fine.

It's all going to be fine.

All quotes are from the varied and various works of the late Charles Bukowski,
who also provided the inspiration for the title.

DOUGALD HINE

Coming to Our (Animal) Senses

a conversation with David Abram

In the opening pages of *The Spell of the Sensuous*, David Abram stands in the night outside his hut in Bali, the stars spread across the sky, mirrored from below in the water of the rice paddies, and countless fireflies dancing in between. This disorientating abundance of wonder is close to what many of his readers have felt on encountering Abram's words and his way of making sense of the world.

Philosopher, ecologist and sleight-of-hand magician: even the barest outline of his work already suggests the webs he spins between worlds, the unexpected patterns of connection that make his books unique. As a college student in the 1970s, he took a year out to travel across Europe as a street magician, ending up in London where he hung out with the radical psychiatrist R. D. Laing, exploring how the magician's craft of playing with the attention might help open connections with people whose levels of distress placed them beyond the reach of clinical practitioners. Later, he travelled to Nepal and Southeast Asia, to study the healing role of traditional magicians; once again, his own craft opened possibilities for conversation where the professional anthropologist would not have been welcome.

From those encounters, he found himself drawn beyond the relationship of magic and medicine into larger questions about the ongoing negotiation between the human and the more-than-human world. This is the landscape he explores in *The Spell of the Sensuous*, which draws together a re-understanding of animism – rejecting the supernatural projections of missionaries and anthropologists – with a distinctive take on the philosophical tradition of phenomenology. If that sounds heavy going, the book is also woven with passages of extraordinary beauty in which Abram relates his own encounters with the wider-than-human world in all its strangeness. And at the heart of it is the deep question of how we became so distanced from our surroundings, so unaware of ourselves as animals in a living world, as to become capable of rationalising the destruction which surrounds us?

Thirteen years passed between the publication of Abram's first book and the arrival of *Becoming Animal: An Earthly Cosmology* (2010). The length of time perhaps reflects the priority he gives to the spoken and the embodied, his refusal to accept the dominance of the written word. (As Anthony McCann, who first introduced me to *The Spell of the Sensuous*, muses, 'Chances are, most of the helpful things that have been thought and spoken throughout our history were never written down, and most of the things that have been written down might not be all that helpful.') When it came, however, the new book was if anything more ambitious.

'A central question was: what if we were to really honour and acknowledge the fact that we are animals?' he explains. 'How would we think, or speak, about even the most ordinary, taken-for-granted aspect of the world, like shadows, or gravity, or houses, or the weather? So much of the language we've inherited is laden with otherworldly assumptions. So many of our patterns of speech, so many of its phrases, so many of the stories embedded in our ways of speaking, hold us in a very cool and aloof relation to the rest of the animate earth that enfolds us. Can we find ways of speaking that call us back into rapport and reciprocity with the other beings, the other shapes and forms of this world?'

We met in Oxford, a strange place for such a conversation; a city which epitomises the heights and the strange coldnesses of 'civilisation'. But from the moment we spot each other across Radcliffe Square, a pocket of warmth and wildness seems to open up. We spend a couple of hours exploring and eating breakfast, before sitting down at last in the gardens of New College, in sight of the old city wall, to film a conversation that would ramble across our mutual fascinations and our desire to make sense of the situation of the world.

What stays with me is the heightened sense of animality which you come away with after spending time with Abram. Later that afternoon, I stepped off the coach in central London and walked down Oxford Street, aware of myself as an animal among other animals, all of us always already reading each other in deep ways which go back thousands of generations.

DH: It's funny that we're sitting where we are, because one of the ways I've talked about Uncivilised writing is as writing which comes from or goes beyond the city limits, which negotiates with the world beyond the human Pale. And in *The Spell of the Sensuous*, you go to meet these traditional sorcerers, to learn about their role within the human community, but you notice how often they live outside or on the edge of human settlements. And it's a stance that recurs in the writers and thinkers who have inspired me – Alan Garner talks about the *mearcstapa*, the boundary-walker, and there is a text in which Ivan Illich calls himself a *zaunreiter*, a hedge-straddler, an old German word for witch.

DA: Ah yes, the *hagazussa* (from whence we get our word 'hag'), which means: she who rides the hedge. The magicians are those who ride the boundary between the human world and the more-than-human world of hawks and spiders and cedar trees, those who tend the boundary between the human community and the wider community in which we're embedded. It seems to me that the human hubbub is always nested within a more-than-human crowd of elementals, a community composed first of the particular geological structures and rocks of our locale. The stones and minerals of each place give rise to certain qualities in the soil, and that soil invites a specific array of plants to seed themselves and take root there. Those shrubs and trees, in turn, provoke particular animals to linger and sometimes settle in that terrain, or at least to feast on their leaves and fruits as they migrate through that landscape. Those animals, plants, and landforms are our real neighbours, the folks with whom we need to be *practicing real* community, if we want to be living well in any place.

DH: One of the things I get from your writing is the sense of the abundance of the natural world. It strikes me that a lot of environmentalism has the opposite quality, that we often describe the world in terms of scarcity. The crises we face are expressed in terms of limits, shortages and scarceness of resources. So how do we make sense of the relationship between the hard walls against which our civilisation is hitting up, and the quality of end-lessness in the world as you invite us to experience it?

DA: It's a puzzle for me, as well. The term 'resource' always befuddles me. If we would simply drop the prefix, "re," whenever we use the term, it would become apparent that we're almost always talking about 'sources', like springs bubbling up from the unseen depths. But when we put that little prefix in front of the word, and speak of things as 'resources', we transform the enigmatic presence of things into a reserve, a stock of materials simply waiting for us to use. When we conceive it as a stock of stuff, then there naturally comes a sense that that stock is limited, and bound to run out.

If I sense the things of this earth not as a resources but as sources, if I feel them as wellsprings bubbling out of the unknown depths, well, this is not to deny that many of those springs seem to be drying up. This is a horrific circumstance that we've gotten ourselves into. But the way beyond this mess has to involve, first, a reconceiving and a re-seeing and sensing of this wild-flowering world as something that cannot ever be fully objectified, a zone of unfoldings that can never be understood within a purely quantitative or measurable frame. This ambiguous biosphere, in its palpable actuality, is not so much a set of quantifiable objects and determinate processes as it is a dynamic tangle of corporeal agencies, of bodies – or beings – that have their own lives independent of ours. To feel this breathing biosphere as something other than an object is to begin to sense that there's something inexhaustibly strange about this world, something uncanny and unfathomable even and especially in its everyday humdrum ordinariness. The way any weed or clump of dirt seems to exceed all of our measurements and our certainties. And it's this resplendence of enigma and otherness, this uncanniness, that we eclipse whenever we speak solely in terms of scarcity and shortage.

DH: When you talk about how this world can never be adequately reduced to the quantitative and the measurable, it strikes me that there is a difficulty for environmentalism since it has become focused on climate change. Because Carbon Dioxide is so inaccessible to our senses, something we can only measure and not experience. So we are trying to train ourselves to a consciousness of something utterly outside of our direct experience.

DA: You point to a genuine problem in the broad environmental movement, one which mimics a tremendous problem within contemporary civilisation: our culture places a primary value on abstractions, on dimensions of the real of which we have no direct visceral or sensorial experience. We are born into a civilisation that straightaway tells us that the world we experience with our unaided senses is not really to be trusted, that the senses are deceptive ...

DH: That *real* reality is this mathematical layer, which you can get at, if you use the right tools to probe beneath the experience of reality.

DA: If we probe beneath the "illusory" appearances. Exactly. So this world that we directly encounter, through its smells and textures and colours, comes to seem an illusory – or at best a secondary – realm, derivative from these more primary dimensions. Like the fascinating but largely abstract dimension of axons and dendrites and neurotransmitters washing across neuronal synapses – all of these hidden occurrences unfolding behind our brows – which many of our colleagues believe is what's *really* going on when we imagine we're experiencing the world: the apparent world that we experience is actually born of processes unfolding within the brain. Meanwhile, other colleagues will insist that what's *really* causing our ways of feeling and tasting and touching are molecular patterns and processes tucked inside the nuclei of our cells; that is to say, our experience is primarily caused and coded for by the nucleotide sequences in our genome, by the way certain strands of DNA are transcribed and translated into the proteins that compose us and catalyse all our behaviours.

Still other comrades of ours, working in laboratories very different from those of the molecular biologists and the neurologists, will insist that what's *really* true about the world is what's happening in the subatomic dimension of mesons and gluons and quarks.

So the world of our direct experience seems always to be explained by these other, ostensibly truer and realer dimensions which are nonetheless hidden behind the scenes, and so our felt encounter with one another and with the ground underfoot, and with the wind gusting past our face, is always marginalised ...

DH: ... and mistrusted.

DA: ... and one can sense, perhaps, that this is the very origin, the secret source of the ecological mayhem and misfortune that has befallen our world. Because it's so hard, even today, to mobilise people to act on behalf of the last dwindling wild river, or the last swath of a great forest that is about to be clear-cut, since people no longer feel any deep affinity with the sensuous, palpable earth. Their allegiance is elsewhere, their fascination is held by these other dimensions, which seem more trustworthy and true than this very ambiguous, difficult, and calamity-prone earth that they share with the other species.

And although many of the experts who speak in this manner – relegating the sensuous world to a kind of secondary or derivative status – are avowed atheists, and although they will rail passionately against the creationists and any others who they think are caught up in a superstitious worldview, this approach that privileges abstract dimensions, whether subatomic or genetic, over the ambiguous world of our direct experience has much in common with old theological notions. It's deeply kindred to the old assumption that the sensuous, earthly world is a sinful, problematic, and derivative realm, fallen away from its truer source – from a heaven hidden beyond all bodily ken, to which the human spirit must aspire.

DH: This reminds me of a conversation that I got into on Twitter last week. Somebody posted: 'All children are born anarchists and atheists.' I sent it on and I said, 'I think they're born anarchists and *animists*.'

DA: Well, there's a lot of evidence that what we call 'animism' – which simply names the intuition that everything is animate, that each thing has its own active agency – that this is a kind of spontaneous experience for the human organism ...

DH: A sort of default state of consciousness?

DA: A default, baseline state for the human creature. It doesn't really seem to be a belief system, but rather a way of speaking in accordance with our spontaneous, animal experience. Since, for all their differences, the various entities I meet – brambles, stormclouds, squirrels, rivers – all seem to be composed of basically the same stuff as myself, well, since I am an experiencing, sensitive creature, so this maple tree must also have its own sensitivities and sensibilities. Doubtless very different from mine (and different even from those of a birch or an oak) but nonetheless this tree seems to have its own agency, its own ability to affect the space around it and the other creatures nearby. And to affect me.

Given the ubiquitous nature of this animistic intuition among the diverse indigenous peoples of this planet – given its commonality among so many exceedingly diverse and divergent cultures – it would seem that this is our birthright as humans. To feel that we are alive within a palpable cosmos that is itself alive through and through. From an indigenous perspective (and even, I would say, from the creaturely perspective of our sensate bodies) there's no getting underneath the felt sense of the world's multiplicitous dynamism to some basically inanimate, inert stratum of matter; rather, to the human animal, matter itself seems to be animate – or self-organising – from the get-go. Such is the most commonplace human experience: in the absence of intervening technologies, we feel ourselves inhabiting a terrain that is shot through with sensitivity and sentience (albeit a sentience curiously different, in many ways, from our own).

DH: And yet to articulate that is immediately to be told that you're projecting: that this is Romantic, sentimental, anthropomorphic nonsense!

DA: The assumption and the knee-jerk objection that comes toward us, over and again, is that such a participatory way of speaking involves merely a projection of human consciousness onto otherwise inanimate, insentient materials or beings. This reaction often seems (at least to me) a kind of wilful blindness and deafness to anything that does not speak in words; a resolute refusal to hear these other voices as anything other than meaningless sounds. Humans alone have meaningful speech; the sounds of birds and humpback whales and crickets (to say nothing of the whoosh of the wind in the willows, or even the night-time hiss of tires rolling along the rain-drenched pavement) cannot possibly carry their own meanings! There is no openness to the likelihood that these other sounds are genuinely expressive, and communicative, although they carry meanings that we humans cannot necessarily interpret or translate. Certainly we cannot know, in any clear way, what these other utterances – of redwing blackbirds, for instance, or of an elk bugling on an autumn evening – are saying. But nonetheless, if we listen with our own animal ears, uncluttered with assumptions, then these other voices do move us as they reverberate through our flesh. And if we listen year after year, watching closely the patterned movements of elk, perhaps apprenticing ourselves to the ways of the herd as it migrates with the seasons, then one day we may find ourselves spontaneously hearing, like an audible glimpse, some new edge of the meaning embodied in that bugling call.

DH: One of the things I become more aware of over time as a speaker is the extent to which language acts as a frequency on which something else is being transmitted. The experience of the audience, or of the other people with whom we're interacting, is as much an experience of something else that passes through words, in the way that music passes through a string on a cello or on a guitar, as it is of the rational, the formal content of language.

DA: Yes, even in this conversation, it's as if the denotative meaning of our words rides on the surface of a much richer, improvisational interchange unfolding between our two animal bodies. There is a rhythm and a tonality and a melody to our speaking, like two birds gradually tuning to one another; via the soundspell of our phrases, and the rise and fall of our singing, our voices affect and inform one another. I suspect that much of the real meaning that arises in any genuine, human dialogue originates in this inchoate layer, far below the dictionary meanings of our words, where our bodies are simply singing with one another.

But also, I was thinking of our brothers and sisters who insist that human consciousness is so profoundly different from anything else we encounter in the surrounding landscape, and that our sense of the life that we meet in a lightning-struck tree or in a lichen-encrusted rock or even a rusting, overgrown bulldozer is entirely just a projection – their insistence that the world be seen from outside, as it were, by a human consciousness that isn't really continuous with the world ...

DH: That echoes the role of God, in a monotheistic cosmology ...

DA: It does, yes, it's a kind of bodiless view from outside the world, one which flattens all of this diverse, multiplicitous otherness into just one kind of presence, the so-called material world, a mass of basically inert or mechanically-determined stuff. But as soon as we allow that things have their own agency, their own interior animation – their own pulse, so to speak – it becomes possible to notice how oddly *different* these various beings are from one another and from ourselves. If I insist that rocks have no life or agency whatsoever, then I can't easily notice or account for the way that a slab of granite affects me very differently than does a sandstone boulder, or the manner in which each influences the space around it in a distinct way. But as soon as I allow that that rock is not entirely inert, then I can begin to feel into the very different style and activity of that sandstone relative to the granite's way of being, or to that of a piece of marble. So this is really a way of beginning to access the irreducible plurality of styles, or velocities, or rhythms of being, of waking up to the manifold otherness that surrounds us, rather than reducing all this multiplicity to one flattened-out thing, 'the environment'.

I can't really feel into, or enter into relationship with, an inert object. I cannot suss out the changing mood of a winter sky if I deny that the sky *has* moods.

DH: It feels like what we're talking about are 'ways of seeing', to use John Berger's phrase – or ways of sensing, since it's not only about the visual. That takes me to something I was thinking about before. It's a painting from 1649 of a man called William Petty, who was Professor of Anatomy here in Oxford, at the ripe age of twenty eight. I've been fascinated by this painting since I stumbled across it in the National Portrait Gallery, years ago. In the painting, he's holding a skull in one hand, and in his other hand is an anatomy textbook open at the drawing of the skull, and from where the hands are it's as if you are watching the scales of the seventeenth-century tipping away from the symbolic and the physical, real skull, towards the new reality – quantitative, measured, anatomised, cut open to reveal its mathematical properties.

DA: Wow.

DH: And what's remarkable is that Petty the anatomist stands between two other phases of Petty's life. Before that, during the Civil War, he had been in Paris with Thomas Hobbes, studying optics. And this is the moment in which, as Illich discusses, you are passing from an earlier optics, in which the gaze is understood as something tactile, a reaching out towards what you are looking at, to a new, lens-based, passive-receptive under-standing, which sees our eyes as cameras in our heads.[2] So that's where Petty was before he was here in Oxford, and afterwards, in the 1650s, he went with Cromwell to Ireland, where he carried out the first econo-metric survey of a country, after the bloody subjugation of Ireland by Cromwell's forces. And so you have, in this one figure, the conjunction of the transition to a new way of seeing; the anatomical cutting open of re-ality to reveal the mathematical new reality, hidden behind the untrust-worthy evidence of our senses; and the foundation of modern economics, which is bounded in the same assumption that the measurable is the real and that the fundamental character of reality is scarcity.

DA: It's amazing to think of that one painting as presenting an image of the hinge between these realities.

DH: Yes. And I suppose where this takes us is back to how on earth we relate these things to the sense of urgency which characterises environmental-ism, and the consciousness of the crises we're facing. Because what I hear people saying is, 'Come on, we've got five years to save the planet. It's hard enough getting people to change their bloody light bulbs, and you want to up-end 350 years of people's worldviews? This is self-indulgence!' So what do we say back?

DA: It's a tough one, because it's trying to speak across such different bodily stances, such different ways of standing in the face of this outrageous event breaking upon us, rolling like a huge wave over the earth. But the idea that we can master this breaking wave, and control it, and figure out how we're going to engineer a way out of this cataclysm, is an extension of the same thinking that has brought us into it.

DH: It presents us with a choice: either we can get control of this reeling system, or we have to give in to despair. To me, what I've been looking for – and what *Dark Mountain* is rooted in – is the search for hope without control. And I know, at the level of my human experience, that it's only when I let go of control that I can find a deep hope, as opposed to a wishful thinking.

DA: Control or despair, it's a false choice. Total certainty or complete hopelessness – they amount to much the same thing, and they're both useless. But also, the insistence that we've got just five years, or we've got twenty years, or two – these are all framed within the mindset of a linear, progressive time that is itself very different from the kind of timing, or rhythm, that the living land itself inhabits. The other animals seem to align themselves within the roundness of time, a curvature that our bodies remain acquainted with, although our thinking minds have become mighty estranged from this cyclical sense of time's roundness. The round dance of the seasons, the large and small cycles of the sun and the moon. Certainly, there's no way through the onrushing instability of climate change and global weirding without at least beginning to recouple our senses into the larger body of the sensuous, without beginning to tune ourselves and our intelligence back into these larger turnings and rhythms, even as the seasonal cycles, in many places, are beginning to shift.

Sensory perception is like a silken thread that binds our separate nervous systems into the wider ecosystem. Perception, beginning to attend to the shifting nuances around us, taking the time to slow down, rather than speeding up to meet the urgency – slowing down to notice what is actually happening in the local terrain, even if it's a buzzing cityscape that we inhabit, noticing whatever weed is breaking up through the pavement at this spot, or on which skyscraper ledge the peregrines are nesting, or why these apples have so much less taste than they did when I was growing up, and what that says about the soils in which these apples are growing, or how they're grown. I won't notice those tastes if I'm motivated only by a frantic sense of urgency and of time running out.

DH: One of the phrases from the manifesto which I've held onto most is when we say, 'The end of the world as we know it is not the end of the world, full stop.' And I'd add to that, that the end of the world as we know it is also the end of a way of knowing the world. Whatever happens, to the extent that we are still going to be here, we're going to live through the end of a lot of the certainties that characterised the ways of knowing the world that have served us for the past few lifetimes. And that's not a utopian goal, that's something that is going to happen whether or not we manage to do anything about climate change.

DA: That's right, and as these very conventional, long-standing ways of know-ing begin to spring leaks – and in many cases the leaks are already turn-ing into floods – this also suggests a replenishment of much older and deeper and more primordial sensibilities that we've cut ourselves off from for many centuries, and in some cases for several millennia.

But how do you approach the shuddering aspect of this turning point that also entails that there will be many, many losses? Not just losses of facile pleasures that we've come to take for granted, but the disappearance or dissolution of whole ecosystems, and the dwindling and vanishing of myriad other species from the lifeworld, other creatures with whom we've sustained a kind of conviviality, throughout the long stretch of our human tenure within this biosphere. We find ourselves living, today, in a world of increasing wounds. In the course of my speaking, hither and yon, I encounter many people who are frightened of their direct, animal experience, who are terrified at the mere thought of trusting their senses, and of stepping into a more full-bodied way of knowing and feeling, be-cause they intuit that a more embodied and sensorial form of awareness would entail waking up to so many grievous losses. People sense that grief and they immediately retreat, they pull back and say 'no, I want to stay more in the abstract.' Or they want to retreat into relation with their smartphone or their iPad, taking refuge in the new technologies with their virtual pleasures. Because they quite rightly sense that there is some grief lurking on the other side of such a corporeal awakening.

What they don't realise is that the grief is just a threshold, a necessary threshold through which each of us needs to step. The first moment of coming to our senses is indeed one of grief. Yet it's as though the parched soil underfoot needs the water of our tears for new life to begin to grow again.

DH: Well, the soil of ourselves needs us to go through that. But one goes through it, into being alive and being present.

DA: It's as if the grief is a gate, and our tears a kind of key, opening a place of wonder that's been locked away. If we step through that gate we find our-selves slowly but with new pleasure being drawn into first one and then another and then a whole host of divergent relationships, each of which nourishes and feeds different aspects of our organism. We abruptly find ourselves in active relation and reciprocity with dragonflies and hooting owls, and with the air flooding in at your nostrils, with streetlamps buzzing as they break down, and with gravity, and beetles. There's a kind of eros that begins to spark up between your body and the other bodies or beings around you.

DH: I think it's about a different relationship to time. Part of the numbness of the way of being in the world which has been orthodox in recent times is the enslavement of the present to the future, which to me is the core of the myth of Progress. So when people attack Dark Mountain for being gloomy and pessimistic, it bemuses me, because to me believing in Progress is absenting yourself from the joy of being alive now. And this is connected to the denial of death that is characteristic of modern culture. Part of the reason we have so much difficulty facing the ecological grief that is part of what it means to be alive right now is because we are terrified of our own deaths. And so much of the activity of our societies is a way of staying busy enough not to pass through the full entry into consciousness of the fact that you are going to die, and that this does not cancel out what makes being alive good.

DA: I think you're right. This great fear and avoidance of our mortality. Not just of our death, however, because there's also a tremendous terror of vulnerability; a real fear of being vulnerable in the present moment. If I'm fully here, where my fingers and my nose and my ears are residing, then I am subject to a world that is much bigger than me, exposed to other beings in it like yourself who can see me and perhaps disdain me. If I acknowledge and affirm my own animal embodiment, then I am vulnerable to the scorn of others, and to all the sorts of breakdowns and diseases and decay to which the body is susceptible. There are so many reasons to take flight from being really bodily here, deeply a part of the same world that we share with the other animals and the plants and the stones. So yes, a fear of being bodily present within a world that's so much bigger than us, a world that has other beings in it that that can eat us, and ultimately *will* eat us. The palpable world, this blooming, buzzing, wild proliferation of shapes and forms that feed upon one another, yes, and yet also jive and dance with one another – this earthly cosmos that our work is trying to coax people into noticing – is not a particularly nice world. It's not a sweet world. It's shot through with shadows and predation and risk – it's fucking dangerous, this place – but it's mighty beautiful, it's shudderingly beautiful precisely *because* it's so shadowed and riven with difficulty.

DH: It's not easy, but it's worth it. Easiness and happiness and convenience are things we seem to have fallen into the habit of believing are worth pursuing. And yet, if we think about our most meaningful relationships, the people we love most closely, even the best of our relationships are not characterised by easiness and they're not characterised by everything being happy ever after. Most of the relationships we will have in our lives are easier than the relationships that will mean most to us.

Notes

1. A spoken remark.
2. Ivan Illich, 'The Scopic Past and the Ethics of the Gaze: A plea for the historical study of ocular perception' (1998) http://www.davidtinapple.com/illich/1998_scopic_past.PDF

VINAY GUPTA

Death and the Human Condition

Lessons from the Kapalika

What new thing can you say about death? Surely it is the oldest topic in the world, examined and reexamined; a daily part of life for our ancestors, now pushed to the edges of our attention, hard up against the skirting boards of society, when not all the way under the rug.

AIDS, among gay men in coastal America, was a holocaust. Every once in a while I will meet somebody who was part of that society, and who did not die; and there's a sadness etched in them from seeing half or more of their friends die, bleached out of reality by a poorly-understood virus. It is bad and bad enough, but then you start looking at Southern Africa. The HIV infection rates in the general population are astonishing: 15 per cent in Zambia, 18 per cent in South Africa, 26 per cent in Swaziland. There's a particularly horrible graph showing life expectancies: a perky upwards slope until AIDS arrives, and then the slope reverses, twice as sharply as it rose, and falls by 20 years in a decade. 45 years was the expected span in 1950, and 45 years is the span in 2010. All the progress in between has been wiped out.

Two score years and five, and a continent of orphans. Protease inhibitors would extend their lives a lot, and are almost available, but too expensive, too little and too late.

Now I want you to stop and think for a moment. Where does this stuff fall in your consciousness as you read it? We run over the dry statistics together, and a picture forms – a picture of horror in poor lands, shanty towns devoid of grandmothers and grandfathers, and all too often parents, and at the bottom of the mental bucket where these images are filed we find some other items: climate, economic collapse, and most important of all, our own deaths. As the topic of conversation creeps closer to our own mortality, the mind becomes increasingly prone to take the blanket which covers our own grave, and stretch it, pulling the cloth thin, but hiding the new issue.

At both ends of life, there is an obscenity we cannot face: our mothers and fathers as sexual beings, creating us in a manner no more enlightened or rational than our own offspring may be – and our own death. The light at either end of the tunnel is completely obscured by our own hands over our eyes, and so we pass between those obscene endpoints, our precious cargo of unknowing, safe and inviolate. This is perhaps not as god intended, but it is a luxury all humans share, unless they have the misfortune of encountering a teacher or an event which wakes them up, tears their eyes open, and hurls them directly into the abyss of knowing. The glassy-eyed stare of a person facing their own impending death is not enlightenment, but it's the step right before it.

They don't tell you these things when you start meditation. In the early days, it's all peace of mind, calmness, dampened instinctive reactions and heightened resistance to trauma and melodrama. You coast gently uphill for the first year or two, learning how to make the time most days to sit, learning about your own instinctive reactions. Eventually Freud and Jung come to visit in turn, as the personal id-ego interface comes up for examination as a series of disturbances in the flow, followed by the superego and his friend, God. The wise meditators kill the Buddha and whoever else they find standing around offering comforting platitudes and continue to sit, searching for some ultimate truth, and if the dedication runs to a decade or so – less for some, more for others – it happens. The third eye or the feedback loop in the cerebellum, or however you want to think of it. Much as a video camera pointed at its own output produces an intense swirl, a vortex of colors, then flat white light, so the mind focussed on itself, the act of perception focused on awareness, dissolves into the union of subject and object, and the feedback loop which produces enlightened awareness.

Here's another thing they don't tell you: life goes on. 'Before Enlightenment, Chop Wood, Carry Water – After Enlightenment, Chop Wood, Carry Water.' That's the saying. Still, something has changed. The blinders are off, the tactful obstructions of consciousness which hide our origins and our ends vanish in a puff of awareness, and while one end of the equation reveals the infinite in a grain of sand, everywhere else you get one-day-I-am-going-to-die. You walk around knowing *life*, feeling, seeing that your body grew inside a woman you know, and hers did too in a continuous stream of Russian dolls going back as far as something that hatched from an egg and then back further, other shells and other relationships, to an invisible and eternal first mystery, the origins of life itself, the First Ancestor from which we are all descended, the replicator at the beginning of biological time, the originator of evolution itself, the molecular Adam.

At the other end, you see clearly how things pass from the world, and it's here that the vital connection is to be made – how our own squeamishness about our own deaths, and the eventual deaths of our children, has closed our minds and our wallets to the actions which would if not save the world, at least keep it for the next generations. You are going to die, but first you are going to live. The clear light at the end of the tunnel is merely the sight of our own creation and end. The Global Dying, the Apocalypse, the great fear of which underlies our environmental helplessness, is a metaphor for one tiny death, your own.

The great mistake of environmentalism was counting backwards from the end of the world, and saying: what if? Couched in terms of the bad thing which will come if we do not change, all effort and energy becomes entangled in what amounts to a spiritual process – to see the end of things clearly enough not to flinch, indeed, to change course early and bring the boat about. Such clear sight is beyond most of those who have dedicated their lives to the pursuit of power, and so even the best of our politicians grasp the issues shallowly, while the voters, as squeamish about the end of the world as they are about their own deaths, remain unmotivated. Had the environmental movement framed its concerns differently on day one, saying instead 'This is wonderful, how may we continue to enjoy it forever?' and drawing on the mythology of heaven on earth, rather than of Apocalypse, perhaps we would have had more traction.

But this is not the cultural decision made, and it is The Moon and not The Sun which rules our environmentalism, much to our limitation.

Back, then, to death.

I am a Kapalika, a bearer of the skull. My life was destroyed when I was a child by the nuclear explosions of my parents madness, and in rebuilding it I opened the doors at both ends of the mind to see clearly my own beginning and my end. Stray yogis are put to work, so I became one whose profession and avocation was to stare at death so hard that death itself flinched, a little, and came back later.

So came a variety of projects based around this work of seeing the beginnings and ends of things, their comings and goings, how they enter and leave the world, and how they spend their stay. This long focus led first to the hexayurt, 'the little hut that could', a free house built on every habitable continent. Then the map, *six ways to die*, whose simple language of 'too hot, too cold, hunger, thirst, illness and injury' lends order to disaster relief coordination. Born out of meditation, these ideas have found a home – among other places – in the Pentagon.

The cold Kingfisher's eye changes as it sees, says Carse.* Who will live forever? You will not die on my watch. I will see.

The bearers of the skull traditionally operated under a simple vow: they could only eat out of a bowl made from the top part of a human skull. It is one way to live intimately with death. There are others, and not living in Nepal, I have my own, but the real question is *what is the social role of one who understands that all this will end?*

It is the same question whether one is an enlightened human living in a culture in which death happens impressionistically every fifteen seconds on the TV screen but far, far off-camera in our real lives, or an environmentalist contemplating the death of this industrial civilization, the end of the mall as the temple of consumerism in which externalized costs can be bought for bargain prices with no accounting for the earth, the future, or the oppressed. To know that you will end, and to know that your culture will end, place one in exactly the same position: staring into the light at the end of the tunnel, knowing that this will end.

So what lesson can we offer you, the Kapalika, the old brethren of the end? The social function of the Kapalika is only to know.

This does not sound so much, only to know, but to live in the awareness of the truth accomplishes dual functions. First, it slowly compels one to act differently, by degrees. Perhaps we say one tonne of carbon each is our real limit and then over ten years try to approach it. Perhaps we say each meal I eat from this bowl is one meal nearer becoming as dead as its donor and then try to live right, whatever that means by our lights. This individual function, to change what we live, to be in accordance with the truth that things end, is the fundamental *satyagraha*.

---

* James P Carse, *Finite and Infinite Games* (New York: Ballantine Books, 1986)

The second function, however, is the one where I want to throw you a bone of hope. The second function of the Kapalika is to strip away the lies about death, the mythology and the avoidance, and to spread hope by a simple fact: The avoidance of the truth of death is worse than death itself. Death cannot be avoided, but its avoidance can be avoided.

Over-consumption and aggression to the planet and other people cannot go on indefinitely, and we will either transform or crash, but the age of the mall-dinosaurs is over and living in the truth strips out the lies. It does so without any bold statement, with no advert in the papers proclaiming that the end is nigh, but with the gentle and gradualist refusal to acknowledge other people's social fictions around consumption. It is the least we can do.

Reincarnation is the fundamental doctrine of the East, present in Hinduism, in Buddhism, and in the background of Taoism. The end of life joins to the beginning, and it's all a single light, death-orgasm-birth, a single psychomortosexual moment, the timelessness which is The Beyond. We live in a culture which has made birth relatively safe, sex less mysterious, and death largely invisible, yet still from all three timeless points, the numinous shines.

So too, there is a strange numinosity around the death of capitalism, the survival challenges we pose the ecosystem, and the green shoots of a new culture which ache to climb the wreckage, and instead find themselves shadowed by dead-while-standing oaks. We sense in it the birth of a new world, not the quiet progression of the new better replacing yesterday's best, but the wracking collapse of everything we have known, and a rebirth, with all the pain and trauma and blood which goes with that sacred mystery.

Things fall apart; the centre cannot hold. In fact, nothing can. To wish for collapse is as foolish as to wish for our own early deaths to see new life. To seek to postpone it may be as rational as eating healthily, or as irrational as a fourth heart transplant. To remain conscious that we seem to be taking a turn much for the worse, and to make sensible preparations, to put our affairs in order, to make a will, and to tell our friends and relatives that we love them, is a sane and sensible way to face the end.

Go to Paris one last time. Enjoy the steak. As you bite off and chew these experiences of the outgoing global order, consuming a little of the death of the world, taste it fully, this life of unbridled excess and borrowing against the accounts of future generations.

It tastes good, regardless of what it means.

And then, one day, in awareness, the bitterness behind the sweetness can be tasted, and we lose all desire to live by the suffering of others, and honest, non-destructive labor becomes enough.

But you will not cheat nature, and we cannot awaken others on our own schedule.

So you live your life in truth, day by day, every meal from the skull bowl, wondering what else there is to learn from it.

EM STRANG

Two poems

The Bonnie Banks of Fordie

Before them there were no other
women, only the wind in their hair
only the wind in their dresses,
and if they cover the ground
with their shade, it's all
for the flowers: loosestrife, iris,
willow-herb.

Three sisters with the river
in their limbs, white arms
like the strong necks of swans,
bare-legged, bootless,
and one of them is singing
into the vortex of tress,
voice like a leaf.

There's no knowing why he comes
only the flash of his coat
on the windy banks and the flash
of his eyes, the white cloth
of his shirt fair torn at the throat,
yellowing, button-less,
collar out of place.

Afterwards, his shirt quite red,
he comes to the third and she shuns him.
The knife like a fish in his hand

and on his shoulders
his long loose hair.
It's when she speaks his name
he remembers

the way the flesh parts
by his own white hand.

The wind lumbers down the bank
like a drunk man or a man
overfull with waking.

The third one takes her brother's knife,
wipes it quite clean. The wind
whistles a song in the river.
The grass is soft and green.

The Miracle

We cross the boundary
carrying the body to where the horses are.
We are bloated with it and the flies test us all,
land on our eyelids like tiny black kisses.

The hearse horse is calm, god bless him,
and we harness up, tie and double knot
until the sky has dimmed
and everybody's hungry.

It's a short ride but the stench is strong
and if the birds had been to eat
we could've saved overselves
the ritual, could've let him lie.

It's at the low copse we notice it:
a strange light coming out of the earth
where the burials are.
It's blue like an ice-hole
or how we might imagine
the inside of the moon.
The horses snort.

Before we realise it,
we've dismounted into the dust.

Someone takes off their hat
and we stand like birds.

The body is up and walking to the light,
arms and legs intact.

if we could speak, words
would climb out of our mouths
and dance all over the trees,
the bushes and horses
and revolving earth.

The Place Looks Back

Next door to our farm on Kootenay Lake, a rich man is building a house. This is happening a lot these days as the baby boomers retire and the price of lake frontage skyrockets. I don't know this man, but I do wonder what he thinks about when he looks out at the pictures his windows make. Sometimes I imagine him as a blind man in a house full of light. The land upon which he has placed his house has been bulldozed, gravelled, levelled, staked, concreted, and underneath, unknown and unseen, the earth is walking, moving, breathing, being born, living and dying, while he sits and stares at a picture he can only understand in a certain way, because he knows almost nothing about it except what it has cost. The land on which he has built his house is land I have walked on since I was five. And now I walk there no longer.

Of course, I am being unfair. I don't know him and I don't know what he sees. Nor do I really know if he is rich. In fact I don't know anything about him, because rural people are no longer neighbours. We pass each other on the road or in our lives, unknown, ungreeted. Once, rural people were neighbours because they depended on each other to survive. Now we live side by side, ignoring each other like people in a too-crowded apartment building, even with a half-mile of space between us.

My father, who was from a different era, a different system and different values, would have gone over and introduced himself. He would probably have annoyed the man by telling him stories, and then he would have ended by charming him. People were charmed by my father because they had never met anyone like him before and probably never would again. My father assumed everyone was his neighbour because he had always survived as a rural pioneer person. For him, neighbours mattered. Who they were and what they thought about things mattered much less than the fact that they were present and available to be neighboured with.

But I'm a writer who imagines things so instead of introducing myself, I imagine the way that this man looks at the pictures his windows make. Perhaps he says to his friends, 'Look at the view,' and they say, 'Isn't it pretty,' and 'Aren't you lucky?' I know some of what I imagine might be true because before he built his enormous summer home, projecting out over the water, he put up a sign naming his place Wood Nymph Trail. His house is on the granite shores of a huge rugged lake. There may be wood nymphs here but it is unlikely. The actual First Nations Ktunaxa story is that there are powerful and ancient spirits here, and certainly the lake itself is a presence, muttering in its deep narrow bed, turbulent, wind driven and cold.

How odd that a view should be worth so much money. The price of lakefront property has risen lately to strange and almost unimaginable heights. Lakeshore in our area is all granite, difficult to build on. Sewage has to be pumped away from the lake. But still people come, crowding in to build anywhere they can see, or even glimpse, the water.

People are buying a view, rather like the way speculators buy gold and diamonds. It's strange that a view should be worth so much money, because it is useless. It is useless other than as a picture, useless other than as a commodity. The world is beautiful, but that term is only human; unlike an ecosystem, or water, or trees or other components of the world, a view means nothing unless it is somehow owned and appreciated by humans. Selling views is like putting the world in a zoo, carving it into pieces, and putting frames around the pieces. The world as art, framed on a wall.

I like views myself, as all humans seem to do. When I was sitting with my daughter this summer on my deck, we stared out at the lake and the clouds rolling by. My father built this house on a cliff; the deck looks out over a pond, green fields, the lake, and the statuesque blue mountains, stoically eternal.

'It's like a very slow movie,' she said. 'It's so entertaining.'

My daughter, who is a landscape architect and a much better gardener than I will ever be – I am a farmer and not a gardener – then told me about the theory that humans want and need to be up high so they can see what and who is coming.

It turns out there is something called prospect-refuge theory; in this theory, humans get 'aesthetic satisfaction' from the 'contemplation of landscape'. According to Jay Appleton, this stems from the 'spontaneous perception of landscape features which, in their shapes, colours, spatial arrangements and other visible attributes, act as sign-stimuli indicative of environmental conditions favourable to survival, whether they really are favourable or not.'

In other words, we like the view because it used to help us survive.

Appleton adds, 'Where he has an unimpeded opportunity to see we can call it a prospect. Where he has an opportunity to hide, a refuge ... [To this] aesthetic hypothesis we can apply the name prospect-refuge theory.'

This doesn't explain why we want so desperately to stare at water. There's also a theory that humans were once cliff dwellers; another that we were shore living inhabitants. Perhaps if we can combine cliff dwelling with water viewing, so that we can be sun-basking cliff dwellers, we get a situation that satisfies some deep biological urge. And then if we can capture this behind glass so we don't actually have to deal with anything, so that we're safe and the prospect before us is only a prospect, then we can relax. The view is no longer about survival but only about aesthetics. A view becomes yet another avenue to satisfy the drive to commodify everything; once it is only a view, it can be sold off to an 'owner'.

But of course the person behind the glass doesn't have a relationship with what he or she is looking at; they only have a view, a concept stripped of challenge, danger, interest, and the possibility of coming to know the other beings who are in this place with you, as well as the possibility of them knowing you.

*

For many years, I have had people come to the farm, look around in wonder, and pronounce it beautiful. After that, they often tell me how lucky I am. And although I smile and nod and agree with them, I am never quite sure that we really understand each other.

Because, after that, we usually go for a walk, and they are also, I find out, afraid, variously, of mosquitoes, wasps, (or bugs in general), bears, cougars, spiders, lightning ... there's always something. They look at the garden, the fruit trees, the fields and the animals with interest but little comprehension, and then we go inside for tea.

I don't want to disparage these people; they are wonderful, caring friends and they mean well. But we sit on either side of a cultural divide that, for me, keeps getting wider and more unbridgeable.

Lately I have been getting a plethora of thirty-something visitors, usually through an international programme called WWOOF (Willing Workers on Organic Farms), who pronounce themselves interested in gardening or organic food or herbs or whatever fad is current. One of these young men asked me the other day if there were whales in the lake. Nope, I said, with some amused despair, didn't think so, never seen any.

What are they seeing, all these varied people and what do they think they are doing here? I have decided, after long experience and some thought, that perhaps what they are seeing must most closely resemble a photograph, and what they are doing is living, temporarily, within that photo. Or perhaps sometimes it's a painting. It doesn't matter. This still doesn't explain the vagueness of the term, beautiful, or why they seem to think they are complimenting me, as well as the place, by saying it. To some extent, it is because of the quality John Berger terms 'glamour'. Glamour, he says, can't exist without envy. Since I, in some mysterious way, now 'own' this expensive view, it is somehow a compliment to me and gives me glamour, that I live in such a beautiful place, that I am so 'lucky'. And, yes, of course, I understand the edge of envy in their voices.

But there our communication tends to stop because although I hear what they are saying, I don't think this way about the farm, nor are our experiences parallel. After all, most of what they know about nature and about 'land' (the word always intoned, somehow) comes from pictures, from movies, or from art – and most of what I know comes from experience. So there is a great gap between their and my understanding of what I am doing here.

That's an understatement. Sometimes I feel like I stand on the other side of a vast canyon, yelling gibberish to people on the other side. To me, their experience seems one-sided and consumptive, whereas my experience is inherently interactive: I engage with plants and animals every day, and I also try, through constant observation and learning and thinking, to understand how I can best live here.

I don't want to be too hard or judgemental of my visitors, who are my friends and often even family. And really, how can my well-meant and caring visitors tell the difference between being here and being in a picture? After all, their experience of nature is that it is something 'outside', outside of the city, outside the house, outside of their experience, and outside of their world. The non-human world, to most people these days, is something one looks at, briefly, or takes a picture of to take home, or uses as a pretty toy, like the summer people who come for two weeks every years, drive around and around in circles in their boats or Seadoos, and leave again.

All of these people, when asked, are sure that they love nature and I am sure they do as well. They love animals, they value peace and quiet, they love the fresh food from the garden, they love the beauty of the farm, they are glad to get out of the city for a while, however briefly, and they are happy to have the experience of being here with me. But it's all about how it makes them feel. I don't denigrate their experience and I believe them when they say they love it here. What I don't understand is what they think they love.

No, that's not true.

When I was a child, living where I still live, I was endlessly swept up, transported and thrilled by the beauty of this place. I tried, as a child, to think how to respond because such beauty seemed to call for a response. I began painting and drawing at an early age; I wanted to capture what I was seeing with paint and canvas but eventually, I realized this was impossible and I stopped painting.

So then I just walked around, looked at it, listened to it, smelled, watched it; I still do.

But when I look out from the deck of my house, these days, what I often see, despite my almost 60 years here, is how little I know or understand. I have come to see that this is not a picture and that 'being' here is an experience of being within an endless number of profound and complex relationships. What I feel is the depth of my own not-knowing, the limit of my ability to get outside of my humanness and begin to understand who or what is looking back at me. Since I have to find my own way to this relationship, I am the confused one, the lost one, the one still learning how to behave.

Although I have both information and experience and am always on the hunt for more, I feel I am just beginning. True, I was seduced into the relationship by beauty. But that's the beginning of understanding, not an end. I also worked on the farm from a very young age, and understood from listening to my parents that my work was necessary to our very survival as family. Or as my father put it, when I complained, "You work or you starve." And in doing the work, I also learned to love it.

Recently I was talking with my friend Evelyn about all this. She lives on a different lake from me, but one where I have spent a lot of time. We were talking about art and its power to communicate. She began telling me about an artist who had spent a week in a cage with a coyote. Why he did this and what he was hoping to communicate is beyond me. I can imagine it and I suppose, if I was really interested, I could look it up. But what amazed me is that someone would do such a stupid thing to an animal. A coyote knows nothing about cages or art because she doesn't care. Why should she? They are meaningless in the coyote's terms. What amazed me is the utter effrontery and rudeness of the artist thinking he could use an animal in that way and have it mean anything to anyone.

My sister is a horse trainer and whenever she is around, we talk about horses, animals we have lived with and loved and danced with and ridden and smooched with all our lives. They're still a mystery to both of us. She knows a lot more than me. Of course, I'm a rank amateur compared to her and now I don't even ride anymore because I have arthritis too badly to even get on a horse. Mostly I like to have them around to look at and play with. Horse people can talk about horses forever and never get tired of the stories or the mystery or the power of being with them.

Sometime I talk to people about horses, because most people are afraid of them. I was, when I was a child, because they were big and powerful and even though I rode all the time, no one ever explained to me how to do it well and how to communicate with my horse. But my sister has been riding for fifty years as well, and all along she has been learning from her horses. She loves her horses but, as she says, she's not nice to them. She's the lead mare and in charge, and when she's around, even I can see that the horses are relieved and glad that she knows what she's doing and they are part of her herd. But they teach her as well, all the time.

I'm not particularly nice to my dogs either. They're working dogs and have jobs to do and that makes both them and me happy. I get to be the pack leader of the dogs because I have the house and the food. It's a useful and ancient agreement and they and I both honour it.

What they and I like best is walking around. My dogs are collies, an extremely moralistic breed. They believe in walks. In the afternoons, if I haven't shown any signs of moving, they start, very determinedly, figuring out how to herd me out the door.

I am never quite sure what it is about walks that is so important but they satisfy something in both of us; they know their territory intimately by smell and sound and touch and taste and I know it somewhat more dimly, by looking around and listening. As Gary Snyder says, "Walking is the great adventure, the first meditation, a practice of heartiness and soul primary to humankind. Walking is the exact balance of spirit and humility."

After our walk, after chores are done and the farm has settled to sleep, they settle in on the rug in the evening for a snooze; we snooze together, in our dog-smelling warm den.

My relationship with the other domesticated inhabitants of this place is fairly peaceful and at least some parts of it make sense, but I want this clarity with our less-seen neighbours. Now, when I go walking, it is often more like wandering, stopping, starting, staring, listening. This kind of walking is one way of greeting the non-human beings where they and I live.

One of the moments I loved most as a child was the passage from the open fields into the trees, and the moments when I would stand inside the tree line, listening to my passage being announced, squirrel by squirrel and raven by raven. I was very young when I figured out that the forest was watching and listening, and that inside the forest, I never felt alone, I felt at home.

The human supposition that we are in some way superior to animals – can use them, impose our metaphors, ideas, experiments, emotions on them – is deeply entrenched among our assumptions. But it is a cultural assumption, not a scientific one. It makes just as much sense to assume that animals and plants are, in their own way, as 'intelligent' as I am, even if communication is a problem.

Our notion of human superiority is a supposition based, in part, on the fact that since we can't speak to animals, they must be stupid. They don't understand us. The same supposition was used by colonisers all over the world. It's a similar supposition to that of those religious people who assume without ever being able to prove it that not only do they know what God looks like, they know what and how He thinks. But I have a suspicion that animals understand us much better than we understand them.

I laugh at myself every time the bear comes to eat 'my' apples. But I still get mad. There's undoubtedly a bit of frustration on both sides. The bear needs those apples, needs the fruit on the trees, needs what he sees as necessary to his survival. How can a bear tell that the wild apple tree down the road, also covered with apples, is any different than this one in my yard? On my part, I want to have some way to tell the bear not to smash the tree down, which to him is the easiest way to get at the apples, and to leave some for me. We're still working it out.

I have spent most of my life in far greater contact with animals than with humans. This summer, I had a lot of young French Canadian visitors. At first they thought the swallow nests above the deck were kind of cute, until they realized there were several wasp nests up there as well. I pontificated on the fact that wasps have a keen sense of smell and a keen sense of neighbourliness as well and would get to know them. They didn't believe me, but since it was my house, they couldn't do much about it. And after a while, they got used to sitting on the deck under a bunch of wasp nests, even if it made them uneasy, not only because of the wasps but at the manifest craziness of their hostess, who made them sit there.

In fact, the chair on the deck in which I sat every morning to drink my coffee also had a wasp nest underneath it. I didn't really notice until my son sat in the same chair. He was indignant and hosed the chair down until all the wasps went away. Then the wasps were probably somewhat indignant, as well, or at least I was on their behalf. But they appeared to accept it as some kind of natural disaster, dried themselves off and went away and when my son was gone, they rebuilt the nest in the chair and we went on having coffee together.

Later this summer, I went on a brief retreat by myself to a camp on a peninsula in the lake. I broke the rules and brought in a can of salmon to this vegetarian camp. The wasps went a bit mad. "Salmon," I could imagine them thinking. "Hey, this stuff is amazing, way better than broccoli."

I sat on a stump and ate my sandwich while they swarmed me in numbers that got a little overwhelming. I laid my plate down for them covered in bits of salmon and juice and they literally licked it clean. But even while I was eating and being swarmed by wasps, I felt no sense of fear. No wasp fixed me with a beady eye and demanded that I share. Instead, they were amazingly polite and hopeful, wanting a share but hesitating, watching me devour this giant sandwich and never interfering except to buzz by my head in constant breathing desire for food.

I walk through this world as both prey and predator. Mostly predator. Chris Irwin, the great horse trainer, says that horses know immediately when you enter their field that you are predator, they are prey and so of course they also know your intentions. If you turn your body and eyes towards them, their immediate instinct is to run. Since most people come into a field to catch horses, the horses' instinct is, obviously correct. But if, in all politeness, you turn your hips and your eyes away from them, they can relax. They're not being attacked. Such small communication allows a bond of understanding to begin, but only begin. I practiced such politeness walking by the wild ducks

that settled in our pond this spring. Turn my eyes down, no staring, don't stop
or point. No predator behaviour. The ducks watched me, and then relaxed
and sailed around the pond unconcerned.

The place looks back. The place has thousands of eyes. The place has morality, courage, a culture, all within a pattern that lives and breathes and dies and
is born and within which I make my own interruption, and my own breathing space. I watch the plants that grow along the road, another interruption,
a clear space within a crowded pattern, how each finds its space in the light so
that although there is crowding, there is lushness; the thimbleberries produce
and produce, the blackcaps twine their way around and through and underneath, the baby maples are putting their feet down, getting ready to make
their own way.

*

And so, yes, the farm is beautiful and I appreciate it. When people get out of
their cars in my yard in the summer, they look out across a grassy windblown
pasture to the blue bulk of Steeple Mountain, and a line of Selkirk Mountain
peaks marching north. There are flowers and birds. It is all lovely. In the
summer mornings, unless it is pouring rain or too thick with mosquitoes, I
take my coffee outside to the deck. I sit and stare out over the glowing green
fields; besides the wasps, there are usually a few mosquitoes, and hundreds of
swallows. At that moment, I am always conscious – I remind myself to be
conscious – that I am here, that this is beautiful, that I am unbelievably privileged and fortunate, and that I love being here. Those are fine reminders
with which I have no quarrel. But I do quarrel with the idea that this is something I could ever, in any way, 'own'.

On the other hand, I used to live in the old house across the yard that my
mother hated because it had no view, and that I loved because it was old and
dusty and full of ghosts, and in the mornings, there, I would sit in my flower
filled, bird-singing small porch at the front of the house, with no view at all,
and feel just as lucky.

John Berger, in *Ways of Seeing*, says two things which I always try to keep
in mind: first, that how we see things is "affected by what we know or believe." And secondly, that the relationship between what we know and what
we see is never settled.

This gives me some hope that the man in his glassed-in house to the north of me might look out of his windows and learn something, might come out of his door one day and notice the ospreys whistling above him and say hello. I can, at least, hope for this.

For my own part, I may still be walking through this landscape I know so well somewhat blind and deaf, but I have, I think, over the years, at least developed better manners. I am always learning; I pay attention; I say hello. Each day I try to walk myself a little deeper into the reality of this living, breathing place, of which I am a small and sometimes lonely participant, somewhat aware, at last, of seeing, and of being seen.

JAY GRIFFITHS

A Love Letter from
a Stray Moon

I

Exiled from Casa Azul

I have always wanted wings. To fly where I belong, to become who I am, to speak my truths winged and moon-swayed.

When I was a small girl, I rehearsed my flight. I dreamt of flying. I jumped off walls and flew, but only down. I wanted to fly up; I needed wings. My hope was winged but it wasn't enough. I jumped when I walked and I photographed myself just by blinking, catching the bright flight of the moment, airborne, between each blink. My friends said that I was graceful, that I made little leaps as I walked, so I floated like a bird;, but they also teased me terribly, my friends, and cut me out of their games because polio had damaged my leg, and they called me peg-leg. I learned to swear and practised on them as much as I could, telling them they were *hijos de puta* and I was going to the fucking moon.

One evening, the moon rising, I was out playing in the courtyard and my father called me in, his eyes intense, brimming with the pleasure he knew he was about to give me. My mother hugged me and set me on the floor in front of her.

'My little angel,' she said, and gave me a wrapped box to open. Never patient, I ripped off the packaging and there inside was a white dress with wings like an angel. I gasped with delight – they knew, *they knew!* It was as if they had looked into my heart and seen what I longed for. I tore off my clothes, flung them into the corner and put on the dress, the wings white and perfect at my shoulders. In the soaring moment, with all the transfixed delight which a child can feel, my spirit as fluent as the Rio Grande and my arms unfurled like an eagle's wings, I ran to the courtyard, knowing that I would fly, so I jumped for the moon. And fell to earth, horribly.

I was shattered and broken-hearted, and I sobbed while my parents laughed kindly, 'Oh, Frida, Frida, of course they are not real wings – how could they be real?' How could they not be real? I thought, because flight is real and hope is real and magic is real, and I cried furiously. These were more real to me than anything, and I had no wish for substitutes. They ask for flight, kids do, they ask for flight and only get straw wings. I could not fly and it felt as if there were ribbons from my skirts which were nailed into the ground. I could not fly but I had to.

My first memory was of the idea of the moon. Our schoolteacher was weird, with a wig and strange clothes, and she was standing in a darkened classroom while we were hushed with surprise as her face was lit from underneath by a candle she was holding. It jagged her features and jangled her face to a skull, like children on the Mexican Day of the Dead turning themselves into spookies by shining torches up under their chins. In her other hand, she held an orange and she told us that the sun (the candle) lit the earth (the orange) and the moon, but she didn't have three hands and the moon was pure idea, an exile present only in its name. (Present in my mind, though, full and shining.) This was the widening universe, so overwhelming that I pissed myself. The teachers made me take off my wet dress and put on some clothes from another girl and I hated that kid from then on. That night I stared unblinking at the moon until my eyes were watering and I knew I would fly there one day.

Before I flew to the moon, though, I dragged that girl across the road and started strangling her and to this day I remember her tongue writhing out of her mouth. The baker came by and yanked me away from her, but I didn't care because I knew I would fly to the moon and she wouldn't.

I recovered from polio, and I grew fierce, boxing, playing football and swimming;, and I remember those days of skates, bicycles and boats as if it was a girl's boyhood, those days when I was as sleek and disobedient as an otter, tempestuously playful and revelling in it. I was sent to catechism class with my sister and we escaped and went to an orchard to eat quinces. I will never forget how sweet was the fruit of our disobedience in that orchard.

I scampered quicksilver through my childhood, out to being a naughty teenager when everything tasted of wine, melons and chilli. I wore a peaked cap and men's suits so they tutted, the neighbours, *who does she think she is?* I scorned them – I scorned all those who scorned me – and I took a cigarette lighter and darted towards the hems of their shawls till they squawked and flapped my hands away. (And the trompetilla sniggered to the cactus.) In my gang at college we played havoc, in all the keys of chaos. Cleverer, quicker, droller and better read than most of the teachers, we exploded with anarchy and mischief. We got hold of a donkey, one day, and rode it through the college, falling about laughing at the stale-faces who tried to tell us off. We caught a stray dog and tied it up with fireworks, and lit them so the dog shot off dementedly around the corridors. Poor dog, I thought later. At the time, I was drunk, giggling like a skellington in wellingtons, flowers sprouting from my skull. What flower? Ix-canan, in its Mayan name, the guardian of the forest, which they also call the firecracker bush.

I was fifteen and I carried a world in my satchel: books, quotes, notebooks, butterflies, drawings and flowers. I cut my hair like a boy, wore overalls, and my eyes shone with devilry and love. The stale-faces called me irreverent. Absolutely not, I snapped, I revere Walt Whitman, Gide, Cocteau and Eliot, Marx, Hegel and Engels, Pushkin, Gogol and Tolstoy. We were terrible show-offs: 'Alejandro, lend me your Spengler, I don't have anything to read on the bus!', I cried to my clandestine lover. We went busking, playing the violin in the Loreto Garden, listening to the organ-grinders and skating at dawn. In imagination, we climbed the Himalayas, rowed down the Amazon and sauntered across Russia. I read the imaginary biography of the painter Paolo Uccello and adored it so much that I learned it off by heart.

We curled up in libraries eating sherbet, we flirted and argued and set fire to everything which offended our souls. That was how Diego Rivera first heard of me. 'Arm yourself to deal with these kids,' he was told by the other painters. He laughed, incredulous, as they told him what had happened to them. The other muralists had come and painted garbage on our walls; they built a scaffold to overreach themselves and underneath them were wood shavings, paper, bits of oily rags, so we'd set them on fire, obviously. The paintings would be ruined;, the painters so pissed off that they took to wearing pistols.

*

I never needed to trace my roots; I could feel them, inside me, my fallopian tubes were grinning like tendrils of vines, my veins as tough as lianas while my legs grew from the earth, twining up into my body, and my fingers were leaves asking questions of the world of spring, those fingers which would one day find his. My heart turned, heliotrope to the sun, wherever sun was. *El ojo verde,* the green eye, all the Amazon was winking within my eyes, and my mouth was full of *Das Kapital* and poetry. Oh, and the faun, I forgot to say, was my friend. I suckled from the breast of Mexico, before gringos, before Columbus, the milk of the Olmec and the Aztec; my blood is the sap of Mexican plants and my mind is metamorphosing from caterpillar to butterfly, symbol of the psyche.

I was drunk on life, drunk on night which was wicked with scent, night which lay across my body like Othello's heavy love over Desdemona's sleeping, breathing, dying body. I sucked all the scent from the orange blossom, and the datura gave itself to me. I could smell everything; I could smell thoughts and words and colours, vanilla days, vermilion nights. Believe me, I could smell the very sky – *with my teeth.*

I grew up in rays of love from the sun, my father. I lived in the sky (why not?) for my father's house was Casa Azul, the blue house, the house of sky. In those days there was enough sky for everything to fly, and I was always the first to jump. *Eh, muchachos, saltar!* My father's town was called the 'father of springtime' and, as he was the father of my springtime, I was sprung. Those were the days when everything could fly. The curled leaf in spring is sprung in its flight to sunlight, and kittens, cantering up gardens, dew drops from long grass all over their noses and paws, felt their kitten-hearts bursting with sun and life because they knew they could fly. To me, all words were winged and all flight was minded and, since I lived in overflow, I overflew. In those days, I understood Icarus, daring, defiant darling, and maybe like him I flew too high, but the Inca doves cooed me, the crested caracara called and I was caught in a cascade of parrots, a whirring of hummingbirds, whose hearts could beat, like mine, over a thousand times per minute.

And, in one hummingbird heartbeat, it was all over.

I was eighteen. Just a day; the sun rose, the earth turned, but something terrible happened. Did the earth turn too fast, or did I?

Alejandro and I were on a bus. 'Dammit,' I said, 'I forgot my parasol. I must've left it somewhere, let's get off.' We did, and leapt on another bus; that was the reason I was on the bus which destroyed me. I was searching for a *para-sol,* something to shade me from the sun. What on earth was I doing searching for a parasol? If only I knew the truths of my own metaphors; I am the moon, and the entire earth is my parasol, protecting me from the sun's rays.

A tiny ex-voto painting, a good-luck charm of the Virgin, swayed by the driver's head till Our Mother was dizzy. It was raining a little outside, and the bus was packed but Alejandro and I managed to find seats at the back. I sat with my hand running dangerously close to his balls, and he was wincing between acute pleasure and acute embarrassment, as several old ladies turned to stare, not quite believing that I was tickling his chestnuts on the bus, and I was starting to giggle at the outraged expressions of the *señoras*.

We were approaching a marketplace which was teeming, even in the rain, and there was a painter on the bus, carrying a packet of gold powder, while a tired child was nudging his nose into the sleeve of one of the cross old ladies, and not one of us knew that this was the moment of scissors, which would cut our lives in two. The route of our bus crossed the tramlines, and a tram – a trolley car – was bearing down on us, as if neither could brake, as if it were all in slow motion, as if it were as inevitable, ineluctable as *La Destina*. *La Destina* held the scissors: one scissor blade the tramlines, one scissor blade the route of the bus.

The bus withstood the impact for a long engulfed moment and then cracked apart, shattering into a thousand pieces, and the handrail broke and speared through my body, piercing my pelvis, and my clothes were torn off me and the painter's gold spilled all over me so I lay like a still life, or an icon, half- dead, half-alive. White skin, red blood and covered with gold, I half-heard someone sob 'look at the dancer,' thinking that I must have just come from a performance, and that the gold was part of my role. A dancer. Never to be that. My Golden Age was over.

The accident was like a hammer breaking my spine, a chisel carving my life to the bone. The steel handrail which entered my stomach came out through my vagina and my screams were louder than the siren of the ambulance.

All of my afterlife referred always to that now, that moment then. Then, when with a shriek, twisted metal and hips, a torture of pulleys and a pool of blood, I was flung away from all I knew and all I had been. The ferocious wrench, the shattering of me. I was flung into the darkness of outer space, injured, lonely, and part of me died – I became the strange and limping moon you see every night. Before, I had been part of earth, as young as life itself and I had known dance and freedom. After, I was unearthed, old as death, and caged in days.

I was taken to hospital, and for long weeks the doctors did not know if I would live. My mind became stale with pain and I could smell no word, no sky, only the horrible hospital opposites of disinfectant and putrefaction. All the green *riqueza* of language in the body was cut down to the dull semaphore of pain while the vultures pecked my liver. If I could never be a dancer, death took on the role, death the dancer curtseying to me all my life as I lived dying. If I was going to fly, from now on it would have to be metaphoric.

Some time after the accident, as I was still in bed, sick and feverish, with paintbrushes in my hand, I suddenly saw in their delicate, feathered tips the tangent of my flight. My soul could fly with each brushstroke and my paintings could make visible all the universes which my soul held within it.

This was the beginning of my age of loneliness, my Age of Silver. Alejandro left me and my exile was extraordinary, my warm soul caged in a cold bedstead across a deserted sky. I paint in blood and silver, in love and exile. For love is my nature and I am red at heart, but my exile is silver. That is my contradiction and the source of my sorrow, the anguish of the Age of Silver, fallen from the Age of Gold.

I was the first exile of the solar system – a slip of earth, hurled into the sky, flung out alone, too young, too far, too dark. I have recurring nightmares of being cast into space once more, entirely alone, my ears ringing with the white noise of galaxies far beyond any hearing. A strange birth it was. The birth of exile, the death of home. The death of mothering and the birth of a stricken art.

11

The moon's instructions for loss

I was born by revolution. According to the register of births, I was born in 1907 but, according to the register of significance, I was the daughter of the Mexican revolution, born in 1910 at the end of dictatorship and the beginning of the peasant revolutions of Zapata.

In the earliest aeons, before she became solid, the earth was a ball of strange gases, and I imagine her like this: if you whistled to the Northern Lights they would swim together, circling in space like a shoal of colours, heat-wraiths stretching, suggesting, dancing backwards, some losing their contact and disappearing, a phantasmic flicker of possibility evaporating into blackness.

And the moon? In the revolution of the earth's turning – and I am a revolutionary – a shard of earth was flung off, coalescing, reforming further and later, far off as the moon. But shard is the wrong word, too hard and substantial; so immaterial was this moment, so unearthly the earth, so unanchored the moon, what word would be better? The moon was more like Idea, more like Metaphor, or Time, Flight or Potential or Longing. A highly strung intensity of latency.

The moon, shining on the Lacandon jungle and Mexico City, on Havana and Madrid, Buenos Aires, Santiago, Montevideo and New York, is wearing a ski-mask and is rolling a cigarette with tobacco she nicked from the subcomandante while she writes a communiqué to earth. 'Instructions for Loss,' it begins. There are many kinds of revolutions and many of these are invisible: when loss has razed the psyche and despair seems to have massacred the spirit, insurgents of hope sometimes arm themselves in the jungles of the heart.

Picasso famously said: 'I do not seek, I find.' What about those whose distinctions are not between seeking and finding but between losing and being lost? Not caught between Picasso's optimism of seeking and success of finding, but stuck terribly between unfinding and breakage?

Instructions for loss: if If you lose something you can find it fractally – and indeed you must find it like this. In order to avoid bitterness, you must find what you lost a thousand times over, in other faces in the moon, other disguises, under other ski-masks, other mountains, not in fractured crystal but in the perfect refraction of a rainbow and the reflection of mirrors, seeing you in myself, myself in you. It is, as it were, a Zapatismo of the human heart, an intuition of plurality which is a salvation, an aesthetic and a rebellion.

PAUL KINGSNORTH

Two poems

Stalker

death will cling to me like frost like the bracken
tick to the skin in high summer I will not smell it
but it will walk with me no love will dissolve it
they will go stonelike will spring back one of them is coming
one of the killers get beneath the rocks behind the thorns
get under the hedges be still do you smell it
one of them is coming he brings the shadow press your body
flat in the hollow press your ears to your back still your wings pray
that he passes

Then we will go to Europe

Then we will go to Europe, go
to Venice or Berlin, and live like Rilke
in communes of verse and there,
maybe there, we will shake off this disease

which dulls our senses and dulls everything
and spreads like aluminium
and clings like a plastic bag in a high branch,
like crude to a gannet's feathers. Or

if not in the cities then in the forests
or in red caves in red deserts
or around the craters of gunungs in the archipelago
or among sandstone towers in the valleys of the West.
Oh —

I don't know. Just take me
somewhere it has not yet reached, somewhere
lonely and still real and let me
stand there and feel nothing
and lose the fear and, finally,
breathe.

A N D R E A   D U L B E R G E R

Parallel Lives

She was an untrained historian
of this instantly messaged moment.
Unblogged by others and not blogging
her own days, she tried to save
her words for what she really
wanted to say   *... The animals are leaving!...*
                    ... hello! Are you free?...
                         ... What does this mean?...

She imagined a Neanderthal
curled up asleep one night in the cave
way back in the days when blood
was the measure of transaction.
An animal life taken in exchange
for more human time. Maybe a
drawing on the wall to celebrate and
sex after dinner, dreams of a substance
like wine? (Felt as an absence
in daily living? A space for some thing
just beyond the tip of the tongue?)

                    Often, she read and wished for space
for the herds of disappearing creatures,
a second earth where the beauty
and bloodletting could continue.
Safe from the evolution
of gadgets, the second earth
would stay.

                    But, hey—
fantasizing about what isn't
there brings heartache, she would
remind herself.

                         Too much pain and
she was the modern single woman's
equivalent of the half-eaten animal:
new messages and news reports pecking
at the sore spots, leaving a gaping place.
So try again, she begged herself and set off.

          What would keep beauty safe amidst the
     unraveling?   Herds of human wanderers
          pouring down on the streets after days
     of rain,   needing free breathing and
          escape from indoor only space   they bask in sun.
     Pockets of the city are jingling
          with its change.

She set off with little tricks
to see her through her days.
Such as the cave-woman she
brought back to life sometimes,
a reverse-forward with her self
as the container for this mental
movie game. How much recognition,
how much a gap of the strange?

          The shaped modern landscape a river of fluxing,
     recycling particles like a million small mouths

killing dinner all at once. Land, food,
objects, and bodies. A life unafraid of other animals,
   barely glimpsed unless on a kitchen floor or a
square moving screen. Space for more than power and
   exchange: a shock in the cave-woman's
body at the endless streams of knowing, idea upon idea,
   detail by detail, the world a flood of worlds
written deep with language, so star-like and dizzying it
   left one almost afraid ...

She sighed and imagined a life
where all the knowings
were here to know each other,
where the living knew their food, the food
knew the land, the land knew the actions
falling down and then up like rain to ocean
to sky ... an earthfull of birth and death
riding its wheel
without knowing why ...

   Who had time to think about it?
time was water   was dollar   was
   migrating each day   through screens
of words and pictures   multiplying like
   a fast-forward of generations   the weather
growing mystery   and she,   she was just an animal
   in a Talking Heads song   looking for home
looking for the Age of Kindness and Loving
   in the exodus of city breathers
downtown doing errands and leisurely
   browsing,   while the disappearances kept ...

What else were we here for?, she
wanted to cry besides knowing
the treeslandanimalswater down to the letters
in their genes – how to get beyond
watching the knowing point at this
earth like a telescope watching
worlds wink out, seeing
creatures without language to transmit
the struggle for their lives.

 pancakeicefrazilgreaseice
rimeanchoricevuggyice
icepipesveinicepencilice
tabularbergsneedleice
growlersbergybitssheetice
icesaddlesicerumples
brashiceicespikesfastice
shoreicerottenicepackice
icewallsiceshelvesicefloes
icelobesicecakesnilas

 Ice is not
mere. Ice is not
silence waiting
to be broken. Ice needs no
token piece of sea
to make it unnaked.

 Here, cold keeps its secrets.
Tales of babies born to women of the north
and white explorers
fail to thaw its lips.

 Ignore the flaw zone and frost boils,
the skin stained red post-kill.
Rejoice, instead, in its willingness to glisten.
Be dazzled by its frazil.
Trust in its diamond dust.

SUSAN RICHARDSON
from Tip of the Icetongue
ILLUSTRATED BY PAT GREGORY

<pre>
        grease
rime   ice
ice   pencil
    bergs
      bergy sheet
          rumples
brashice   fast
     rotten   packice
  walls
    ice   nilas
</pre>

 Winter's on the critical list.
Nilfheim's Great Cow no longer has frost
crusting her udders.
The Pole's had its tongue cut out.
December's on hunger strike.

 Here, two thousand caribou
                fell through
their migration route,
while I trudged two thousand miles,
                spewing
algal bloom.

 Lonely floe
would like to meet pagophile,
for polar drifts, shipwrecks,
maybe something more serious.

Bergs, massive as misunderstanding,
begin to shrink. My breaths strain
to be solid but barely make
mist. My nipples stiffen
with craving to explain.
As I cling to this listing throne,
I will scratch what I know to be true
on the Mirror of Reason
for as long as it remains.

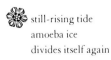 still-rising tide
amoeba ice
divides itself again

 Unice blusters
with rusted wrecks
and whales, brays
salt-laden gales.
It's the opposite
of tongue-tied.

 Here, hosts of ghost bears roam, make
fake-winter homes in phantom lairs, seek
spirit seals' breathing holes carved
from air.

 i am lost for bergs
all i can do is belch
       kelp   spit
copepods and cod
       exhale
methane trails of grief
          and pain

 If you must thaw,
why can't you be a mowed lawn?
Why can't you let sheep graze
and be

       fragrant with daisies?
Why must you be this brazen sea,
more blatant than

            Tesco?

the arctic's forgotten the words for ice it
gropes for terms like polar and frozen it
doesn't recognise its visitors those who take
samples and analyse it calls them all Peary
and Hensen it dribbles back to its youth
…*unblue*… *igloos*… *whitely*… it's been told
it used to thrive at minus thirty-five but now
it can't even find the start of its own circle

MAT OSMOND

Drawing on Water

He traces her name in the dark water
and a million suns break and scatter.
As the words drift apart in widening circles,
a shower of sparks runs down his skin
falling from his hand.

In a bottomless mirror
the well of stars opens beneath him.
The words re-gather, her name whispered
over and over:
a bright forest, its teeming canopy
suspended in the dark water.

LUANNE ARMSTRONG

Farmer

I am walking to the barn, a daily ritual. It's winter now, so twice a day I carry grain and warm water to the chickens, and throw hay to the cows. In the late dusk, after chores, I go for a final wander with the dogs. When I come inside to warmth and peace, the dogs digesting their dinner as they snooze on the rug, I have a satisfying sense of the farm settling to peace with me.

I have always thought of myself as a 'farmer', but this is a self-chosen identity and doesn't have that much to do with how I make a living. Labels about things to do with land are various. My landscape architect daughter says she is a gardener; my neighbourhood-friend, K. Linda, calls herself a peasant; it's all vaguely to do with mucking around in dirt and playing with plants. I call myself farmer and am content. My son laughs at me for thinking I have a farm, and he's right. It's not much of a farm, really, where I live and wander; no big machines or agribusiness connections, just a bit of a clear cut beside a lake, gardens, fruit trees, a few animals.

The first white man who lived here and owned the land was serious; he ploughed and planted trees, ditched and drained and built a house, a barn, a chicken shed, a woodshed, and fenced and cross-fenced the whole place. I have tried to imagine him, but I know little other than that I still benefit from his work.

Later, this place fed our whole family for over fifty years, my father, my mother, my three siblings and myself, and then my children and my brother and my sister's children as well. And yes, it was and is, always, a lot of work and I did much of that work, both when I was a child and then when I was a single parent with four kids to feed. So I feel I have fairly earned the label.

Farmer is a word with odd implications; it is one of those words, like Indian, with romantic stereotypes attached to it. Indeed, it comes with a similar duality of stereotypes: on the one hand, a farmer is someone close to nature, wise in the ways of animals and plants, who can fix anything, turn a hand to anything, and encapsulate a mystical view of the universe in a few well chosen words. On the other hand, the word dumb seems to be always silently appended to farmer: dumb, redneck, slow, prejudiced, the butt of jokes. And male.

The other odd thing about farming and gardening is that as long as you do it as a hobby, you don't get labelled with the pejorative, dumb farmer. You can be a gentleman farmer, that's different from being a real farmer because you have money; or you can be a 'hobby farmer' – you can have your place in the country where you garden obsessively and even keep a few happy cows and be indulged by society in your eccentricity.

But a real farmer is forever, no matter how wealthy, in the lowest class one can be in. People don't want to be farmers anymore; Western civilisation has been a lot about crawling out of the rural peasant class and into something more respectable. Becoming a farmer means going down a long notch in the class war, taking on a complex and contradictory image. Despite the romance and the beauty and the great food and other benefits, being a farmer has a very old and very venerable image problem. Somehow shit on the boots translates into shit in the brain.

When I walk to the barn, I walk like my father; I walk in his footsteps, I walk in his life, I walk on his land. There is, I think a farmer's walk, slow, bent, but steady. Farming is walking, working, stooping, lifting, it is very physical. And there is no point in rushing, the trick in farm work is to keep going at a slow and steady pace that will carry you through from morning to night.

As I get older, I have become more like my father and probably, much like his father and his father and his father. Gender doesn't much enter into it. Superficially, in every way, I am utterly unlike them: I am female, a writer, an academic, an environmentalist, a feminist, and yet none of this really matters on the way to the barn. The ritual and the rule bred into my bones, as old as human beings: you take care of animals before you feed yourself, you check on everything, you put the farm to bed before you come in for the night.

It always amuses me that prostitution gets labelled the oldest profession; the obvious oldest profession is farming. Farming is about food and survival, any romance about it is just that, furbelows and frills added on to the substantive nature of the task that is really only about feeding yourself, your family or clan, and thus staying alive. Farming is fundamental. It is about food. Thus it is also about dirt, physical hard work, being outside in every kind of weather, and of course, birth and death. It is also relentless. Farming never stops, although it does slow down in winter. There's nothing that can be put on hold; fruit can be green one day, ripe the next and rotten the day after, depending on weather, heat, water, soil temperature, and light. Animals always have to be cared for first, plus keeping animals means that you get to love and care for them and then you have to kill them. My father loved his animals, although he never let his children see that; we only knew it accidentally, by coming on him crying when a calf died, or when he had to shoot an old dying dog. But he was fast and skilled at butchering. When I was a child it was an exciting time, killing things. I never connected the fall butchering time with death; to me it was about work and food and curiosity, about the gleaming mysterious insides of cows and pigs, and the fascination with which I watched my all-powerful father dismember the carcass. I think I was probably a teenager before I stopped being fascinated with all this and began to avoid it, not with disgust, but with confusion. I wasn't sure how I felt anymore about killing things.

Then, last year, my brother (with whom I now share the farm) and I had to come to terms with killing things because our father had died and there is now only us to do the killing and butchering. We had raised a bunch of pigs; we've always liked pigs. They're smart and funny and we always get attached to them. We take them for walks, scratch their ears, give them names. They are also easy to feed and delicious to eat. The day my brother decided to butcher was pouring rain. It was late November. He'd been putting it off and now it was getting late in the season. He's a logging contractor in his working life and like me, he loves the farm. But it's hard for him to make enough time for it all.

He fed the first pig a mixture of grain and beer, thinking this would calm it down and make it sleepy. He would shoot it in its sleep; somehow that might make it easier. But the beer made the pig happy. I went over to the barn to see how things were progressing and there was my tall silent brother standing ankle deep in the mud, head bare to the pissing rain, while the pig galloped clumsily and happily from one end of the pen to the other. I left and when I got back to the house, I heard the shot. I went back out but there wasn't much I could do to help. My brother skinned out the pig and threw the legs to the dogs and loaded the carcass in his truck to take to the butcher. It took him about two hours and then he came in the house to get warm and dry off. I made the tea while he sat silent at the table that was once our parents and our grandparents.

Finally he said, (my brother never says much), 'Dad was so fast.' And then he said, 'I like to be alone to do this.' All of which I understood. The subtext was there, missing our father and the feeling of being alone and grown up and responsible adults, even at fifty, and the harshness and the duty and the beauty of killing the pig, good meat for winter, safe healthy meat, and work we could feel good about. We exchanged some small talk about the butcher and when the meat would be ready and then he left.

My work at the farm is primarily growing vegetables and fruit. I grow flowers, but they don't get my attention like the vegetable garden does. Every year, the vegetable garden is a journey into adventure, very small adventures, to be sure, but always interesting. This year, we were invaded by voles, small brown furry creatures with enormous appetites. Since we had never had voles before, it took a while before I began to catch on why the tomatoes were disappearing and the eggplants were hollow and the quinoa stalks were chewed to stubs. I couldn't even decide how to react; should I kill them all, wait for winter to kill them instead, put up with them? In the end, we shared the garden, they ate half and I got the other half and then winter came and ate them up. Or something did.

I contend that there are really two kinds of people in the world: the people who grow food, and the people who cook it. What I like about growing food is texture, colour, shape, the sense of abundance, the sensuousness of it all; for example, the way the late August light glints off a basket of pink and purple eggplants, red and green peppers and yellow and orange tomatoes. I revel in the satisfaction of picking things, but then I try to find someone else to help turn it into something; to can, pickle, dry, bake, juice, and freeze the summer harvest. I like this process as well, but mostly I like the sense of community and shared effort when there's a bunch of us around the table, peeling peaches and slicing them onto trays for the dryer.

Because small scale agriculture is mostly tedious physical work, the more people there are, the more food can be produced. A small farm can feed a lot of people easily, but all the work is intense and the adage of many hands make light work is exactly right. This means that a small subsistence farm is also about community, whether you want it to be or not. It's about geographical community and it's about family; you don't choose who you're related to or who moves in next door to be your neighbour. If you all live there and you have to do the work to feed yourselves, you have to get along. Or leave. Small farming is about depending on your family and neighbours; it's at once both oddly dependent and a powerful source of independence from systems, corporations, governments, and grocery stores.

Industrial agriculture replaced that sense of community and freed us from all that neighbourliness and getting along, through mechanisation and industrialisation. It freed people from the downside of the stigma of being farmers. Consequently, these days, rural community has mostly lost an ethic of neighbourliness, because most rural people aren't farmers, they're either middle class people who have retired, or people who have bought a second home in the country, or wealthy people busy fending off poor people and gating off the countryside. Instead of being the place where people work, the country is now where people play.

But with the rising price of everything – oil, energy, food and land – there is currently, in my part of the world, a faint buzz about farming and whether small farms, subsistence farming and local agriculture, might make a comeback. On a broader scale, in parts of North America, the new movement has all kind of recombinant parts and labels, re-localisation, the one-hundred mile diet, local organic food. But it seems, still, to be far less about farming than about urban or formerly urban people acquiring good food. Those of us who remember the 'back to the land' movement of the seventies are trying not to be too cynical. People like me, who were never anything but local, are waiting to see if this actually translates into more actual money for farmers. But not many people that I've talked to are thinking of going back to farming themselves. For some reason, urbanites tend to see farming as mysterious and difficult, more about some mysterious alchemy than just plain work.

Farming is complex but it's also simple. Farming is basically about things growing and since things really want to grow, a lot of farming happens almost accidentally. Seeds in fertile ground will do their best to grow and reproduce; given enough water, warmth, and light and not too much competition, they'll do just that. Animals want to have babies and reproduce; there's always too many male animals and nothing else to do but eat them. And of course to do that, someone has to kill them. There's also a lot of work involved in eating meat; things have to be butchered, preserved, put by to last, somehow.

If you're not trying to make money or produce picture perfect fruit, farming can be a story of amazing abundance. But of course, it is also a story of weather, animals, weeds, insects, disease and frustration. Perhaps this is why my father saw his farm as his enemy, surrounded by other enemies. He was depending on the place for income and survival and I'm not, at least not at the moment.

So why do I call myself a farmer and why have I stuck to this label so fiercely? I have asked myself this question for years with no real answer. I have asked myself this not only walking to the barn in winter, but standing in the muddy freshly turned garden soil in early April, planting seeds, or in early June, stuffing my mouth full of new spinach, or wandering the peach trees, bucket in one hand, looking for the first, earliest, just-getting-ready peaches, or in the fall, putting the garden away, pulling onions, cutting cornstalks, with the chill breeze rattling the leaves. I have never made any money farming and I never expect to; mostly I give food away, plus I eat really well.

My complicity here is that I don't identify as 'just' a farmer, I have all those other labels to fall back on, depending on where I am and who I'm talking to. But farmer is a word that tugs at my heart, or perhaps my feet. It's there, digging manure out of the pigpen, that I find my own particular and peculiar sense of freedom within the boundaries of belonging, of connection, of work that is fundamental because it is just that, work that feeds me and my family.

I am well aware that all of this right now is an intellectual luxury, that, even though I don't have enough money, I have enough to buy packaged food if I need to, that on nights when I am feeling lazy, I can go to the local pub for pizza. And I am also aware that for several thousand years, it wasn't a luxury, that small farming was the way that generation after generation of people survived, that small farmers were often an independent and hardheaded lot, as long as they clung to the land, separate from politics, armies, and the changing fortunes of whatever kind of nation state they happened to be in.

Perhaps that's the connection. That's why, as a writer, I cling to this word, this label, this old-fashioned, outmoded, roots-in-antiquity lifestyle. It's that hardheaded independence, that sense of being outside, of not having to care about the latest whatever-it-might-be, being outside of history, even outside of time itself. It's the ultimate in arrogance, in fact. I think what I want and I live how I want and my feet come down on the earth in tune with some ancient rhythm of which even I am only dimly conscious. But one that lets me live and breathe inside an empire of time and beauty, abundance and space.

MATT SZABO

Sustainable Energy Will Destroy The Environment: Discuss

What I mean in making this statement is this: the current emphasis on climate change, renewable energy, and carbon counting has not only closed down broader environmental debate, it has also undermined or devalued a range of ecological and social concerns which might be grouped as 'green issues.' As of 2011, in the wake of 'Climategate', amidst the ongoing financial crisis, and post the damp squibs of Copenhagen and Cancun, climate change seems to have gone off the boil as public concern number one. An increasing number of people now seem to doubt climate change 'rhetoric'[1] per se, and in this discussion paper I will suggest this means one of three things:

1. 'Old school' environmental worries are now legitimately back on the agenda. Clearly, they never went away.

2. Not only has climate change rhetoric devalued 'old school' environmental worries, the new master-narrative of climate change is currently, for some people at least, heading down the sliding scale of politically cogent or scientifically believable ideas. This may mean a rising tide of denial or hubris regarding *all* forms of environmental concern, including climate change, is washing up on our collective cultural shores. This would be an own-goal for environmentally concerned activists, thinkers, policymakers and professionals of all stripes. By collectively buying into the climate change agenda lock, stock and smoking barrel – to the exclusion of other environmental concerns – 'we' (the environmentalists) have potentially kicked the entire green agenda into a long grass of popular and political malaise.

3. What remains of the climate change agenda (and other remaining environmental issues which are now subsumed under its umbrella) is

increasingly, if not exclusively, couched in free-market points of reference. In particular, this applies to the high-tech, renewable energy 'solutions' which are now touted as both saviours of the planet *and* guarantors of 'sustainable' economic growth.

As little as five years ago, environmental concern wasn't framed only in terms of 'tackling climate change' or creating a 'carbon neutral economy'. It embraced many other concerns, none of which have gone away. In fact, it seems depressingly safe to assume that most if not all of these issues, some of which I list below, have got worse since the collective obsession of the state, NGO, and scientific establishment with climate change became the only environmental game in town. Some of these 'traditional' ecological concerns are included in the following lists.[2] I have split these concerns into two sections. First, *active concerns,* which include real, tangible, physical things people used to judge important enough to get involved with or even go to prison for; secondly, *ideologies,* by which I mean clusters of environmentalist ideas with political and ethical ramifications nestled within them. (Reality is more blurred than this of course, but please bear with me.)

Active Concerns

Protecting wildlife and wildlife habitats locally and globally. This manifested (and hopefully still does) in countless local fights over valued pockets of green space in many countries (not just rich ones), against development on the part of big business, the state, or both. Road protesting is one UK example.

Concern over deforestation and conserving the world's tropical rainforests in particular.

'Saving whales' and protecting marine ecosystems from pollution and over-fishing.

Attempting to control or simply trying to map and understand extinction rates and biodiversity loss.[3]

Fighting for democratic control of the food chain and soil. Challenging agribusiness and genetic technology companies, and exploring non-industrial farming methods and/or local production and supply.

Lobbying for better networks of public transport and reduced car usage, rather than making cars more efficient. In other words, fewer cars and less road building, not more 'clean' cars.

Attempting to legitimise concern over global population levels.

Ideologies

Localisation of politics, food production, and personal work-life arrangements.

Treating small as beautiful in as many aspects of life as possible including the economic; advocating 'downshifting' or 'dropping out' as genuinely sustainable lifestyle options.

Making environmental ethics tangible in some way. For example, extending ethical consideration to nonhuman life via animal rights; Deep Ecology-inspired direct action movements like Earth First!; attempting to think in bioregional terms via locally grown food and local conservation projects; envisioning, establishing or visiting 'alternative' communities which reflect principles of social ecology, e.g. Global Ecovillage Network.

Exploring the ethical dimension of vegetarianism, semi-vegetarianism, veganism or ethical meat-eating as realistic long-term diet options, not fads. (This is perhaps the most political thing some people do; hence it probably warrants *ideology* status.)

Questioning industrialisation per se, and attempting to envision personal, local, and societal alternatives.

Questioning consumer-based capitalism per se, and attempting to envision personal, local and societal alternatives.

Since climate change rhetoric, as opposed to climate change as a 'reality', i.e. a measurable, actually-happening, meteorological, geological, ecological and anthropogenic process, took over all aspects of state- and market-compatible environmental discourse, many of these environmental actions and narratives seem to have miraculously evaporated; as if boiled off the face of the planet by increasing levels of climatic radiation. The ideologies listed above, in particular the radical discourses which contain anti-state and/or anti-market implications, have either been side-lined, in some cases criminalised as terrorist activities, or been rejected as redundant, hair-shirt strategies of environmental yore. (This period of 'radical environmental yore', I suggest, stretched from its beginnings in 1960s radicalism until some point in the late 1980s or early 1990s when sustainable development became wedded to growth economics.[4] Its demise was completed when Climate Change officially 'began' as a mainstream political discourse – let's say when the *Kyoto Protocol* was (sort of) agreed, circa 2005.)

Through the twin filter cycles of sustainable development and climate change discourse, the ideological concerns which once played an important role have been rinsed out of mainstream political, and to some extent, hard-core environmentalist conversation. However, I suggest it is these discourses which gave 'old-school' environmentalism both a distinct point-of departure from growth-based capitalism and some intellectual basis from which to envisage and possibly build new cultural possibilities.

I want to suggest – knowing that I am not alone in doing so – that the dramatic cultural shifts the world needs to survive climate change, overpopulation, water and food shortages, economic instability, creeping urbanisation and the loss of biodiversity will require experimental and possibly uncharted social visions. New survival strategies need to be trialled and hopefully 'mainstreamed' with speed and agility. Instead, the mainstreaming of climate change rhetoric has taken us in a destructive, anti-environmental, market-compatible direction, dragging a lot of untested but ecologically-attuned survival strategies into a morass of free-market 'solution speak'; i.e. conceptual subordination to a process I have previously described as 'normative economic rationalization' (Szabo 2004).

No doubt serious, systematic and radical environmental or 'post-environmental' thinking still exists in some embattled university departments, but I see no mention of such discourse – or even watered down, populist versions thereof – anywhere in the mainstream UK media. Things may be different in a North American, Latin America, Asian, European or African context, but in 'Great Britain' at least it currently feels like hard times for anyone who discusses ecological and social issues outside the parameters of a market-friendly, carbon management format.

Some have argued that as green discourse (i.e. climate change rhetoric) becomes mainstream, it has had to lose all trappings of radicalism and grow up politically. But I suggest this is not what we are seeing. Rather, all the challenging dimensions of environmental theory which held the potential for cultural change (as alluded to in the ideologies listed above), have simply been filtered out, watered down, or fluffed up as 'win-win' market-compatible sound-bites. For example, *bioregionalism* was once a somewhat crazy, but nonetheless novel idea proposing a radically localized communitarian politics built upon local points of ecological reference – both totemic and real. Run a search-engine past this word now and you will come up with any number of management consultancies, 'sustainable development businesses' and the like with 'bioregional' somewhere in their mission statements. You could say this is a case of bioregionalism 'maturing as a brand' – or you could say it is a case of a once 'radical' environmental idea being co-opted, politically sterilised, and relaunched as a hollow, marketing soundbite.

Mainstream politics has not nurtured more 'grown up' forms of green ideology; rather, the more challenging forms of 'old school, firebrand' green ideology have simply been excluded from the table of acceptable debate. Further, the rhetoric of climate change – and, more specifically, the profitable forms of sustainable energy which can be utilised to 'tackle' climate change while supposedly propping up current levels and targets for economic growth – is now the main mechanism behind this expulsion procedure. Sustainable energy is currently a bullying teacher of environmental thinking, which forces all other potential ways of 'tackling' climate change into the corner, with a dunce hat thrown in for good measure.

For example, it seems fairly obvious to most people that dramatic cuts in energy usage and carbon emissions could be achieved on a massive and near instantaneous scale if people were encouraged (or forced) to purchase less products per se, or use their existing stuff more sparingly. However, instead of prioritising thrift or self control on the part of 'consumers', most if not all market-led sustainable energy 'solutions' require massive spending on R&D and marketing to offer replacement products which simply maintain or enable increasing levels of usage. "If I buy a low energy wall-screen, I can leave it on for more of the time."

Low energy products and renewable energy generating technologies maintain or even intensify the growth-based, business-as-usual mentality which free-market proponents and (most) politicians accept as a natural state of social reality. Clearly, low energy products and renewable energy sources are a crucial component of any sustainable future society, but the way they are currently being pitched as saviours of global economic growth appears massively unsustainable. Alternative and possibly simpler solutions to cutting carbon – like an ethic of thrift, or enforcing radical energy reduction via law or policy – terrify free market ideologues, because they fundamentally challenge the mantra that economic growth is a prerequisite for a healthy society.

In the environmentalism of the 1960s through to the 1990s, the ideological visions of anarchist, utopian and radical socialist traditions (think flowing Victorian beards) were rewoven by the likes of Rachel Carson (1962), Murray Bookchin (1971), Ivan Illich (1973–74), E.F. Schumacher (1973), Amory Lovins (1977), Kirkpatrick Sale (1985) and Arne Naess (1989) (think clipped beards).[5] Today, such thinking has been dumbed down to the conceptual equivalent of brand-loving teenagers bopping around the mall of green consumerism (think facial piercings and accessories). We now know what this latter, market friendly version of a green utopia is meant to look like: Imagine, if you will, a (professionally-envisioned) sky line, populated by silhouettes of slowly turning wind-turbine blades. Beneath it, green-collar workers riding designer bicycles wend their way to cosy geodesic-dome, mini power-station houses. In this corporate lo-energy future, we will drive hybrid cars, eat free range meats (or perhaps 'animal free' meat grown in vats), and live much of our lives in virtual retreat, as enabled by mobile infotainment technology. Think Luke Skywalker's desert home in Star Wars meets The Matrix meets Apple's current design ethos. On the one hand we will soon all be living in stylish eco-housing and pretty much carry on as now only with better gadgets, cleaner cars, and high-tech sources of food. On the other hand, It doesn't take much imagination to envisage that this heavily branded green utopia of turbines, hybrid cars, and buzzing technology could easily evolve into an over-developed hell of total suburbanisation – albeit a low-energy hell. Animals, trees, insects, and farmyard manure don't really feature in this brave new world, although one would like to think spaces of pastoral rebellion were still available for those who might choose (or could afford) to rebel against the 'profitable *and* sustainable' future currently under construction.

However ... in present day reality, for those of us in the "over-developed world" (Carmen 1996), the reality of the above vision actually manifests via a plethora of recycled mouse mats, pens, fleece jackets or cotton shopping bags, generally advertising a worthy local cause or government campaign. More ambitiously, we find it embodied in the occasional and invariably short cycle-lane running alongside a lethal road, the fly-by-night energy company (unsuccessfully) applying to build unwanted wind-turbines in a sensitive location, the box full of unused CFL light bulbs lurking at the back of a cupboard, kindly supplied free of charge by our caring utility company. It rolls off the garage forecourt in the form of a 'hybrid' car, which has no less capacity to crush people and animals, consume bio-fuel, and maintain the construction of an expanding road network. To borrow Ivan Illich's terminology (1974), hybrid cars remain a 'faulty technology' which can 'render the environment uninhabitable' by sheer scale of production and the 'radical monopoly' of their 'entrenched and structuring nature'.

Alas, now that climate change has been successfully branded as *the* driver for 'green' sustainable economic growth, nothing much else will cut it as an alternative big green idea to the free-market low energy dystopia presented above. The wilder and more potent ideologies I have touched on seem largely forgotten, criminalised or rendered 'safe and sane' by a combination of climate change rhetoric and market solutions speak. The climate science that indicates we are heading for some kind of catastrophic shift is almost certainly or 'near-as-damn-it' true. We must separate this from the manner in which the science has been adopted by a mainstream politics, entirely encircled by capitalist thinking. It has become the new meta-narrative, overarching the next wave of sustainable economic growth, propping up the kamikaze economics which are pushing the world into an unstable ecological and climatic state. Darker green changes are needed in thinking and action, but the conceptual stranglehold of market-compatible climate change 'solutions' has undermined the ground on which alternative visions of the future might take shape.

Yet, as I said at the beginning, things are in flux. To return to my opening gambit: Even if market-based solutions to climate change were ever likely to work, the fact that climate change has now gone out of fashion makes the current position even more ridiculous. And so we move from theory to *realpolitik*.

Anyone who works in or near the energy sector is aware of the political apathy, economic under-investment, and absence of any enforceable policy which would enable a 'market led solution to climate change' to be made real – at least any time soon. The energy landscape is complex to say the least, mainly because (I would argue) of the Reagan-Thatcher privatisation legacy.

Neoliberalism diverted control of energy production, water supply and
public transport away from nation states and into the hands and pockets of big
business, and we live with the legacy of this capitalist sucker-punch to this
day. In other words, as long as energy sources, water supplies, and transportation systems are driven by the logic of short-term private profits as
opposed to the logic of long-term collective management aimed at protecting
both the climate *and* the environment, all the rhetoric surrounding market-
based solutions to climate change will remain environmentally disastrous,
disjointed, PR bullshit.

*

In conclusion, let me offer a reality check on the situation here in the UK:
Our government's current attempts to rein in the 'Big Six' utility companies
and force them to part with some of their profits for the sake of energy
efficiency and renewable energy via CERT or CESP funding are painfully
slow, disproportionately small, and so completely insignificant in terms of carbon reduction. Like all other 'free' governments, it appears to be beholden to
the utility companies and lacks either the ability or, perhaps more truthfully,
the political will to reclaim power over those who currently provide power.
Instead of clawing back control of the production of basic utilities for the good
of society via strong changes in policy, the UK government is utterly under the
yoke of free market trade rules and tied into public-private deal-making
shenanigans. As a result, all we can currently hope for is the mishmash of
approaches the energy landscape currently exhibits: stop-start Research &
Development programmes funded by speculative venture capitalists (i.e. if
they don't work instantly, or provide shareholders with a quick payback, end
of R&D); clandestine oil and coal industry lobbying and corporate green-
washing; unachievable carbon reduction targets unsupported by technology,
staff time, or sufficiently strong policy; third sector and local government
hand-wringing over their inability to 'deliver' on said targets, and a few
concerned citizens assisted by charity workers attempting to catalyse a disin-
terested and sceptical public. The combined carbon-busting 'force' of these
various strands is like trying to crack a sledge hammer-sized issue with a very
small bag of (mixed) nuts. I think we can guess the outcome of the 'fight
against climate change', if things continue in this vein for much longer.

There are of course some emerging 'grass roots' trends like the Transition
movement which offer an alternative ray of hope, but I suspect that without

serious political and popular support these loose affiliations of well-meaning and (occasionally) influential local idealists will tend to fall into ineffective feel-good activities, or else get hijacked by local entrepreneurs who want to make a fast buck out of renewable energy – albeit in the name of 'the community'. Without strong support from national and international forms of democratic governance (i.e. national government, the EU, and ideally the UN) that are open to non-market approaches, these initiatives cannot stand up to free market trends, resist the lure of investments which may not be ethically or ecologically kosher, or address consumer-based apathies and addictions.

Still, as government doesn't seem able to understand climate change outside of a market-paradigm, assuming that Transition groups (or the 'grassroots' let us say) are our current best hope, I sincerely hope the membership of such groups rediscovers elements of the radical thinking around bioregionalism, social ecology, deep ecology and other older schools of thought, and starts to create radical local alternatives to globalised supply systems. This project will entail discovering (or rediscovering) a militant ethos around autonomous food production, lifestyle simplicity, energy production and wildlife protection at a transparent,[6] community level. While a revamping of old-school environmentalist discourses may frighten off local business sharks with a vested interest in renewable energy or green building developments, they would at least give people ideas to play with – or, better, an ideological platform to build on.

These ideas won't necessarily fit in with the market-friendly 'win-win' hokum we have now grown used to accepting as correct or inevitable. Climate change, food supply, population growth and wildlife protection are too important to be left to a combination of market forces, energy entrepreneurs, and the pipe dreams of advertising/PR con artists. It is time to dig out, dust off and redevelop old-school environmentalist alternatives which need to be redefined within the post-environmental[7] 'new reality' of the climate change era. This is a fight for ideas and language, but also for physical space and future political possibility. Road protests and animal rights activism are now terrorist activities in the eyes of the British state; hence, to revisit these or to develop new, equally radical, post-environmental discourses focused on energy, local food supply and protecting wildlife habitats may entail similar if not higher levels of orchestrated civil disobedience. This is probably now too risky for most people to consider – what with the threat of a 'terror'-based criminal record hanging over your future career.

Will green thinkers be silenced by the law, consumer indifference, or political indignation if we dare to question the potential nightmare the free market version of a 'sustainable' future might deliver? It is time to define and pitch what the alternatives might be.

Bibliography

Blühdorn, Ingolfur. *Post-Ecologist Politics: Social Theory and the Abdication of the Ecologist Paradigm*. London & New York: Routledge, 2000.

Bookchin, Murray. *Post Scarcity Anarchism*. Berkeley CA: Ramparts Press, 1971.

Carmen, Raff. *Autonomous Development: humanizing the landscape: an excursion into radical thinking and practice*. London & Atlantic NJ: Zed Books, 1996.

Carson, Rachel. *Silent Spring*. New York: Fawcett Crest, 1962.

Illich, Ivan. *Tools for Conviviality*. London: Calder and Boyars, 1973.

Illich, Ivan. *Energy and Equity*. London: Calder and Boyars, 1974.

Lewis, Sian and Naomi Antony. 'Poor want biomass, not biodiversity', 30/4/2010. http://scidev.net/en/news/poor-want-biomass-not-biodiversity-finds-study.html.

Lovins, Amory. *Soft Energy Paths: Toward a Durable Peace* (1977).

Kingsnorth, Paul. 'Why I stopped believing in environmentalism and started the Dark Mountain Project', *The Guardian*, 29 April 2010. http://guardian.co.uk/environment/2010/apr/29/environmentalism-dark-mountain-project.

Naess, Arne. *Ecology, Community and Lifestyle: Outline of an Ecosophy*. Cambridge: Cambridge University Press, 1989.

Sale, Kirkpatrick. *Dwellers in the Land: The Bioregional Vision*. San Francisco: Sierra Club Books, 1985.

Schumacher, E. F. *Small Is Beautiful: A Study of Economics as if People Mattered*. London: Vintage, 1993.

Szabo, Matt. *Seeking an Environmental Morality: Bauman, Weber, Levinas and Nonhuman Nature*. PhD thesis, 2004.

Notes

1. When I say climate change 'rhetoric', I mean a combination of good science, propagandised science, press scare-mongering, political opportunism/confusion, academic lobbying, vested business interests, and legitimate popular concern. In other words a conflagration of different narratives which, in combination, have created a complex set of cross-referenced 'truths' which have their own self-referential logic, high levels of political credibility, and a healthy media presence.

2. Please note this is just a personal ad hoc list written from a UK perspective. My apologies to people whose 'favourite' ecocide topics are not contained within this list. Hopefully you catch my drift.

3. A recent article published by the Science & Development Network indicates a tension: 'Preserving biodiversity may be the goal of conservationists and environmental activists, but preserving biomass is a more important priority for the poor, says a literature review. "People just don't care about biodiversity," Craig Leisher, of the US-based Nature Conservancy, told SciDev.Net ... Leisher, who conducted the research with Neil Larsen, also from the Nature Conservancy, gave the example of a poor fisherman, for whom the route out of poverty is to catch more fish – not more *kinds* of fish.' (S. Lewis and N. Antony, 'Poor want biomass, not biodiversity', 2010.)

4. Before climate change discourse took over environmental thinking, another simplification process had already been set in motion by the free-market co-option of the term 'sustainability'. Despite noble intentions set out in the *Brundtland Report,* where the concept 'sustainable development' was first floated in a major way, the term sustainability has now become a near meaningless catch-all term. 'Sustainability' is now a concept 100 per cent steeped in free-market 'solutions speak' which homogenises various green ideas into one big soup of political concern, while simultaneously filtering out 'deviant' ideas (like animal rights or downshifting) that are clearly unsustainable in terms of mainstream capitalist politics.

    The best this vision can offer is something along the lines: sustainable economic growth will be built upon sustainable energy solutions and a scientifically managed sustainable food supply, which will sustain society through the worst effects of climate change (and all other 'bad', unsustainable crises). Ideally, current standards of living can be sustained in the first world while simultaneously expanded in a sustainable way to developing countries. Is any of this vaguely true or vaguely likely? The term sustainability is politically redundant – at least in ecological terms as it now essentially refers to sustaining economic growth.

5. See bibliography for full publication details.

6. The democratic dimension of Transition Towns groups is a different issue, one which I will not broach here. My impression is that they are not very democratic in their current structure. This may not be bad thing in all respects, but it needs analysis.

7. I use the term 'post-environmental' in reference to recent comments made by members of the Dark Mountain Project, which suggest the environmental/green agenda is no longer relevant and has now moved into (or needs to find) another realm of meaning. See, for example, Paul Kingsnorth's article 'Why I stopped believing in environmentalism and started the Dark Mountain Project', published by the Guardian in April 2010. Similar ideas were being floated ten years ago in Ingolfur Blühdorn's *Post-Ecologist Politics* (2000).

HEATHCOTE WILLIAMS

Wasp Honey

'Everyone hates wasps,' people insist with self-righteous fury
As if anyone who thought otherwise was beyond reason:
'What on earth was God doing making wasps?' a child exclaims,
At a picnic or in a kitchen, or anywhere. 'We hate them'.

Then the child seems to imply that the whole of creation's at fault
Because of this unwelcome bug in the system, 'Oh go away!
'Why are they so annoying? What use are they? And they sting!
'You're horrible. You're completely pointless. So just go.'

'Okay, I've told you; now you've had it,' and someone tries to kill one
Then, as if in a self-fulfilling prophecy, someone gets stung —
For a threatened wasp's signal, if it should be picked up by its fellows,
Urges them to come to its defense, whereupon they sting.

Wasps then leave to pollinate a wild orchid, their speciality; or to farm aphids
For honeydew; or to make their waterproof paper nests —
This latter skill giving the Chinese the idea of turning chewed pulp into paper
According to Needham's 'Science and Civilization in China'.

This bio-mimetic act, or plagiarism, changed the course of history:
Without the wasp, paper might have been a rarity
And communication confined to papyrus or cuneiform marks
On mud and wax tablets or graveyard inscriptions.

'I still hate them,' a voice persists. 'It doesn't matter what you say,
'They're hateful. Absolutely anybody sensible knows that …'
After the Falklands (which Borges said was as sensible as two bald men
Squabbling over a comb), I was in a library in Buenos Aires —

The library of the University on the banks of the River Plata
Which had been trashed by the Argentine junta.
Everything was still in disarray; books strewn about the floor;
Journals trampled, torn and out of sequence.

'This is what happened when we had our meetings here,' said Ana Cordoba
'They'd burst in. Then they'd throw red paint at us and leave.'
She pointed to telltale traces: glossy red drips on books and metal shelving,
'Then they'd watch us when we left the library buildings.

'They would know who'd been attending the meetings here, you see,
'Because of indelible splashes of paint on us. They took us in.
'Then we were locked up and, you know… torture. Many people died.
'So you mustn't talk to any of the police here, whatever you do.

'You know Eduardo? What they did to him? The police bribed a boy
'To run past him quickly. Plant something on him incriminating.
'So then they arrest Eduardo. Take him to their place in a Villa Miseria.
'Looks like a police station, but it's not a police station. It's a fake.

'Total fake. Set up especially for police robbery. 'So, what you got, señor?
''Money? Credit cards? we take them, then we let you go. Maybe.'
'Then', she added darkly, 'if you're lucky, they don't have bad fun with you.
'They're not what they seem. They sting you. Worse than your wasp.'

Her city was a place where human beings persistently stung each other.
Seeing a beautiful woman through the peephole in his door
A friend responded, only to have three men enter, one with a machete —
Its blade pressed on his genitalia till he gave them his money.

In England I'd once seen a striking picture of a South American wasps' nest
In a Victorian book on unusual habitations of the world's wildlife.
The spiky nest hung from a tree and it was covered in fierce protrusions
Shaped like inch-long thorns, seemingly to protect the contents.

Remarkable, haunting contents I'd not heard of before: this wasp made honey.
Its weird nest belonged to a species called *polybia scutellaris*
Which was only found on the Argentine pampas in its pendulous paper castles.
The honey was said to be almost solid, and black as obsidian.

'Did you find any articles yet?' Ana said, after more time in the library,
Studying the remains of painstakingly comprehensive journals
Relating to her country's flora and fauna before the place was rubbished
By Galtieri's Junta, and indirectly by the wasp-woman, Thatcher.

Two centuries before, Dr Johnson had expressed wiser thoughts than theirs About
the Falklands: he'd said that there were just and unjust wars,
And wars which were just not worth fighting for, and that the Falklands
Fell into the latter category, being the sovereign domain of sheep.

In two hundred years little had been learnt. People still hated people
And people still hated wasps, to no useful purpose.
It occurred that if it was more widely known that wasps made honey
They'd be seen in a different light, and redeemed.

The first account of it by the naturalist, Don Félix de Azara, was ridiculed
As 'a pure concoction of the Baron Munchausen class'.
Undeterred Azara sent a wasp's nest to London, to the British Museum,
Where a Dr. Adam White found dry honey in its combs.

So if a wasps, with its mechanical space mask, really makes honey
And thus disrupts the settled rigour of scientists' categories,
How does it taste? Does it cure stings? Like dock-leaves and nettles —
Might it even allay the fear of wasps, namely spheksophobia?

Then if one wasp can make honey why don't all wasps make honey
And improve their public standing?
Perhaps this one's a mutant species designed not to die off like bees? —
A hardcore hymenoptera producing punk honey;

As bees are dying off (thanks, it would seem, to global pollution
With smog interfering with the bee's ability to find nectar)
Then this steelier wasp might be replacing its loveable hippy cousin
By manufacturing the sweetest stuff that life has to offer.

When I chanced to unearth a metallic wasp, near where I'd ended up,
One which had a transparent abdomen like a portable honey-pot
With antennae-like reindeer-antlers looking more than usually alien —
Its outlandishness suggested that wasps were capable of anything.

Then Jorge Godoy told me of a Guaraní Indian in the north-east,
On the borders of Paraguay, in the region of Gran Chaco.
'He knows the biography of every blade of grass. So he'll know.
'He speaks good Spanish ... Guaraní means forest people.

'Originally they came from the Amazon Basin seven centuries ago
To look for Iwy Mara' Eye, 'a land without evil.'
They were guided by their prophets, wearing their sacred feathers,
And by their Ava Yumpa which means 'God man'.'

Jorge and I travelled to meet Manu on a tributary of the Río Paraná.
He greeted us with a brief word, sucked on his *maté* gourd
Then fell silent. 'The spikes on the nest,' I asked, 'of the *camoati*'
(The indigenous name) — 'they're protection from jaguars?'

Manu looked puzzled. I opened up the book I'd brought to show him,
'The Romance Of Animal Arts and Crafts'
With its picture of a wasp's nest attacked by a snarling jungle cat
And the swarm of honey-wasps defending it.

Manu furrowed his brow. 'No. Para ventilar. Caliente aqui.' —
The book evidently over-dramatized the nest's spikes
They were there simply to ventilate the nest and keep it cool.
He grinned. 'I'm more danger to this wasp than a cat.'

He explained this was because the *camoati* honey made him feel good
And when he felt good this reduced his hatred
For those who'd stolen his land: Brazilians, Bolivians, North Americans
And Paraguayans. It was a consuming hatred.

The *pytagua*, or foreigners, had edged him from the land he'd lived on
For generations, reducing his people to living by roadsides,
But when he saw the wasp's spiny fortress he could still feel happy,
For it held one secret which sustained him.

It was that 'even this wicked wasp, he has learnt to make honey
And the wasp has to do this – despite his bad nature —
Because all those who want to live, have to be good in some way
But you must learn how to discover this goodness.'

He climbed up to prise clear a tiny portion of the elusive comb,
'I borrow a little for you. I don't steal. It's their honey.'
A squad of black creatures moved out of their thorny scrotal sac
To crawl all over him during this suspenseful inspection.

A surviving article in the library had spoken of Guaraní wasp-honey shamen
Who made a 'mouth music' while collecting it and were never stung.
'They know I already have 'mad honey disease", Manu laughed at our concern
Then he turned back to continue delving while he vibrantly hummed.

'These wasps feed on jimson weed. So their honey contains atropine —
That lets you know how you going to die.' He handed us some comb
 Then he added, out of the blue, 'Stupid people cause a lot of damage. Why?'
'Will this cure them?' I asked, 'I'm still testing it,' he smiled.

It tasted strange, this paradigm-shifting honey produced by creatures
The world always feels justified in so intractably hating ...
An intriguing after-effect was an old enemy buzzing my consciousness.
He appeared to lean forward, to smile gently, then wave.

Darwin would make many references to Don Azara's work,
To his studies of woodpeckers and black-necked swans
And the five hundred other birds of Argentina's River Plata
That Azara had captured and then pickled in brandy.

Darwin had also drawn on Azara's studies of small Indian tribes
And on their methods of sexual selection:
Researches that found their way into Darwin's 'Descent of Man'
To fuel fascist doctrines of the survival of the fittest.

Oddly however, Darwin overlooked Azara's discovery
Of polybia scutellaris, the counterintuitive wasp —
Still inconceivable to those who like things cut and dried,
To whom wasps are evil and so cannot make honey.

On returning to Buenos Aires I bought a new blank book,
A black Moleskine, and made a whimsical note
Of the irony that man's intellectual dependence on paper
Made him a kind of Mowgli – civilized by wasps.

In San Telmo market, a frail, ailing couple with a wind-up gramophone
Elegantly tango to *Milonga de mis amores* —
Both parents of a young boy on the Belgrano, torpedoed by the British,
They collect money by telling strangers their story.

I see a graffiti, 'LAS MALVINAS SON ARGENTINAS', at the Recoleta cemetery
Where a family's mausoleum has electricity, so the bereaved
May boil a kettle and spend the day playing their loved one records.
The war graves show a human wasp's sting lasts the longest.

Illustration by Jonathan Penney

WARREN DRAPER

Myths of civilisation #2

The Shuttle Exchanged for the Sword

Continuing our series examining propagandist narratives innocently posing as Facts, which help underpin our civilisation's view of the world and itself.

As the liberty lads o'er the sea
Bought their freedom, and cheaply, with blood,
So we, boys, we
Will die fighting, or live free,
And down with all kings but King Ludd!

When the web that we weave is complete,
And the shuttle exchanged for the sword,
We will fling the winding sheet
O'er the despot at our feet,
And dye it deep in the gore he has pour'd.

Though black as his heart its hue,
Since his veins are corrupted to mud,
Yet this is the dew
Which the tree shall renew
Of Liberty, planted by Ludd!

– Lord Byron, 'Song for the Luddites'

Chant no more your old rhymes about bold Robin Hood
His feats I but little admire
I will sing the Achievements of General Ludd
Now the hero of Nottinghamshire

– Anon, from the files of the Home Office

If you visit York Castle – and I highly recommend that you do – you will encounter the romanticised celebration of the life of one John Palmer, a violent thief and murderer whose early exploits include the pistol-whipping and torture of a 70-year-old man, and the aiding and abetting of the rape of two women. Palmer is better known today for his later exploits, and by his real name: Richard Turpin.

The Dick Turpin we have come to know was originally popularised in Richard Bayes' semi-fictional biography, *The Genuine History of the Life of Richard Turpin, the noted Highwayman*. This account of Turpin's exploits was hurriedly published in 1739 shortly after Turpin was hanged for horse theft. Biographies of condemned villains were highly popular in the seventeenth and eighteenth centuries and, at a time when the premeditated murder that so saturates our own fiction was relatively rare, a known murderer and horse-thief was considered to be the worst criminal imaginable.

Bayes' described Turpin as a highwayman, even though he was not famed as such in his own lifetime (then he was better known as 'Turpin the Butcher'). This encouraged later authors to further embellish Turpin's exploits. In his 1834 novel, *Rockwood*, William Harrison Ainsworth gives Dick Turpin his legendary horse, Black Bess. Ainsworth borrows from a famous folk-story surrounding the highwayman John Nevison, who was said to have ridden the 200 miles from Kent to York non-stop, in order to establish an alibi for a crime he had committed. In Ainsworth's novel, Turpin has Black Bess gallop overnight from London to York, where his beloved mare promptly dies of exhaustion. The story of Turpin and Bess was so well received that it became popular fodder for the Penny Dreadfuls of the nineteenth century, and thus a powerful (but inaccurate and exaggerated) legend was born.

On the 16th of January 1813, some three quarters of a century after Turpin was hanged, fourteen more lives would end on the gallows at York Castle. The crimes for which these young men died would be recorded variously as 'riot, breaking and entering and attempting to demolish William Cartwright's water mill (for finishing cloth by machinery)'. Unlike Turpin, their actions

were motivated by much more than common greed – indeed it was the greed
of other men that sent them to their deaths. But no gravestone, plaque or
waxwork exhibit marks the passing of their lives. Instead their legacy is a
shallow, overused and inappropriate insult thrown around by those who go
into battle on behalf of the myth of inevitable, beneficent industrial progress.

*

All mythologies must have their monsters, and for modern industrial civilisation it can sometimes seem that there is no more terrifying beast than the
Luddite. The word has today become one of those tame insults which are used
to suggest the superiority of the user without being deemed overly offensive
to the intended recipient. In his *Tips for Transhumanist Activists* (transhumanists study and promote opportunities for enhancing the human organism, and
thereby the human condition, through the use of technology), Michael
Anissimov says:

> Don't use harsh, insulting, unkind words to describe people who
> disagree with your views. … Using words like 'stupid', 'ignorant',
> and 'daft' smack of elitism, and reflect negatively on the speaker,
> only making it clear to everyone that their brain is firmly stuck
> within the pathology of name-calling and tribalistic thinking. If we
> must use some sort of adjective to describe the people we think are
> our 'opponents', then 'Luddite' should do. [1]

By implication Anissimov suggests – intentionally or not – that the Luddites
were not only opposed to new technology, but were 'stupid', 'ignorant' and/or
'daft' to hold such a position in the first place. Unfortunately this attitude is not
unusual. Even academics are prone to treating the historical Luddites as
little more than a naïve and reactionary backlash against the inevitability of
change. As Eric Hobsbawm observed sixty years ago:

> [A]n excellent work … can still describe Luddism simply as a 'point-
> less, frenzied, industrial Jacquerie', and an eminent authority, who
> has contributed more than most to our knowledge of it, passes over
> the endemic rioting of the eighteenth century with the suggestion
> that it was the overflow of excitement and high spirits. Such
> misconceptions are, I think, due to the persistence of views about

the introduction of machinery elaborated in the early nineteenth
century, and of views about labour and trade union history formu-
lated in the late nineteenth century, chiefly by the Webbs and their
Fabian followers. Perhaps we should distinguish views and
assumptions. In much of the discussion of machine-breaking one
can still detect the assumption of nineteenth-century middle-class
economic apologists, that the workers must be taught not to run
their heads against economic truth, however unpalatable; of Fabians
and Liberals, that strong-arm methods in labour action are less
effective than peaceful negotiation; of both, that the early labour
movement did not know what it was doing, but merely reacted,
blindly and gropingly, to the pressure of misery, as animals in the
laboratory react to electric currents. The conscious views of most
students may be summed up as follows: the triumph of mechaniza-
tion was inevitable.[2]

The truth about the Luddites was very different to the clumsy appropriation
of their name for the purposes of contemporary propaganda. Far from being
a naïve, disorganised mob, they were highly-skilled independent craftsmen
whose way of life had been under attack for decades. The mechanical loom
was to these artisans what Twitter is to Homeric poetry.

The tragic story of the men hanged at York began during the winter of
1811, in the village of Bulwell, four miles north of the city of Nottingham.
On the night of November 4th (traditionally known as 'Mischief Night' in
the north of England because children were allowed to play tricks on the rest
of the community – a practice akin to the US tradition of 'Trick or Treat') a
band of men with blackened faces marched through the streets of Bulwell to
the workshop of a 'master weaver' named Hollingsworth, whom they said:
'had rendered himself obnoxious to the workmen.' The men, armed with
a variety of hammers, axes, pitch forks and pistols, forced entry into
Hollingsworth's premises and smashed up a half-dozen wide-lace-frames –
new machines which were said to do the work of many men in a fraction of
the time.

Not content with their actions, the men returned on the following Sunday
night to finish the job, but this time Hollingsworth had a team of gunmen
lying in wait. John Wesley (or Westley), a young weaver from the nearby
village of Arnold, was shot as he tried to gain entry to the premises. With his
dying breath he exclaimed, 'Proceed, my brave fellows, I die with a willing

heart', which so enraged the mob that they pushed forward regardless of the gunfire. Hollingsworth's gunmen fled and the workshop was promptly burnt to the ground.

On the same night, other frames were destroyed in nearby Kimberley, with similar attacks taking place throughout the surrounding areas on the following Monday, Tuesday and Wednesday nights. On the Thursday, the body of John Wesley was carried through the streets of Arnold by a procession of a thousand men. They were met by six armed magistrates, a company of mounted Dragoon guards, a local militia, and a posse of volunteer constables. One of the magistrates read the Riot Act, whereby people were supposed to disperse under threat of immediate arrest. The procession ignored him, and after a scuffle many of them were taken into custody. But if the authorities thought that this might put an end to the matter, they couldn't have been more wrong; Nottinghamshire erupted.

Despite the presence of thousands of troops in the area, over eight-hundred looms were broken in Nottinghamshire during the final months of 1811. And each act of resistance, so it was claimed, was conceived and conducted under the order of one man. As Kirkpatrick Sale observes in his classic work, *Rebels Against the Future*:

> [A]nger was seething in the district, and a rebellion had begun which would not be smothered by Dragoons and magistrates. It was now that anonymous letters explaining the causes of the machine breaking and threatening more of it started appearing throughout the district, mailed to or slipped under the doors of hated hosiers, sent to local newspapers, or posted in the night on public boards – 'many hundreds' of them ... reported one manufacturer. All announced that a new concerted movement was afoot; all were signed by, or invoked the name of Edward (Ned) Ludd, 'King,' 'Captain in Chief,' or 'General.' ... Luddism had begun.[3]

There has been much speculation as to the origins of the name Ned Ludd, but the most popular theory also seems to be the most likely. Edward Ludd (or Ludlum) is said to have been a boy from the village of Anstey, just outside Leicester. In 1779 he was employed as a weaver's apprentice, but was beaten for 'idleness' by his master. Not much caring for being whipped like a dog, young Ned took a hammer to two of his master's knitting frames and promptly 'beat them into a heap'. From that moment on, whenever anyone damaged a loom, whether by accident or with malicious intent, it was common for people to say, 'Ned Ludd did it'. We cannot know the truth behind the story of Ned Ludd, but we do know that 1779 marked the beginning of the end of the traditional weaving trade. In the closing years of the eighteenth century, the weaver's profession would come under threat; not only from the introduction of new technology, but also from the newly emerging capitalist attitudes towards production. To return to Kirkpatrick Sale:

> Lancashire, say 1780:
> The workshop of the weaver was a rural cottage, from which when he was tired of sedentary labour he could sally forth into his little garden, and with the spade or the hoe tend its culinary productions. The cotton wool which was to form his weft was picked clean for him by the fingers of his younger children, and was carded and spun by the older girls assisted by his wife, and the yarn was woven by himself assisted by his sons. When he could not procure within his family a supply of yarn adequate to the demands of his loom, he had recourse to the spinsters of his neighbourhood. One good weaver could keep three active women at work upon the wheel, spinning weft [although] he was often obliged to treat the females with presents in order to quicken their diligence at the wheel.[4]

> Lancashire, say 1814:
> There are hundreds of factories in Manchester which are five or six storeys high. At the side of each factory there is a great chimney which belches forth black smoke and indicates the presence of powerful steam engines. The smoke from the chimneys forms a great cloud which can be seen for miles around the town. The houses have become black on account of the smoke. The river on which Manchester stands is so tainted with colouring matter that the water resembles the contents of a dye-vat ... To save wages mule jennies have actually been built so that no less than 600 spindles can be operated by one adult and two children. Two mules, each with 300 spindles, face each other. The carriages of these machines are moved in one direction by steam and in the other direction by hand. This is done by an adult worker who stands between two mules. Broken threads are repaired by children (piecers) who stand either side of

the mules ... In the large spinning mills machines of different kinds stand in rows like regiments in an army.[5]

It was, make no mistake about it, an industrial revolution, an alteration of such speed and complexity and scale as to dwarf even the considerable upheavals that had come in the centuries before.[6]

The 'considerable upheavals' of the 'centuries before' of course include the enclosure of land, and the enforced urbanisation and loss of commons which went with it. As Simon Fairlie demonstrated in the first issue of *Dark Mountain*,[7] a significant percentage of the population either made a good living directly from the commons or depended upon them for food and vital resources when times were hard. The increased levels of autonomy and self-sufficiency offered by the commons also meant that people were not as susceptible to exploitation. If you had free and open access to food, grazing pasture and materials for shelter and/or energy, i.e. wood, then you did not have to be at the constant beck and call of farmers, proprietors and landowners. Indeed, many labourers and artisans worked only as long as was needed to ensure that the immediate needs of their families were met; the idea of working to the clock for extra surplus value (profit) would have seemed somewhat ludicrous, as Kirkpatrick Sale observes:

Time was a medium, not a commodity, and the workers were not its slaves; in dozens of trades the tradition of 'St Monday', as important a day of rest as sainted Sunday, was inviolable – and as like as not Tuesday too (and even Wednesday) if the tasks were not too pressing ... Work usually involved some bodily skill and some mental agility, often a craft in which a person would take some pride, usually with the family pitching in.[8]

It wasn't just family ties that were closer thanks to pre-capitalist production methods, community life benefited as well. Of the weaving communities, E. P. Thompson says:

A unique blend of social conservatism, local pride, and cultural attainment made up the way of life of the Yorkshire or Lancashire weaving community. In one sense these communities were certainly 'backward' – they clung with equal tenacity to their dialect traditions and regional customs and to gross medical ignorance and superstitions. But the closer we look at their way of life, the more inadequate simple notions of economic progress and 'backwardness' appear. Moreover there was certainly a leaven amongst the northern weavers of self-educated and articulate men of considerable attainments. Every weaving district had its weaver-poets, biologists, mathematicians, musicians, geologists, botanists: ... [T]here are accounts of weavers in isolated villages who taught themselves geometry by chalking on their flagstones, and who were eager to discuss the differential calculus. In some kinds of plain work with strong yarn a book could actually be propped on the loom and read at work.[9]

Compare this to today's time-bound, ultra-specialised (politely referred to as 'professional'), careerist, who is such a slave to the clock that they are more likely to consume than create whenever they have any spare time; indeed, excess time is sold back to the workforce in the form of 'leisure' which leads to the creation of yet more 'careers' and – more importantly for the capitalists – a whole lot of extra profit. As capitalism has progressed, knowledge has been reduced to a meritocratic means-to-an-end (qualification) rather than an end in its own right; and in wealthier countries the self-educated polymath has become an endangered species.

Robbed of their traditional land-rights, and divorced from communal production methods, the artisans and peasantry were forced instead to rely on the wage-labour system; and the newly dominant mercantile classes took full advantage of the situation. It is easy to forget that the mythologies which shape the attitudes and actions of a culture – in our case beliefs like wage-labour, the work ethic, proprietary ownership, profit and progress – needed to be invented, developed, endorsed and enforced like any other man-made product. The patterns of life we now consider normal could only come to dominate at the expense of traditional beliefs. And so the industrial revolution brought with it new attitudes towards work which would prove as devastating to communal life as enclosure itself.[10]

*

By January 1812, the area north of Nottingham was awash with troops sent from around the country. Armed deployments on this scale were unprecedented and the local population lived in anxious fear. Lines from the 1812 Nottingham *Annual Register* read 'It is impossible to convey a proper idea of the state of the public mind in this town during ... the constant parading of the military in the night, and their movements in various directions both night and day, giving us the appearance of a state of warfare.' Indeed, as is often the case when forced to choose between trade and people, the government treated the Luddites as a direct enemy of the state (what Margaret Thatcher would have described as 'the enemy within'), and on 14th February, the Tory government introduced a bill to make loom-breaking punishable by death. When the bill was read to the House of Lords on 27th February, it was received with what is perhaps the most eloquent and impassioned speech in the history of the British parliament; understandable when the man delivering it was Lord Byron.

Byron's speech was loaded with sarcastic references as to the 'benefits' of progress. He questioned the inferior quality of the items produced through automation when compared to similar items produced by the hands of artisans. He argued that the men in question had never had a fair hearing from the government (no less than three petitions from some eighty-thousand weavers had been delivered to parliament in the build up to the events of 1811), and that the area could have easily been restored to 'tranquillity ... had proper meeting been held in the earlier stages of the riots'. Instead, 'your Dragoons and executioners must be let loose against your fellow citizens ... Can you commit a whole country to their own prisons? Will you erect a gibbet in every field and hang up men like scarecrows? ... Are these remedies for a starving and desperate populace? Will the famished wretches who have braved your bayonets be appalled by your gibbets? When death is a relief, and the only relief it appears you will afford him, will he be dragooned into tranquillity?'

Unfortunately, capital and the state – inseparable aspects of what William Cobbett called 'The Thing' – are driven solely by motives of profit and power, and are therefore impervious to arguments based on knowledgeable reason or impassioned intuition (Byron being one of the only Lords ever to offer both). And so, somewhat predictably, the bill was passed into law. As is ever the case with government, that which cannot be subdued must be destroyed.

Fortunately, those arrested in November and December were exempt from the death penalty having committed their 'crimes' before this new law was

passed. But having escaped hanging, those convicted were instead transported
to Australia. One of the men singled out as a 'ringleader', twenty-two year
old William Carnell, was described as having 'the merit of protecting the
occupier of the House, an old man of 70 from any personal violence' – in stark
contrast to Turpin's pistol-whipping exploits.

The strong military presence and the threat of judicial murder did appear
to have an immediate effect on the local population, with only thirty frames
being broken in February compared to over 300 in January. After this, frame-
breaking in Nottinghamshire became even less frequent, although 1812 did
see regular food riots in the area which were themselves a by-product of the
hardship created by the introduction of the mechanical looms. But this was by
no means the end of General Ludd's war.

On 12th January 1812, a finishing machine was destroyed in Leeds, and on
the 15th of January, Leeds' magistrates raided a meeting of men with 'blackened faces'. Then, on the morning of Sunday 19th January, the finishing mill
of Oates, Woods and Smithson, just north of Leeds, was found to be ablaze.
Yorkshire, it seemed, was in the thrall of King Ludd. On the 9th of February,
he further extended his reign when the Manchester warehouse of the textile
manufacturing firm, Haigh, Marshal & Co., was set on fire, destroying the
machine-manufactured cloth stored inside.

When we consider the hell that the industrial revolution had unleashed in
a single generation, it is small wonder that the thoughts and actions of the
Luddites found fertile ground in the smoke-blackened streets of the industrialised north. Having borne the brunt of industrialisation for three decades,
they knew better than most what factories and machines could do to the
welfare of the local population. In living memory the vast majority of the well-
fed peasantry and relatively wealthy artisans had been reduced to a powerless,
starving proletariat – and all in the name of progress.

As the Luddite influence moved north it became clear that far from being
reactionary, the Luddites were an insurrectionary movement. In Yorkshire
and Lancashire they became more highly disciplined and more overtly political than before. Here, for the first time, there is evidence of oath-taking; oaths
(from the Old English ð) were considered so serious that an echo of the practice can still be found in the modern judicial process (swearing on the Bible)
and in parliamentary ceremonies (where tradition has always been held in
higher regard than reason). Under British law, the act of oath-taking was punishable by transportation, no matter which cause was being pledged or who
was involved. In Luddite circles, taking an oath was known as 'twisting-in',

in reference to the twisting of separate threads to form a single, stronger yarn. This sworn bond was further strengthened by military-style, night-time drills. Kirkpatrick Sale elaborates:

> Along with oathing, a greater emphasis on training and marching surfaces in the Lancashire and Yorkshire accounts, suggesting that the intensity was ratcheted higher there. The report of the Committee of the House of Lords that investigated Luddism later that year may be somewhat florid, but the details are mostly corroborated elsewhere:
>
> They assemble in large numbers, in general by night, upon heaths or commons, which are numerous and extensive in some of the districts where the disturbances have been most serious; so assembled they take the military precautions of paroles and countersigns; then muster rolls are called over by numbers, not by names; they are directed by leaders sometimes in disguise; they place sentries to give alarm ... and they disperse instantly at the firing of a gun, or other signal agreed upon, so as to avoid detection.
>
> Whether or not such training was going on in every area of the counties, certainly stories of 'midnight drills' and 'the measured tramp of feet' and 'mysterious shots in the moors' were common enough.[11]

Sale also observes another tendency of the Yorkshire and Lancashire Luddites:

> Ratcheted higher, too, was the violence. ... [T]he attacks now focused on the large factories – the power-loom mills of Lancashire, the finishing mills of Yorkshire – since they were the source of the most immediate grievances. And as the targets were larger so the forces amassed were greater, the weapons more numerous, and the damage more extensive.[12]

On the night of 12th April 1812, an armed band of some six-score Yorkshiremen made their way to Rawfolds Mill, a factory owned by the hated William Cartwright. Inside the mill stood fifty steam-powered finishing machines which had put at least two-hundred croppers out of work. Inside too was William Cartwright, four armed workers and five soldiers from the Cumberland militia. The factory itself was built like a fortress, with an ingenious system of pulleys and flagstones that allowed marksmen to take aim from the second floor whilst remaining concealed and protected from gunfire themselves.

As they arrived at the factory, several men came forward and used hatchets and blacksmith's Enoch-hammers to break down the factory's outer gates, which fell 'with a fearful crash, like the felling of great trees.' Spurred on by this, the men rushed forward and began to smash the factory windows. Then the gunfire started. Despite one Cumberland militiaman refusing to fire 'because I might hit one of my brothers' – for which Cartwright would have him publicly flogged outside the mill on 21st April – volley after volley was fired into the assembled crowd. Undeterred, the men took their hammers to the factory doors; but tight metal studs deeply embedded in the timbers made progress painfully slow. All the while an alarm bell rang out from the rooftop. Aware that a cavalry brigade was stationed at nearby Huddersfield, the men must have known that time was against them, but still they hammered at the factory doors.

John Booth, a saddler's apprentice and clergyman's son, was first to be shot when the doors finally gave way, his leg shattered by a musket ball. A black-smith named Jonathan Dean was then wounded in the hand as he wielded his hammer. Knowing the game was up, the Luddites began to retreat, but as they withdrew Samuel Hartley, a 24 year old cropper, was hit in the chest. The men had little choice but to leave the mortally wounded Booth and Hartley where they lay, if they were to have any hope of avoiding capture themselves.

Booth and Hartley were still alive when Cartwright emerged from the mill, but he refused them any aid until they gave the names of their comrades. The men refused. Booth died at six in the morning; Hartley survived until the next day. Neither gave testimony against their Luddite brethren.

Other men must also have received mortal wounds that night, for a local minister, Reverend Patrick Brontë, records that two days after the event he came across a group of known Luddites burying two corpses in the corner of his churchyard. Of the Reverend, Sale says:

> Although this was clearly the act of criminals and the churchman had an obligation to tell the authorities forthwith, he said nothing, watching it all in a silence that he kept – for, as he said later, he would not betray his flock over a Christian burial. This kind-hearted man ... was the father of three rather famous daughters,

one of whom [Charlotte] attended and then taught at a school only
a few miles away that overlooked the field where the Luddite army
had gathered before the Rawfolds raid.[13]

Following the failed attack on Cartwright's mill, and with the much despised
West Riding magistrate Joseph Radcliffe (famed for ordering poor and or-
phaned children as young as seven to work in the factories of Huddersfield)
'scouring the district for Luds', Luddites in Huddersfield began to target
smaller, less well-defended premises. But the large, factory-owning manu-
facturers were still regarded as the real enemy, so a new tactic came into being.

On 18th April, an attempt was made on the life of William Cartwright.
Shots were fired, but he was unhurt. Ten days later William Horsfall, owner
of Ottiwells Mills, who famously declared that he 'would ride up to his
saddle girths in Luddite Blood', was ambushed by four men as he rode home.
Horsfall was shot in the thigh and died later that night of his wounds. It is
widely accepted that this murder marked a turning point for the Luddite
rebellion; previously widespread support for their cause began to dwindle in
light of this murder. George Mellor (a 24 year old cropper who would also be
cited as one of the ringleaders in the attack on Cartwright's mill), William
Thorpe and Thomas Smith would later be hanged for the murder of William
Horsfall on Friday 8th January, 1813.

The first Luddite executions, however, took place in June 1812, over the
Pennines in Manchester. Indeed, Lancashire and Cheshire saw the greatest
loss of life during the whole rising. At the end of April, a series of food riots
erupted in Manchester and the surrounding towns of Bolton, Rochdale,
Oldham and Ashton. Similar riots, and some loom-breaking, took place in
the north Derbyshire village of Tintwhistle and the Cheshire village of Gee
Cross – where one man, later deported for his actions, wore a paper hat bearing the words 'General Ludd'.

The unrest came to a head on 20th April in the town of Middleton, 10 miles
north of Manchester. A crowd gathered in Wood Street, at the steam-powered
calico printing factory owned by Daniel Burton & Sons. The crowd threw
stones at the factory windows, and in response a volley of shots was fired from
somewhere within the factory. Somebody in the crowd said that they were
only firing blanks, and the stoning continued. But the rounds were live, and
four members of the crowd, Daniel Knott, Joseph Jackson, George Albinson
and John Siddall, were shot dead.

The next day the enraged crowd returned, bent on avenging the blood of their fellows, to find a troop of Cumberland militia posted outside the factory. Instead of attacking it directly, they responded by ransacking the cottages of men who worked at the factory, and burnt Emmanuel Burton's stately mansion to the ground. They intended to do the same to Daniel Burton's property, but cavalry troops turned up and started firing into the crowd. At least four more people died that day, but there were also several reports of bodies being found in the woods in the following weeks.

On 24th May, fifty-eight defendants were brought to trial in Lancaster in association with the food riots, loom-breaking and attacks on property that had taken place throughout April. The trial resulted in eight hangings, seventeen transportations and thirteen imprisonments. On the same day a 'Special Commission' was held in Chester to deal with more of the rioters and Luddites. Here fifteen were condemned to death, eight transported and five imprisoned. On 12th June, eight of the Luddites convicted in Lancaster were hanged in Manchester. None were repentant. Three days later, two Luddites convicted in Chester marched to their place of execution, 'followed by an immense crowd of people'.

The 'Luddite triangle' was now completely flooded with troops; some 6,900 in Lancashire and Cheshire and 4,000 in Yorkshire. The magistrates had dozens of spies working in those areas known to be sympathetic to the Luddite cause, and the government had sent a clear message that Luddism was now punishable by death. In the face of all this, the Yorkshire Luddites began to raid any properties which were known to store arms, for the Luddites were amassing weaponry. Was the insurrection about to turn into full scale revolution?

We shall never know. The government had seen the benefits of its own tactics in Lancashire and was determined to repeat this success in Yorkshire. By December 1812, on the evidence of paid spies and some very questionable witnesses, sixty-four men had been arrested and held for trial at York Castle. Of these sixty-four, only seven would be acquitted. Fourteen men were transported and twenty-six were imprisoned. The aforementioned Mellor, Thorpe and Smith were executed on 8th January 1813 and fourteen more men – with an average age of 25 – were sentenced to die at York castle on 16th January.

Of their execution it has been written:

> The criminal records of Yorkshire do not, perhaps, afford an
> instance of so many victims having been offered, in one day, to the
> injured laws of the country. The scene was inexpressibly awful, and

the large body of soldiers, both horse and foot, who guarded the approach to the castle, and were planted in front of the fatal tree, gave the scene a peculiar degree of horror.[14]

*

That, in effect, was the end of the Luddite rising. There was still some recorded Luddite activity in the months and years following the York trial, but there was a marked change in motives. Prior to 1813, the Luddites had wanted to save an autonomous, communal way of life based on self-sufficiency and skilled craftsmanship. Later loom-breaking incidents were almost exclusively centred around disputes regarding levels of pay; reflecting the later (and modern) labour movement, which claimed to stand against capitalism, but failed to question the central tenets of the 'progressive' production system.

This was the beginning of the marked shift from pre-modern to modern – or perhaps pre-industrial to industrial – forms of rebellion. Put simply, pre-modern resistance was a fight against enclosure – a battle to save independent, self-sufficient ways of life from destruction; to prevent the industrial machine from enslaving the people. Modern industrial unrest was a battle waged after this war had been lost. Now the focus was on justice for the proletarian victims of the Industrial Revolution: better wages, better living conditions, the right for factory workers to form unions, the right to be looked after by a beneficent state.

Despite the wars, tensions and revolutions that cost millions of human lives during the twentieth century, every dominant 'ism' – no matter how revolutionary it claimed to be – had the powerful, Western-industrial mythologies of progress, the work ethic, profit and growth at its heart. In Europe, the only revolution to offer any noticeable hope of something different was that of Spain in 1936. The Spanish peasantry of the time still lived the kind of autonomous, self-sufficient lives that the northern English weavers had enjoyed until the end of the seventeenth century. They were, to put it bluntly, far less domesticated than their counterparts in the urbanised, industrialised proletariat. So, when anarchist-inspired ideas of a free society – free that is from hierarchy, economic inequality and exploitation – were introduced to their communities, they were largely welcomed because they were, to a large degree, already being practised. Small wonder then that the Spain George Orwell visited in 1936 was 'the only community of any size in Western Europe where political consciousness and disbelief in capitalism were more normal than their opposites' and 'the normal motives of civilized life – snobbishness, money-grubbing, fear of the boss, etc – had simply ceased to exist'.

Today, in the West, the ideas that the Luddites fought for look prehistoric. Our societies have been so comprehensively remade in the image of capital that it is hard to talk about concepts like self-sufficiency, independence and the land without being immediately dismissed by progressives on right and left as Romantics – and, of course, 'Luddites'. Elsewhere in the world, though, these ideas still have some purchase. Arguably, in fact, the only viable alternatives to the dominant progressive ideology today are peasant-based. Movements like Brazil's Movimento sem Terra (MST), Mexico's EZLN (Zapatistas), South Africa's Landless People's Movement or India's Bhumi Uchhed Pratirodh Committee, question the standard mythology of an increasingly global civilisation and offer something a little different from the usual progressive rhetoric.[15] The land-based movements of the twenty-first century may have little hope of becoming a worldwide revolution – certainly not within the time-scale dictated by catastrophic climate change or peak-oil – but these communities may yet prove to be the most resilient in the face of an unfolding collapse.

Here in Britain, where the Luddites took their doomed stand, we can no longer seek to emulate them. It is too late for that. But it is not too late to take some lessons away from the rebellion of the weavers, and apply them to our times.

This should start with accepting that the Luddites were right. The Thing – the state-industrial nexus which Cobbett identified in its infancy – is now the dominant force in the world, and its mythology shapes the times we live in. Today the mill owners are global brands. On their own terms, and according to their own stories, this should mean that we all benefit from the bounty their markets give us. But we don't:

> Today of the approximately 6 billion people in the world, it is esti-
> mated that at least a billion live in abject poverty, lives cruel, empty,
> and mercifully short. Another 2 billion eke out life on a bare sub-
> sistence level, usually sustained only by one or another starch, the
> majority without potable drinking water or sanitary toilets. More
> than 2 million more live at the bottom edges of the money economy
> but with incomes less than $5,000 a year and no property or savings,
> no net worth to pass on to their children. That leaves less than a
> billion people who even come close to struggling for lives of comfort,

with jobs and salaries of some regularity, and a quite small minority at the top of that scale who could really be said to have achieved comfortable lives; in the world, some 350 people can be considered (US dollar) billionaires (with slightly more than 3 million millionaires), and their total net worth is estimated to exceed that of 45 per cent of the world's population.[16]

This is before we even begin to explore how genuinely free and satisfied the enclosed masses of the industrialised world really are, and it is also before we start to discuss the ecocide that has been unleashed on the non-human world by the industrial machine. The Luddites may not have seen this coming, but they certainly knew what the consequences would be for them, their families and their way of life.

From this we can take away a realistic assessment of the powerful, perhaps unstoppable nature of the global industrial machine. But we can take away too an understanding of the role of technology in our lives, and start to think a little more clearly about what that role should be in the early twenty-first century.

The word 'Luddite' today is easily and instantly identified with one thing: rejection of new technology. The fact that this is a travesty of the historical reality of the Luddite movement does not make it any less true. You are a Luddite today if you turn up your nose at using a Satnav or Twitter or an iPhone or a laptop, or if you object to nuclear power or wind turbines or smart meters, and the implication carried within the insult is clear: you are reactionary and backward-looking and have nothing to offer the modern world. In turn, another assumption is clear within this one: all new technology is good; all change is good; all progress is good, and all else is mumbo jumbo.

In reality, instinctive resistance to technology and its mindless embrace are two sides of the same coin, and neither are especially helpful. I actually have a lot of time for Anissimov's Transhumanists, in that I share their belief that our species can be made 'better by design'. What I don't share is their assumption about what this means. Improving the human lot through the use of technology is not going to be achieved through a combination of surveillance camera and warheads, nor through a combination of nuclear power stations and carbon capture, nor through a transhumanist Singularity in which those who can afford to pay for it become immortal semi-robots.

Instead, it's going to mean developing and using human-scale technologies which can augment our liberty and self-sufficiency rather than enslaving us to a grid. It's going to mean hand-looms rather than wide-frames; control by the people rather than control of them. The best way to avoid being controlled by technology is to be in control of the technology you use.

If this sounds idealistic, it's actually already becoming a reality. If you take a visit to one of the many websites which encourage a little technical-tinkering (instructables.com, hacknmod.com or makezine.com, to name but a few) you'll find that a combination of free and open information, Open Source software, reduced material costs, high volumes of useful waste, and micro-innovations have made it possible to develop and create projects at home – from bicycle trailers to slow cookers to mini robots – that would have needed highly specialised multi-million-dollar factories just a few years ago. The amazing Afrigadget website chronicles stories of remarkably creative individuals who seem to be able to build a range of tools from next to nothing (such as the inspirational Frederick Msiska,[17] a Malawi peasant farmer who built a mobile phone charger from his toilet and some leaves.)

We are now, in other words, approaching a position where it may be possible to create once again an infrastructure built upon localised, craft-orientated, community-based, ecologically sensitive, production techniques – in other words to potentially return to the pre-capitalist idea of the cottage industry which the Luddites fought so hard to defend. It's a world in which not only is it easier to work in and from your home, but it is easier to work away from the growth-addicted world of capitalist production. Traditional crafts are also experiencing a renaissance as people look for more ecologically sound and more self-reliant ways to live. The artisan, it seems, is coming back from the brink of extinction – just as progressive civilisation itself begins to tip over the brink.

Writing of the legacy of the appropriate technology movement of the 1970s, John Michael Greer says:

> The appropriate tech movement, with some exceptions, tended to avoid the kind of high-cost, high-profile eco-chic projects so common today. Much of it focused instead on simple technologies that could be put to work by ordinary people without six-figure incomes, doing the work themselves, using ordinary tools and readily available resources. Most of these technologies were evolved by basement-shop craftspeople and small nonprofits working on shoestring budgets, and ruthlessly field-tested by thousands of people who built their own versions in their backyards and wrote about the results

in the letters column of Mother Earth News ... The resulting toolkit was a remarkably well integrated, effective, and cost-effective set of approaches that individuals, families, and communities could use to sharply reduce their dependence on fossil fuels and the industrial system in general.[18]

Such a toolkit is needed again, and is starting to appear, in response to the crisis of consumer civilisation. I see at least some spark of a hopeful future in the development, practice and sharing of what I call ADApT (Anticipatory Design and Appropriate Technology) initiatives, which can help us to distance ourselves from the corporate leviathan and restore some of the freedom of action and creativity that the Luddites went to their graves to protect.

†

In memory of

James Haigh, Jonathan Dean, John Ogden,
Thomas Brook, John Walker, John Swallow,
John Batley, Joseph Fisher, Job Hey,
James Hey, John Hill, William Hartley,
Joseph Crowther and Nathan Hoyle.

*Murdered in the name of Progress
on 16th January, 1813.*

Notes

1. Anissimov, M. 'Tips for Transhumanist Activists', August 2003.
   [http://acceleratingfuture.com/michael/works/transhumanisttips.htm.]
2. Hobsbawm, E. 'The Machine Breakers', *Past & Present* 1 (1952), pp. 57-70.
3. Sale, K. *Rebels Against the Future: Lessons for the Computer Age* (Quartet Books Ltd, 1996).
4. Ure, A. *Cotton Manufacture of Great Britain*, volume 1, (C. Wright, 1835), p. 191;
   cited in K. Sale, *Rebels* (1996).
5. Henderson, W. O. *Industrial Britain Under the Regency* (Frank Cass, 1968); cited in K. Sale,
   Rebels (1996).
6. Sale, K. *Rebels* (1996).
7. Fairlie, S. 'The tragedy of the Tragedy of the Commons', *Dark Mountain: Issue 1* (Dark
   Mountain Project, 2010).
8. Sale, K. *Rebels* (1996).
9. Thompson, E. P. *The Making of the English Working Class* (Penguin Books, 1980).
10. I expand upon the 'mind forg'd manacles' created during the Industrial Revolution – and
    offer hope to would-be polymaths – in a partner article to this one. See W. Draper,
    'The Work Aesthetic', *The Idler No. 44* (2011). [http://idler.co.uk.]
11. Sale, K. *Rebels* (1996).
12. Sale, K. *Rebels* (1996), pp. 109–110.
13. Sale, K. *Rebels* (1996).
14. Peel, F. *The Risings of the Luddites, Chartists and Plug-drawers* (Frank Cass, 1968); cited in
    K. Sale, *Rebels* (1996).
15. For more information on these important, but widely ignored, peasant movements, visit:
    http://viacampesina.org.
16. Sale, K. 'Five Facets of a Myth', (no date). [http://primitivism.com/facets-myth.htm.]
17. Msiska's story features in 'Rural people more creative than townfolk!', part of a planned
    documentary by M. Gondwe (*African Science Heroes,* unfinished). 'Rural people …' was
    published on YouTube by 'Afriscihero', 22 March 2010.
    [http://youtube.com/watch?v=J7bQm3hZioc&feature=player_embedded#!]
    See also the African Science Heroes blog. [http://afrisciheroes.wordpress.com/.]
18. Greer, J. M. 'Merlin's Time', *The Archdruid Report* [blog], 30 June 2010.
    [http://thearchdruidreport.blogspot.com/2010/06/merlins-time.html.]

STEPHEN WHEELER

American Road Movie

Passing by Bristol (again), where the M5
  Siphons seamlessly off of the M4 – because,
    Apparently, no-one really wants to stop —

And dull burrs of hill struggle upward from the soil
  In vain attempt at relief amidst the gentle rotundity of
    English quiltwork green – whilst, above, almost touching,

Massed thunderheads glower uneasily
  Like hurt cloddings of dim putty —
    We are ferried past, along the slick tarmac,

The Last Manufactory in Great Britain; twin slanted squares
  Of corrugated white, clinging stubborn to the
    Clay, and guttering memories of piecework and clamour.

And holding the plain across its flanks, the
  Serried armies of hatchbacks, vast parking lot
    Of painted units, flocked like steely sheep

In white and red, their noses facing the ridge of our transit,
  In challenge or in eager solidarity; and to their left,
    The vanguard, a fresh cohort of commercial vehicles,

Highsided, impatient, edging towards the silted
  Conduits of speed, saying: We too will join you,
    We too will plough the new furrows of the age,

Pouring more sound into the sky, pelting the green
  With visions of grey, draining more black
    From the deeps of the earth – We too, we soon ...

Little knowing that their ranks are already in retreat,
  Exhausting, depleted, supplicant to the rule of
    Returning, to circle, and the rusting bones of the land.

And so we pass, towards villages, and green, and older ways,
  Up into the fastnesses of the bevelled hills
    And out, into the choiceless plains beyond.

The General Assembly
Dark Mountain Music

We followed the fires until we finally found it – too nervous to talk, too scared to be silent. It's black and it's bitter but it breathes us in. We were made in the mountains now they're drawing us back. There's bells on the branches and paint on the track. We've marked out the way but we're not coming back.

We're howling in the mountains, burning bones, firing off flares, calling you home. The moon is rising, the night is closing in. The darkness breathes and draws us in again. The story starts at the end of everything.

download your four songs by
The General Assembly at:
tgamusic.bandcamp.com

BENJAMIN MORRIS

Three poems

Dzud

The blizzard's never seen the desert sands...
  – Kristian Matsson

Oh, but it has. Imagine winter for most
of the year on the steppes, where death
is a cough bearing ice on its breath.
See: livestock piled in heaps, pyres of waste
frozen into place until the spring thaw
which every year recedes into the distance.
Were there some form of landward sextant
you would sail away from, and I back towards,
this season with no name. It's all I know,
these encyclicals of snow and dirt
encrusted on the heart, so why desert
the hurt that heart calls home? Last you wrote
you dreamed of beaches south – of sun,
of warm sand. Oh, how I would run, will run.

Torrey Canyon

I would hate to know how many are underneath it.
 – Jayne Le Cras

One million and four. Since 1967
they've seen the slick as a place to land,
a smooth patch of soil that worms and
time have made slick as glass. Even
the sunlight is confused, its rays sinking
down into the muck past the water's
surface. In the night-stained sludge an otter
dreams eternally of oysters, of drinking
anything but mud. Its bones melt into
one another, buffeted by creatures
who saw water for oil, this new feature
the landscape itself and not the window.
No bird flies except towards its death.
One million and five, gasping for breath.

Low Country

All I have ever wanted
is a mountain,
         a rock
where rivers are born,
on which bracken clusters
and scree falls, where
the map must be built,
not splayed: a jagged line
for the eye to grasp onto
in this endless ocean
of sky—

         not these fens
flat as paper from the press,
broken only by canals
and rails signing the fields
in steel. To tower over them
we must only stand up,
to rinse the one tree
from the horizon we need
but squint and it is gone.

Were this landscape a lover
I would leave it without mercy—
no wet letter or backwards glance,
no matter how full its eyes of dew.
It could chase me with storms,
send tornadoes to spin me around,
but still I would shun it
in search of my mind's desire:

the savage join of crag
and cloud, cove of goat,
proof of gravity spurned,

where smoke tendrils north
in the morning and shadows
lay stiff on the slate – where,
this far up, this near to the sun,
the only way out is *in*—

SIMON LYS

Fragments of a Shared Madness

My thick gloved fingers are twirling a dance of absentminded twists in the dead rope when the mountain tricks me, the petrified king in all his majesty, dark black eyes staring out from under his fringe of white. I see him shift and rise in his throne

Then the scream shatters everything. The scream, the slip, the screech of the rope, the body of my companion plummeting down. (Companion is easier to say than friend.)

And the laugh of the king in the silence.

I cut myself out from the tangles and burns and fall into the soft white, aware that I have buried myself, aware that my friend will have no burial, that he will lie undigested in the gaping mouth forever.

I scurry as injured prey from the drift, bewildered at this life I still have beating inside of me. My body starts to shake, to expel the shock. I tear at my coat, my shirt, my vest, throwing them off but I cannot free the shaking. Nothing is enough. It has frozen inside of me.

My bare arms turn purple and goosefleshed and I welcome the raw pain.

I go on, out into the white void, wind and sky for company. I leave my pack, my tent, my water, my food. I try to leave it all behind. All I take is a length of rope, looped around my shoulders; a reminder of negligence, of cost. I can smell blood in the hemp.

I dream this walk over the mountains. It itches between my shoulder blades, I think wings may be trying to grow. I am heading down, but down does not go in one direction and there is much that I must climb. I trek through the sleep realm where the hungry ghosts dwell ready to latch ticklike into my imaginings, burying their heads down into my soul.

The crevasse is not three foot wide – jumpable and unremarkable but for the brilliant turquoise it gives off in this morning light. It is long, a bright blue gash across the mountainside. It stops me and I know I have to look in it. Black ragged shapes in the blue. My stomach sees abandoned packs; my brain sees dead bodies.

Hold and pull, pull tight, handflesh burns, rough rope slices against raw skin. I drag, reeling the catch in. Her fingers come over the lip. They are colder even than the snow. Iced bones curl like damp wood, they clasp around my mittenless flesh.

I want to feel a pulse through her wet paper skin, a reassurance that I am not holding a ghost. I do not want to have dragged a demon from the depths.

I lift her body free from the abyss. It is as stiff and unwieldy as a sack of logs dragged in on a winter's day. I let her fall soft to the snow. She is wrapped, bundled in many layers, things tied tight to her. I lean close. My breath hangs its chilled smoke like a shroud over her face. I watch her neck for signs of life. Shadows fall on us.

A dark angel is hovering. Wings thick and leathery, with a frail body wasted, the angel sings to me as she circles. She touches to the earth beside us and rubs between her old legs to make it wet, to get one last gasp of moisture. She rubs the stickiness between her fingers, blows softly on it, then she bends down over the bandaged woman. She rubs the wetness on her closed eyelids, streaks one lid then the other, daubing her.

The woman's eyes open, a bright blue surrounded by a golden halo. She see us, me and the angel. She blinks. I help her up to standing. There is a thump of heavy wings and we are alone.

The sky is greying; the crevasse has lost its brightness. We stand and face each other.

'Please look away,' she says. I nod and turn out into the sea of the snow.

'Night will not come this evening,' I say. 'The moon will be too bright, too big to let any darkness fall. We must use it, keep going, as far as we can. Get down to lower ground. Get away from the bite of the cold.'

She says nothing, I can hear wrapping and unbinding. I keep my eyes down into the mist of the valley. There are soft murmurings, like tiny birds, I do not know if they lie with the wind or with her.

'I am ready to go,' she announces. She has retied the cloths; they are radiant and rainbowed, like a tropical bird. Bound to her back are two bundles, like the humps of a camel. 'My children,' she says. I take a step towards her.

'They are sleeping,' she says. 'We will go gently. I do not want to wake them. They need their sleep. After what they have seen, what they have been through, it has made them ill. They must sleep. It is the way to get better.'

We walk through the day and through the darkless night, until the moon shines purple in a coloured world I have never seen before. She keeps beside me, she does not slip a footing, she sings soft songs under her breath, barely formed lullabies. We walk as if in a trance through a soft drizzle of rain.

The sun bleeds her morning and births the day. We are down in the foothills. We make a pile of sticks and wood and leaves. The land is verdant here, a stream courses life down from above. Soft thunder rolls and lightning dances. The wet sticks leap and catch the flame. A sizzling burn, a magician's flash of smoke. And there is warmth. We are in paradise.

She unties one of the bundles from her back and lays it on the earth beside the fire. She unwraps the coloured cloth. The little boy within is still and silent, his lips are blue and his eyelids frosted shut. She strokes his forehead. She lifts him in a cradle.

She bares her breast and holds him to her.

I stare into the fire. In the charred wood teeth snap angry bites. The wind blows soft in the sunlight. It is beautiful here.

She takes the child from her breast. The movement makes me turn. Her breast is withered, the nipple a dark flush of maroon petals. Thick blackness drips in clods from it. She places a hand over, to cover it, hide it away, but she sees I have seen. She turns from me. I start to cry.

I look at the boy. His face is now streaked with this thick black. Painted for a war that he will never grow to be soldier for.

Birds circle, ready to peck.

She swaddles the child again and slings him to her back.

'It is time to move on,' she says. 'It is dangerous to stop.'

But my body has accustomed itself to sitting. 'We have walked for hours,' I say. 'Let us rest a while longer.'

'No!' She is on her feet and walking away from the fire, out towards the trees.

I jog after her. She talks as we go. I stumble to keep up, sliding on the loose scree.

'They came in the night,' she says. 'There was no warning. They smashed the door with the butts of their rifles. They crushed skulls with the steel of their boots. Fire fled in screams through the city. But our ancestors lie in this land generations deep. We are the land, we are its richness and its food. How dare they say it is not ours?

'I saw them stick flaming torches up inside young girls until their bellies glowed like lanterns. I saw them bite at prepubescent penises, tearing them off in their teeth. They ran through the streets, jackal-faced, bearded in blood. When the churn of chaos spilt and matter formed hard in the sun, it had no idea of the horror that would be unleashed.

'I knew I must run. I took the children, tied them to my body and headed for the higher ground.

'When we started up through the mountains, they cried so much the sound filled the range, screaming from the hills themselves. I kept telling them to be quiet. I did not want to be cross with them, but I knew people were following. Uniforms, guns. I sang soft songs to try to soothe them.

'They have been sleeping for days. I am beginning to worry. They are tired. They are hungry. But what they most need is sleep.'

The woodland has grown thick, tall over arching trees. We come to a clearing, in it a wooden shack raised on stilt legs. It is simply made, cut and bound timber, grass roof – a basic shelter against the harshness of the world. We circle around it. A shovel leans against one of the legs, the metal of the spade stained in bright brown shit flecked with red.

She climbs up the ladder first and perches motionless, half on the platform by the open doorway. She peers into the dark.

'Where is my grandmother?' she calls.

There is no response. I hover at the bottom, one foot on the earth.

Then a soft moan from within the hut. She climbs up and in, I scramble after her.

He sits naked in the dark shadows away from the light of the door. There is a line of medals pinned to the flesh above his nipple, along a fissure of thick scar tissue. His eyes burn red, shining like monsters' teeth in the moonlight.

'Where is my grandmother?'

She pushes back past me and down the steps into the clearing.

I go in to the hut. The air inside is a solid fetid thing, acrid ammonia hangs like jungle flies in his hair.

I crouch down next to him. He rocks back and forth. It is some while before he notices me, then he turns his head slowly.

'I could not sleep for the light last night.' His voice is quiet. He talks past me into the air. 'And the wind blew so loud. It told such frightening tales, fearful demonic songs that crawled like nursery rhymes into my bones and shook the frost from my eyes.'

I help him to his feet and walk him out of this hut that faces the trees, and down to a fire that she is now sitting by. A kettle swings above the flames. His eyes scrunch shut as we come out. Eyeballs flick and click below the lids. There is black ooze leaking from the sockets.

I sit him down and she makes us hot drinks. The warmth in my throat is so beautiful.

'I was rich once, the richest of men,' he says. His hands tremble around a tin cup, a wedding ring clinks the metal.

'I'd get back from the fighting,' he says, 'and I'd hit my wife. I'd throw her across the room like a rag toy. I'd push her through the door, down the stairs, make her crumple on the ground. I'd take my fists and pummel, I'd kick her with my boots, I'd beat her with sticks. I'd dig down into her. I'd get the shovel and I'd hollow her out.'

He drops the cup, his hands are shaking too much.

'Since the fever left me I have not stopped shaking.' He tries to shrug. 'I was so good a soldier once, the sharpest of shots. I rose through the ranks on skill alone. I was a general. I led armies.'

She has untied her children from her back. The inert bodies lie beside the fire. She is stroking the smaller of the two. It is a girl, her face is yellow and violet. 'The monsters will come soon, little one,' she says. 'They will come and fight for you, rise up from the earth and the seas. And you will live again.'

The general starts to laugh. 'You are too late,' he says. 'I have slayed the monsters. I have cut them all down. Stuck spears in their heels and felled them like rotten oaks. I buried her sons back in her womb and I stitched her closed.'

The mother looks up from her children. She smiles at the general. 'There are creatures from the deep that are coming too,' she says softly, 'rising from their long slumbers in the icy depths.'

The general's shaking increases. He tries to laugh but it sticks in his throat.

He coughs, wipes the dark sputum on the back of his hand.

'I murdered the leviathans in their bed chambers,' he says. 'I snuck in while they slept and doused them in my poison.'

'Blood will drop from heaven and give them life once more,' she says with surety. 'They will rise.' She turns back to her child. 'Do not worry little one,' she says. 'Listen – do you hear them sound the charge? Listen, my sweet, you can hear them on the wind.'

The loose skin on the general's cheek shudders. His head trembles and spasms. 'I hear nothing,' he says. The scar where the medals hang starts to run pus, black lumps in red stain down his chest. 'I will form an army,' he says. 'We will defend our castles. And my gods will fight with me. We have ways of killing that you have not dreamed of.' He coughs again and spits into the fire. It shoots up like a flare. And he is gone.

'He murdered my grandmother,' she says. 'And I will be revenged.' The earth begins to shake. I hear the howling on the wind. The bodies of the children grow snaked in vines. Insects scurry and flutter over the corpses until there is nothing left but the coloured cloth in which they were wrapped.

Flowers sprout and bloom from a washed-out rainbow.

She walks over to me, sits me on the earth by the ashes.

I touch her softly and slowly. She moans, her eyes sparkle. I feel it pulse inside me deeper than if I were touching myself. I watch it shoot out.

Golden geyser spraying, the fountain lessens with each pump, turning to thicker blacker crude.

She looks at me with disgust.

'The war is coming,' she says. 'I am birthing my soldiers. Yet you are not fit to be one of them.'

Her belly starts to swell.

I fall to my knees in front of her, 'Let me crawl back inside.' She shakes her head.

'You must finish crossing the mountain. You must take the journey back. Say what you have seen. Be scorned for your madness. You have duties that must be fulfilled first, to the family of the friend you have killed. Only when you are clean will you be ready. Only then can you prepare for war.'

I leave her by the embers of the fire clutching her belly. I walk back alone, waiting for the lights of the village to appear out of the mist, waiting to awake.

The Science of Imaginary Solutions

I suffer from chronic cluster headache and chronic migraine. I have to take lethal doses of medicine to cope. (Thank you, National Health Service and Astra Zeneca. I mean that sincerely.) Just as I come to a decision to do a particular thing, the headache intrudes and takes over my being. People complain about a migraine a month. They might like to try one every day, for years and years, decades, and if that sounds intolerable, consider conditions some people endure that are so very much worse. Life itself is a terminal disease: the brief, shocking, astonishing, painful interval between birth and death.

So, the famous journey of a thousand miles begins with the first step ... but, but, but, before I can take that step, what *is* this obliterating pain? What is this mental confusion and dizziness? What is this illness? What is this urgent need to collapse and curl up and dissolve into oblivion in the dark, to escape from my own existence?

Solipsism. The self is the only thing that can be known and verified. Know self. Forget self. Forget the pain. Play, dance, skip, in the moonlit garden of the semi-conscious, the sub-conscious, the sublime subliminal, the Perfect Place, paradise for pataphysics.

Pataphysics? Often referred to as a 'pseudoscience', it was invented by French absurdist writer Alfred Jarry, who called it 'the science of imaginary solutions, which symbolically attributes the properties of objects, described by their virtuality, to their lineaments'.[1] Like Jarry, tricksterish, finding all thought deficient and inadequate, allowed only to see and think in short bursts, I must prod at the periphery of the thinkable, the knowable, with a sharp stick.

*

Zone: A locality, a circumscribed place, characterised by some distinctive features. A region or area, distinguished from surrounding or adjoining parts.

In permaculture, the zone system is a theoretical design tool which describes concentric areas:

> Zone 00 is the person at the centre of the system.
>
> Zone 0 is the person's home.
>
> Zone 1 is the immediate surroundings of the home.
>
> Zones 2 to 4 accommodate the areas for growing food and keeping fowls and all the other paraphernalia which sustain human existence.
>
> Zone 5 is left as natural wilderness, without human intervention other than observation.
>
> Zone 6 is the larger totality, the global commons, the Gaian system, the biosphere.

Permaculture is popular amongst the growing army of eco-minded folk who can see what the industrial machine is doing and who want out. Yet permaculture is another manifestation of human solipsism. Permaculture is anthropocentric: a system designed by people for people to provide for people's needs.

Every living thing requires a place to be. A place to exist and a place to find food and to reproduce. When you take over an area for your own use, you take away that area from other living creatures. Habitat loss is the greatest threat to species worldwide. So, the wise permaculturalist tries to design Zones 1 to 4 in such a way as to maximise opportunities for species to co-exist. The ideal is to produce an artificial ecosystem which mimics natural systems whilst providing for human needs.

Zone 5 is, theoretically, the area where humans don't intervene. The words 'wilderness' or 'left to nature' are frequently used. But what does this mean, in practical terms? I'm thinking now of the British Isles, where I live and farm. And in the British Isles, unlike some other parts of the world, there are no genuinely wild or natural areas.

Some people dispute this, so, it is necessary to consider the definition of terms. By 'natural' I mean the opposite of 'artificially created by humans'. An example might be an island discovered by a voyager, which had never previously been visited or populated by *homo sapiens*. That would be pristine, virgin nature. The condition of fauna, flora and geology in the absence of human interference.

That is what we do not have in the UK or Ireland. Every square inch has suffered the effects of human activity over the last nine or ten thousand years, since the glaciers retreated and the sea level rose. Even remote hilltops, although not covered in obvious stuff like plastic, tarmac, concrete, fields or streetlights, have been subjected to air pollution and soot, radioactive fallout, acid rain, and now altered weather due to manmade climate change.

The only people who appear to have lived in anything like harmony with the original wild landscape and its natural features were the mesolithic hunter-gatherers, who can be thought of as a component of their ecosystem, like bears, wolves, beavers and aurochs. When the neolithic farmers arrived, the first thing they did was to cut down the wildwood and begin killing off the competing species. Strictly speaking, wild, pristine nature began its retreat, its defeat, at that time – around ten thousand years ago – and the speed and degree of destruction has increased ever since.

So, although it may suit some Romantic city dwellers to imagine that there must be, out there somewhere, a truly remote patch of untamed wilderness, where they can commune with Nature as she once was, this is a fanciful illusion. Of course, Glen Affric is closer to true wilderness than is central London or Leeds. But Glen Affric is, despite the remnants of ancient forest, not anything like an original intact ecosystem. Most of the original forest cover is long gone. Bears, wolves, lynx, eagles and many other species, which would have made for a different ecology if they had remained, have been wiped out by humans. People have lived there, grazed their animals, encouraged deer for hunting and much more over millennia. The semblance of wild nature remains, but not the real thing.

In most of the rest of the British Isles, not even the semblance remains. What we have is pastiche, 'mock-natural', a faux idea of the wild which convinces those who know no better. Our beautiful rolling mountains were denuded of trees during the stone age and the bronze age and the iron age, the soil was washed away, and they've remained bare ever since because of the grazing of goats, sheep and cattle. The landscape is Manmade. If Britain had never seen people, it would be unrecognisable – a lost world.

Where is my Zone 5? There is no Zone 5.

If you are an urban permaculturalist, then, where – among the streets, houses, bus depots, factories, motorways, airports – will you go, to find your Zone 5? What would you be looking for? And if you don't know what you're looking for, how will you recognise it if you find it?

The British countryside is a wonderful palimpsest, the work of hundreds of generations of humans, from those who mined flint and copper or built the megaliths, the hilltop camps and forts, the Roman villas, the drove roads. Our ancient, green, troubled rural landscape is like a vast dilapidated cathedral, full of wonders and symbolic of the human quest in so very many ways. But that's not nature. That's people.

Meanwhile, the manifestation of the human quest in most of today's countryside – modern agribusiness – is fascistic, a totalitarian regime which allows no opposition or dissent. The land is a factory floor, to be swept clean of anything which might intrude, anything which might be an interference with the machinery that makes the money. Organic farming is a more tolerant, liberal, regime. It welcomes a sprinkling of weeds and wildflowers, and is kinder to the soil and the stock. But it's still not nature.

Permaculture is a huge philosophical advance on the dominant mainstream industrial techno-culture-religion, where nature is seen as irrelevant and short-term human interests and advantages are taken for granted as 'obvious' priorities. But it's still about people. What about the destiny of all the species which play no part in permacultural design? What about otters? What about leeches? What about Scottish wildcats? What about stoats and weasels and mink? Permaculture shoves all these off into Zone 5.

Then what?

*

If you were a natterjack toad, a sand lizard or a smooth snake intent upon constructing a perfect heathland permaculture design, you would probably want to leave out a few predatory species, like the domestic cat, or the carrion crow. But would you omit humans? Probably not: you'd need them. Heathland is a manmade habitat, maintained by the grazing of domesticated livestock, sheep, cattle, ponies. 'No human management' equals 'no more heathland' equals 'no more habitat for heathland species'.

The same goes for many other landscape features – hedgerows, traditional orchards, water meadows, hay meadows, marsh, moorland, machair – which, in the absence of grazing by domesticated animals, would go through successional changes, turning into a different habitat, typically scrubland and forest. Scrubland and forest are good for wildlife, but not necessarily good for the species that pattern our landscape today.

Many species have co-evolved with humans over the millennia. The corn-crake is a good example. Ask a corncrake to design a permaculture system for corncrakes and it would say yes, we need humans in our system, but we need them to behave differently, we need them to return to the old agricultural methods, when we were common everywhere, not the modern ways which have driven us off the land and to the brink of extinction, clinging to the machair. Ask the harvest mouse, the partridge, the peewit, the sparrow, the swift and they'd say the same.

But ask the human permaculture designer if they need corncrakes and, of course, they don't. Ask them if they include lichens and bryophytes in their de-sign. Ask them if they include foxes and otters. Or peregrines or polecats or ptarmigan. The permaculturalist is, of course, content that such organisms have liberty to exist. Somewhere. That's when you get the wave of the arm that depicts an imaginary 'out there', over the hills and far away, in hypo-thetical Zone-Five-Land.

Perhaps we could envisage re-establishing a more authentic 'wilderness' as an ideal to move towards: an artificially reconstructed British Zone 5 involv-ing the re-introduction of the 100 or more species which have become extinct over the last 8000 years or so? Wolves, lions, brown bears, elk, beaver, wolver-ine, walrus, bison, lynx, cranes, pelicans, bustards and many more. Even this would not be nature or wilderness, of course – it would be a heritage project. But the average permie on their smallholding or allotment is likely to flinch at the idea of a Zone 5 featuring lions and bears. How much real, live, dan-gerous, disobedient nature do we – even those of us who think of ourselves as 'green' – really want to have contact with?

The tamed, manmade British countryside is beautiful – landscape painters, photographers and poets testify to that over generations. But real nature isn't just pretty, and it is not necessarily welcoming either. It has power and feroc-ity, and that scares us in our urban and suburban enclaves, where we sleep safe from the growls and snarls of things with big teeth and sharp claws. Perhaps only in nightmares do we understand the primeval fear, the primary fear, of being torn apart and devoured.

> I soon heard a man's strong voice in a stern, commanding tone
> telling someone to leave immediately. The Ju/wasi never took that
> tone with one another. I came out of the tent to see what was hap-
> pening, and behind some of the shelters I saw four very large lions,
> each three times the size of a person … The speaker was ≠Toma.

Without taking his eyes off the lions, he repeated his command while reaching one hand back to grasp a flaming branch that some-one behind him was handing to him. He slowly raised it shoulder-high and shook it. Sparks showered down around him. 'Old lions,' he was saying firmly and clearly, 'you can't be here. If you come nearer we will hurt you. So go now! Go!'... The lions watched ≠Toma for a moment longer, then gracefully they turned and van-ished into the night.[2]

That is an extract from Elizabeth Marshall Thomas's account, in her book *The Old Way*, of her life with the Kalahari Bushmen. For 35,000 years, the Bushmen constituted the world's longest-lived and arguably most successful human culture, before it was destroyed in the twentieth century by the nation state and the global market. In all of that time the Bushmen lived with, and were forced to accommodate the needs of, genuine wild nature.

In the West, we can no longer even imagine this. The closest some of us get to being threatened by nature is the hysterical response one sometimes wit-nesses at the appearance of a wasp. I recall reading in a newspaper that some Buddhists were taking over a building for a retreat centre. They called the council pest control officer to come and destroy a wasps nest they'd found. I read the item to the woman I was with, remarking contemptuously that they must be pretty crap Buddhists to be afraid of wasps, and anyway, as it was autumn, the wasps would all be dead in a few days. The woman responded, scornfully, 'Huh! You wouldn't want wasps living in your house!'

The next year, when I left an upstairs window open, a queen wasp entered in the spring and made her nest inside an Epiphone acoustic guitar that was leaning against my wall. The wasps kept coming and going, until the fabulous papery structure of their nest had filled the guitar and extended in an im-pressive mound out of the soundhole. They were there all summer. I didn't trouble them, they didn't trouble me. The guitar was ruined.

*

I keep rheas. Rheas are South American ratites, smaller than their better-known African cousins, the ostriches. Because I've found most humans to be idiots (some are very charming and pleasant company, of course: if you're one of those, please don't be offended) I was forced to turn elsewhere for wisdom. Rheas are wise.

The ratites are thought to be of Gondwanan origin. They have been around since the Cretaceous Period, more than sixty five million years ago – considerably longer than we naked apes. It seems fair to suggest that they might have learned a thing or two about survival.

Consider their sex life: The males make the nest. The male courts the female, steering her towards the nest site, where she will deposit an egg. When sufficient eggs are accumulated, the male settles down to incubating them. When they hatch he takes care of the youngsters. The females take no interest in the proceedings. It works for them.

Rheas also know how to meditate. Like Bodhidharma facing the blank wall, if times are hard, if it's cold or pouring with rain, they settle themselves down, gather their *chi*, tuck their long necks between their wings, fix their gaze on the ground about a metre in front of them, and enter a trance state until things improve. When the youngsters do this, they keep their spirits up by singing a round, each taking a turn to vocalise, as the song circulates around the group.

Rheas have a good memory for the rhythm of the year. There is a damson tree on my land which fruits prolifically, and having once gorged on the fruit for a week or two, they are ready and eager the same time the following year. This led me to an interesting observation. Bill Mollison's vision, (which grew into what we now call permaculture), was the insight that it might be possible to build artificial ecosystems which mimic natural ecology. The concept views plants and animals as components which are arranged in such a way as to produce beneficial relationships.

What I find fascinating is that these kinds of systems seem to arise spontaneously. They don't require a human designer. They don't require long periods of time to evolve. The damson is the product of human selection – the Damascus plum, introduced from Syria by the Romans. Rheas have been in Britain for about 300 years, so they can't be considered part of the native ecology, but they seem to slot into that ecology just as if they were a native species.

So they eat the damsons off the trees, then excrete the kernel with their dung. The dung lays on the ground providing a fertilised patch of soil for the damson seed. The large native dung beetle, the Dor beetle, the British scarab, comes along, drills a hole down into the soil and takes some dung down the vertical tunnel, where it lays its eggs. Mated pairs together work as a team to find suitable dung, usually at night. The female then digs a hole underneath it, about sixty centimetres deep, with some small chambers off to the sides. The male helps to clear the excavated soil, and brings small bundles of dung into the chambers. The female then lays an egg in each chamber. When the egg hatches, the larva has enough dung to eat for the first few months of its life. When fully grown the larva pupates underground, and the following year it emerges as an adult beetle.

When the damson seed sprouts, it already has this ready-made beetle hole full of soft soil and manure into which to extend its tap root. Eventually, it will grow into a damson tree, providing more fruits for rheas. The rheas gathering beneath the damson tree, reaching up to pluck fruits, trample down all competing vegetation and cover the ground with a layer of broken vegetation and copious rhea droppings, which make a splendid fertile soil for the tree's roots.

This is not a system that has evolved over millennia. The damsons are man-made; a selected, cultivated species. The rheas came from a different continent quite recently. Yet they slot into a sort of archetypal pattern, with the soil and the dung beetles, where all gain mutual advantage. Everything happens by itself.

*

What is the meaning of 'land'? I can look out of my window at a panorama, a land-scape. There are features: a standing stone, a Bronze Age cairn, telegraph poles, haylage wrapped in black polythene, clouds, sky... but all I am doing here is letting words trickle through my mind, and what does that amount to? Neuro-chemical activity. I overlay a verbal description upon the ... well, that's the crux of the matter: upon the what?

It seems that the original meaning of the word 'land' was 'a definite portion of the Earth's surface owned by an individual or home of a nation'. The trouble is that nobody knows what the Earth is. We've named it and studied it and exploited it, and yet we have no idea, really, what it actually is, or why it is, or why we are ... All we have is stories.

We use words, tell stories, so that we can function. So that we can navigate and communicate. So that we can 'make sense' of our surroundings. And, in doing so, we destroy all the magic, the awe. Because the cultural window we inherit, and are taught, and pass on, is deadening, moronic – the neuroses, the ideas, the concepts of a thousand generations of small-minded psychopaths lusting for power and control and riches: the culture that created William Blake's 'mind-forged manacles' and laid them upon the Earth. A description is not an explanation.

So. Break the manacles. Sit. Look. Jolt yourself into awakeness. Discard every idea you ever had, throw out all knowing. Rheas can help. I look at them and bring myself onto another level of consciousness. Completely in the moment, I am able to see everything as if for the very first time, as if I'd just parachuted onto an alien planet. It's easy for an instant, but it's hard to sustain. It takes practice and training and effort. Build the new habit of no-habit. Just see. Rediscover the child's awe which has been stolen by education and in-doctrination and a culture which mis-interprets everything to suit somebody else's way of seeing.

Zone oo is inside your head. The only place. The place where the idea of place is conceived and considered. The 'Know thyself' place. My Zone o is this room. I reserve my right to exclude nature from it. I don't like snails eating my books. Over the years I have thrown out toads and newts, hedgehogs, at least three species of bat, beetles, spiders, moths, butterflies, mice, rats, shrews, a sheep, robins and chickens on a daily basis. But once I step over the threshold, outside, the land belongs to nature, and I am merely a guest. I try to behave accordingly.

Despite the headaches, despite it all, I am blessed. Someone, a better writer than myself, and a lifetime ago, looked up towards my home and wrote down his thoughts:

> We are apt to pity the small farmers of the mountains, and think they lead a poor sort of life, forever in the clouds, while we dwell in the sun and the mild sea air, to the song of the white horses upon our steep northern cliffs. It is a surprise to us when, at rare intervals, the clouds glide from the proud empurpled contours of the mountains, leaving the skyline sharp and naked and we see that the hill cabins are not swept away after all, but stand there, whitewashed and dazzling in the rare sunlight. Truly a hardy and tenacious race are these smallholders with their black cows, their patches of rhubarb and cabbage, their mountain sheep and the little dark red ponies they ride in the stony lanes. Up there, we say, what are they thinking of us? Do the poor devils envy our wide smiling fields?[3]

Consider the lilies of the field ... except that there are no lilies to consider. Nor even any field, anymore. Contractors came. Machines eliminated the tadpole pool and the fallen rotten willow tree. Men and machines dug drains, brought concrete and tarmac, raised structures of brick and glass with revolving doors. Landscape contractors brought turf and planted exotic well-behaved shabby shrubs, hardened by prior life in a harsh desert so they can withstand the exhaust fumes, the discarded plastic bags, newspaper, cigarette packets, used condoms congregating beside the rusty 'Keep off the grass' sign and the bent 'No litter' sign.

What is to be done? Remember pataphysics – the science of imaginary solutions? In the absence of any real solutions, I suggest the pataphysical route is the only realistic option for a sensitive, caring individual to take on an island populated by criminals and willing amnesiacs. Choose your place. Find your spark of wildness. I don't mean Golding's *Lord of the Flies* wildness, I mean Ian Niall's *Poacher's Handbook* wildness:

> It is not a new thing. It is old, old like the scent of peat smoke from the lonely cottage; the cairn on the hill; the flight of geese in late October. In the flat country of East Anglia a man rose at five today to take a pheasant, and last night, in Wiltshire, kindred spirits were running out the long net, stopping to recognise the yelp of the fox and the cry of the owl.[4]

I think the bottleneck is coming. I think each person should look into their own heart and see if there's something they love, and then take that thing and cherish it, so that maybe there will be a chance that it gets through. It could be a bluebell wood, a reed bed, an estuary, a wildflower meadow, or playing the uilleann pipes or archery or knitting, or the skills of the blacksmith or stone mason, or rare breeds of poultry or sheep or fruit trees, or anything that resonates with grace and integrity which merits preserving and handing on.

What can be abandoned and discarded? What don't we need? I believe that the ship is sinking. For smart people, that means gathering up whatever few things seem useful and precious. When you can't take it all, you must make choices. May you choose wisely.

Notes

1. Wikipedia, 'Pataphysics', last modified: 17 March 2011.
   http://en.wikipedia.org/wiki/'Pataphysics.

2. Elizabeth Marshall Thomas *The Old Way: A Story of the First People* (New York: Farrar, Straus and Giroux, 2006).

3. R. M. Lockley, *The Golden Year* (London: Witherby, 1948).

4. Ian Niall, *The Poacher's Handbook: For the Man with the Hare-Pocket and the Boy with the Snare* (London: William Heinemann, 1950; reissued Ludlow: Merlin Unwin, 2003).

ALBERT PIERCE BALES

Three poems

The New Masses

The man of the future has arrived in Kalifornia
He's a little bit deracinated, middle class
White man's burden gone to seed
More computer virtual
Than blood, guts, mind and soul
He's wired, modular, circumscribed, clean
And pure of any extreme feelings or notions
He scans consumer-positive, non-idiosyncratic
He's eighteen to twenty three percent female
He has never tasted of the tree of good and evil
The law, the courts, the banks and great institutions
Revere him as the solid, clearly defined cipheroid
A fully operational component of the revenue stream

I think of this guy at those moments
When I must attend to some
Homeland security duty in the bureaucratic jungle
With my bad attitude, my universally abhorrent
Opinions, my puzzling official record, my
Ugly looking rap sheet
I am often the tallest, strongest
Smelling citizen in the line
In steel toed boots, workmanlike meathooks, earthy
Bestial, unsophisticated, a reader of Dos, Buk, Jung, Mencken
The higher misanthropic pantheon

I clash with the government clerks
Squandering precious time and paper
Screwing up the computers by my very presence
Amused, smiling, enjoying some private joke
A revolutionary without a
Revolution

Why Industrial Electricians Get Up Earlier
Than Students of Gender Studies

Wind driven rain through the refinery fume and smoke
Is a constant condition, a fact of life here
This project goes 6:00am to 6:30pm seven days a week
Only lightning and flood stops work
Tuesday morning break in the smoke pit
Men too bone damp, beat and weary to converse
Cupping cigarettes against the weather
This little Comanche fella, John, the foreman,
Head prankster
Walks up, looking for mischief
Stone faced, he stands rocking on his heels
Tugging at his whiskers
No one speaks, no one has anything to say
They just listen to the rain on their hardhats
Finally John says, Hey Bub
Where wuz ye yesterday?
Thought ya mighta gone soft on us
You thinkin of quittin us?
This guy who took a day off
Hunkered down in the corner, black stogie in his teeth
Puffing smoke out of the recesses of his rain hood,
expressionless
Everyone looks his way
Well John, he says, I was ah … I woke up with a … ya know, A
young woman in my, um … bed
As laconic and straight up a retort as ever was heard
A lovely comic moment
John is silent amid the laughter
He pivots in the gravel to leave

Thinking, he would say later; that there
Is the A-1
First class excuse
And no
Argument about it

The Velvet Meat Grinder

Into the velvet meat grinder of the 20th century
All but forgotten now
Place a heart, brains and balls
Add a blast of the blues, *con alma*
A whiff of class, a little blood sweat and laughter
For nothing human is so grim that it doesn't want
For some aspect of the absurd
Drop in nine pounds of $100.00 bills
For luck
Salt with the tears of a saint
Put in something you learned from your grandpa
Throw in a quart of the best bourbon
Squeeze the juice of one pedestrian lifetime into the mess
Stir with the barrel of a shotgun
Place the mixture in a man sized box
Press with stones
Truth will drain from the corners
Remove and pour into a Gladstone bag
Lower bag into a 3'x6'x6' pit
Shovel dirt over it and tamp it up solid
Uncover it in one hundred years
Place in a furnace heated to 1,800 degrees centigrade
For a month of Sundays
Garnish with homemade sin
Serve with a bill for incalculable damages
And eat without hope of digesting

NICK HUNT

The Horse Latitudes

The ocean is white and pink and purple and red and yellow and brown and green. After weeks at sea, the captain clambers up the mast of his yacht and scans the horizon with binoculars, rotating himself degree by degree until he has turned full circle.

There are nothing but plastic bottles, plastic bottles as far as he can see.

The yacht slides on, carving a V-shaped wake through the bottles as it goes. The captain turns to watch the gash, brief glimpses of a dirty blue, slowly filling in behind, erasing all trace of his passing.

He hugs the mast and shuts his eyes. He feels nothing, not even the wind.

The bottles clunk gently against one another, so softly he can hardly hear them.

Down on deck, he opens the ice-box and takes out a miniature bottle of champagne. He pours the champagne into a plastic cup, which he raises towards the sky. He drinks the champagne in tiny sips, gazing at the bottle-covered ocean.

All the colours in the world are here, worn dull by the waves.

When the last drop of champagne is gone, he tosses the bottle over the side. Then he tosses the cup over too. Within seconds, he can no longer see them.

The yacht drifts on for an hour. Half a day. The ocean's surface changes. The plastic bottles become interspersed with other items of debris: footballs, tangled carrier bags, crumbled hunks of polystyrene, flip-flops, bergs of packaging foam. The captain watches them slip by with a sense of awe. He spots flower pots, fragments of fishing crates, once the half-submerged torso of a doll. He wonders if the head is here too, and if so, whether the motion of the waves will ever bring them back together.

The yacht travels on. Its prow cuts a swathe through Tupperware boxes, lids, foil wrapping, crisp packets, objects he can't identify. Always plastic bottles, in their hundreds and thousands. He squints overboard to read the names, or recognises brands from faded blocks of colour: Coca-Cola, Pepsi, 7-Up, Schweppes, Sunkist, Mountain Dew.

Occasionally something larger bumps against the hull: half a green plastic garden chair, a refrigerator door. They could have come from anywhere, from any land in the world.

Later, the captain goes below and heats a ready-meal in the microwave. He eats chicken chow-mein from a greasy plastic tub, and, after wiping it clean, tosses the tub over the side, along with its plastic fork.

The act of returning these things to their own satisfies him, somehow.

Night falls over the plastic sea. The captain wraps up and sits on deck, watching the sunset with a bottle of wine and a packet of cigarettes. The ocean is calm, its gentle undulations spreading slow ripples through the trash, giving it almost the effect of breathing. The falling sun catches on pieces of foil and shards of bright PVC. Gradually all colour leaches from the scene, leaving only spots of white that appear to glow, as if holding the light, as everything else goes dark.

Alone on his yacht, it seems to the captain as if he's never seen anything so lovely.

The horse latitudes are situated between thirty and thirty-five degrees either side of the equator. Wind and rain are uncommon here. The ocean is subdued. The captain has always enjoyed the name as much as the legend from which it sprung: that Spanish ships, becalmed for weeks on the glassy millpond sea, would be forced to throw their horses overboard when water supplies ran low.

Of course, this theory is contested, like all wonderful things. Scholars and historians suggest more prosaic etymologies. But to the captain, the name is apt. In the days before plastic was conceived of, he imagines an ocean of abandoned horses, bobbing gently up and down, their hooves sticking up towards the sky.

The North Pacific Gyre, through which the northern horse latitude runs, is located in the Pacific Ocean between the equator and fifty degrees north. A gyre is a vortex caused by a system of rotating ocean currents; in the case of the North Pacific, the currents that turn this vast wheel of water are the North Pacific Current, the California Current, the North Equatorial Current and the Kuroshio Current, which between them spin the ocean clockwise, channelling debris to a central point from which it cannot escape.

The existence of the rubbish patch through which the captain is drifting now – wrapped up in his sleeping-bag, one arm dangling over the bunk, dreaming of nothing that he will recall – was hypothesised before it was actually observed. Experts on oceanic currents predicted such an effect. It wasn't until the closing years of the garbage-strewn twentieth century that a sailing ship, cutting through the subtropical high between Hawaii and California, entered an uncharted ocean of plastic that took a full week to traverse.

The area's true size is unknown. Estimates range from three hundred thousand to almost six million square miles.

It seems unbelievable, in these times, that such a vastness of pollution could have remained unseen for so long. But these are seas seldom travelled. They lie thousands of miles from the nearest landmass, their emptiness unbroken by islands. They lie on no trade routes, shipping lanes or important fishing grounds. This is an ocean en route to nowhere. A convenient vanishing zone for lost, unwanted things.

Also, all is not visible, not to the naked eye. There's more to the patch than rafts of Pepsi bottles and atolls of Styrofoam. Mostly it consists of particles that have been ground by the action of the waves to a minute, multicoloured sand, partially suspended below the surface, in the higher reaches of the water column. Plastic cannot biodegrade. Its tightly-bound polymers cannot unravel. It can only reduce and reduce, growing tinier with each passing year, from the miniscule to the molecular level, changing the very composition of the sea.

At the end of his first week in the gyre, the captain sees a boat on the horizon. At first he thinks he is mistaken. But the boat comes closer. It's a curious kind of boat, with a long, sharp prow like a canoe, and two fine grilles extending like wings from its port and starboard sides.

The boat is crewed by two men and a woman wearing red t-shirts displaying the logo of an oceanographic institute.

The captain watches with amusement as they squint and stare.

'What are you doing?' asks one of the men when they are within talking distance.

'Nothing. What are you doing?' says the captain.

The man explains they have built this vessel as part of an investigation into pelagic plastic pollution in the North Pacific. He says this craft will pioneer a future clean-up operation, to be shared between responsible nations, in which hundreds of thousands of tonnes of waste will be skimmed from the ocean's surface.

The captain doesn't say anything. He takes a chocolate bar from the icebox and snaps off a square.

The woman continues from where the man left off. She tells the captain of their studies into the effect of plastic pollution on the marine ecosystem. She opens a container on deck and produces a sodden albatross, its throat tangled with nylon fibre, polystyrene wedged in its gullet. In parts of the North Pacific, she says, plastic micro-pellets outnumber zooplankton six or seven times over. Plastic has crept into the food chain, is being ingested by everything from jellyfish to large mammals. Nothing on this scale has been observed before. No-one yet has the slightest idea what impact it might have.

The captain watches as the woman displays her other exhibits: a triggerfish with three bottle caps in its belly, a guillemot full of foam.

When the researchers are concluded, he finishes his chocolate. He holds the wrapper between thumb and forefinger, watching it tug like a hooked fish, then lets the wind pull it away. It soars into the sky and drops, coming to rest against a battered polyethylene milk jug.

The researchers stare at him from their boat.

'Asshole,' says the woman.

'You expect to clean an ocean with a boat like that?' says the captain, without any malice.

'Come on, let's go,' says the woman. She slams the lid of her albatross box.

'Even if you skim off a tonne, a thousand tonnes, what will you do with it? Burn it? Bury it in the ground? I don't understand.'

The woman ignores him. She puts on a baseball cap that matches the logo on her red t-shirt.

'What are you doing here? Where are you headed?' calls one of the men as their craft pulls away.

The captain doesn't answer him, but he shields his eyes to watch the boat go, growing gradually more indistinguishable, and finally raises his hand in a motionless salute.

That evening he smokes three cigarettes and drinks half a bottle of wine. He lies on his back on deck and watches the daylight disappear. He makes noises, of varying pitches and depths. The stars are brilliant here.

The plastic age began in 1855 with the invention of Parkesine, soon developed into celluloid in the quest to find a substitute for ivory in the making of billiard balls. The first entirely synthetic plastic was polyoxybenzylmethylenglycolanhydride, better known as Bakelite, half a century later.

This was followed by epoxy, polystyrene and polyvinyl chloride, polyethylene, polypropylene, polycarbonate, polymethyl methacrylate, melamine formaldehyde. Plastics, like plant and animal species, have scientific and common names: nylon, Perspex, PVC, Styrofoam, Plexiglas, Teflon. The products were mated with themselves to develop ever-stronger bonds; polymers that could not be broken, resistant to heat, friction, crystallisation and biodegradation.

With the dawn of the plastic age, the human race at last succeeded in tearing itself free from organic strictures. As a substance that cannot decay, plastic freezes time. The plastic age, thinks the captain, six weeks floating in the gyre, was mankind's first convincing stab at the eternal.

He mumbles their names, makes songs out of them. Polyester, polybutylene, polysulfone, polytetrafluoroethylene. He recites them to the motion of the swell, watching the colours merge and bloom. Surely the very first particles are here, in the centre of the North Pacific Gyre. Fragments of celluloid billiard balls, nylon toothbrush bristles. Ground to a microscopic dust. They have been here for over a hundred years, waiting for man to catch them up.

Going to the centre of the gyre is like travelling back in time. Back to the dead hub of everything, from which nothing can escape.

The engine is silent. The sail is furled. The yacht rests, curlicued with foam. The captain spends his days on deck, reading old sailing magazines, observing small changes in the sky, making inventories and counting his rations. Sometimes the rain falls lightly, lasting an hour or so. It seems to the captain that rain on the ocean is a waste of water.

He doesn't have much need to eat, and he sleeps surprisingly little.

He has seen no other boats. He doesn't expect to see them.

One day he puts his hand to his face and has the impression his skin has thickened, salted and hardened by the sun. The lines on his forehead seem more defined. He traces the wrinkles around his eyes and the edges of his mouth. Hair has colonised the cracks, and he wonders if the spots of grey he last observed back on land have spread and merged together. His lips are chapped, and flakes of dead skin swirl when he rubs his nose. He reads his features like a blind man, but there is little to tell. There are no mirrors on the yacht, and his appearance doesn't matter. He is just a man, after all; there are billions of them.

With ever-decreasing frequency, he thinks about his life. Drifting images of his wife, the house in which they lived, his son, the jobs he did, the friends he knew, the people who once liked him. All the things he threw away. They can follow him if they like. They are welcome to find him here, to cast adrift, if they so choose, but only if they are content to let the gyre take them.

Even more infrequently, he thinks of the other things in the world. The movements of people, the great pronouncements, the setbacks and the disappointments, the breakthroughs, the catastrophes, the advancements and the despairs. These things will not find him here. This, at least, he knows.

The captain has enough supplies, carefully stacked in the hold, to last out here for years. Assuming he eats just once a day, and collects enough rainwater. The alcohol, chocolate and cigarettes will run out after six months or so, but he hopes that by that point, he won't have the need.

He has also brought deep-sea fishing lines, hooks and nets and sinkers. The ocean contains fish of all shapes and sizes, even here, amongst so much waste. The fish will be saturated with plastic, infinitesimal nurdles. He will ingest vinyl chloride and di-2-ethylhexyl phthalate, carcinogenic and mutagenic, substances banned by responsible nations. In this way, he will enter the food chain. The plastic sea will pass into him, changing his very composition.

But for now he leaves the lines alone. It occurs to him that he packed no bait. Until he catches his first fish, he will have to bait his hooks with pieces of chicken chow-mein.

It is hard to tell, without instruments, whether the yacht is drifting on the waves or whether the ocean's surface is changing, subtly shifting its patterns. The depths are far too great to drop anchor, but, without wind, he assumes he will simply remain where he is, slowly revolving around the same point. There are no other factors to act upon him now. He came here to go nowhere.

He has the image in his mind of the plastic ceaselessly spreading around him, expanding like a summer bloom of algae. Every scrap, every fragment that finds a route from the land to the sea, from Japan to Mexico, is making its way towards him now, inevitably honing in. He sits at the centre of an orbit, dragging in lost things.

Sometimes, if the captain squints, if he has drunk a bottle of wine, if he has spent the night on deck, making noises at the stars, he sees things in the pattern of the seas. Amorphous pictures that break apart and blend, dotted masses of colour. Sometimes it looks like grazing flamingos, seen from an aeroplane through clouds. Sometimes it looks like thousands of faces, all the races of the world, crowds at a great political rally at which he is centre stage. Sometimes it looks like old film footage, slowly zooming into the grain. Sometimes it looks like a pointillist painting. Meadows of spring flowers.

He has been six months in the North Pacific Gyre. It doesn't seem so long.

He has come to recognise familiar landmarks in the structure of the sea. An island of polyurethane foam. Tangled reefs of purple twine. Archipelagos of bottle caps.

He thinks about the horses long ago, pitched overboard like polystyrene cups. Bobbing gently up and down, their hooves sticking up towards the sky.

He spends long hours making diagrams, charting the uncharted spaces of this ocean. Inventing names for things unnamed. Making maps of a strange new world.

PAUL KINGSNORTH

The Salmon God

a conversation with Glyn Hughes

I can't remember exactly how I first came into contact with the poet and novelist Glyn Hughes, but I first met him at a launch of his last-but-one poetry collection in Hebden Bridge in Yorkshire. I arrived at the venue expecting to find the handful of intense afficianados that make up most poetry launches, and was surprised to find a big room packed to the gills with appreciative readers.

Hughes, it turned out, has a big following in Calderdale, the West Yorkshire valley where he has spent forty years tracking through his words; and his writing about the area, running to more than a dozen books and as many stage and radio plays, has resonated far beyond its confines. His first novel won two major awards, as did his first collection of poetry, and in the years since he has been shortlisted for most of the big literary prizes and has seen two of his books selected by *Guardian* readers as 'great classics of British nature writing'. The *Times* has called him one of the 'best authors ever on the north of England.'

Looking back on his career now, Glyn sums up his work – the historical novels, the travel books, the semi-autobiographies, the volumes of poetry – as 'a protest on behalf of nature'. It's a career that most writers would be happy with (assuming writers were the sort of people who were ever happy about anything); but it's one which is now coming to an end. In 2010, Glyn was diagnosed with terminal lymphoma, and given two years to live. Early this year, he published a moving response to this, a poetry collection entitled *A Year in the Bull Box*. Flitting between hospital cancer wards and a small, remote former cattle byre in Yorkshire, which is his green retreat from the world, it's an uplifting poetic essay on the approaching end of a life.

In the mid-1960s, Glyn bought a collapsing, condemned terraced house from a local mill owner for £50 and spent decades restoring it. He still lives there, and plans to die there, looking out over the valley he loves. I spent some time there earlier this year, talking to him about his life and work, as spring came up over Calderdale.

*

PK: Your new poetry collection, *A Year in the Bull Box*, starts with a foreword which explains that you've been diagnosed with terminal cancer. And yet this is actually one of the most life-affirming books of poetry that I've read for a long time. In 'Salmon in Twiston Beck,' for example, you have these lines:

> *in the virtue of sight before it dies*
> *I have come into my self*

There's a striking sense of peace and acceptance all through this volume, and I wondered how you'd come to that?

GH: Well, there's only two choices. You either face up to it and say 'this is where I am, I've got this limited time left and I've got to go through this', or you capitulate to being miserable. It's not like the other miseries of life in which you can afford to feel sorry for yourself. The choice between, as it were, self-indulgent sadness and being glad of what life you have is much more stark.

I was ill a long time before they diagnosed it, perhaps a year or perhaps two. I knew I was ill. I remember sitting outside the consultant's office in Halifax towards the end of this period, waiting for the cardiologist, and Liz, my friend, started crying, because she was afraid of what the doctor might say. And Liz doesn't cry very much; she's very strong. And I said to her – and this came without thinking about it – I said I'm not afraid of death at all, not the slightest bit afraid of it; all I'm frightened of is pain. I said it before I'd really thought about it, but I've held to that. I just see dying as part of the huge cycle that we all belong to. You become part of nature again. So I suddenly felt very calm about it all.

And so this place that I found, this hut, the Bull Box – I had it before I was ill, and I'd just about got the doors and windows in it when I collapsed.

PK: It's an old cattle shed, isn't it, as the name suggests?

GH: Yes, that's right. It's very small; it's on an estate – it doesn't belong to me. A stream runs just past the front of it, and the whole valley is so beautiful, so fresh. It's so different to here. It's not such a sharp and deep valley as here; it's open countryside, much more pastoral. Here I'm hemmed in by houses.

There's such a powerful history to this place where I have lived for so long. This is what I've written about so much, Calderdale; it's my world and I know it so very well. The Bull Box is in a very different place; it has a very different history and it's a great contrast to this place, which is dark and brooding. It's very like going back to the landscape of my boyhood in north Cheshire. Cheshire is very different now of course – big industrial farms and the cottages all turned into Manchester homes. But the Bull Box is on an old country estate, and they're very preservationist, they've kept much of it as it was. There's no road to it. It's like a trip back in time. It's paradise for me, really.

PK: In one poem in this book, 'Village Haven', the last line talks of 'the last act, which is not death but *dying*.' That's what you're talking about, isn't it, when you talk about being afraid of pain but not being afraid of death?

GH: Death comes after the last act. Dying is the last act, the last thing you know about. There's nothing really to be known about death. We can wonder about it and speculate on it, and wonder about our purpose and what our personal dying will be. I don't have any theories about that. But what I do know is that the world is so very, very beautiful, and that my visits to this little place – every time I've been I've felt more well, much younger.

PK: That comes across strongly in the book, this sense that being there, being surrounded by nature does bring that life to you.

GH: One of the people at one of the launches I've given for the book wanted to know why I had nothing to say about the other people around there. I know them – the farmer and the shepherd and the people in the nearby house – I know them alright, and they're lovely people, but they're not of any particular concern to me. It's the natural world there that thrills me. I mean, the salmon come up the beck …

PK: There are a lot of mentions of salmon in the book.

GH: Yes, the symbolism of the salmon. These creatures, these fish, swim two or three thousand miles across the Atlantic to come back to the place they're born in. And they're such a mystery. What fascinates me is that they live these extraordinary lives and nobody has the faintest idea why. We have a few faint clues as to *how* they do it, but there's no understanding of *why*. How can we say that we understand life and death when we can't even understand these strange creatures that occupy the nearby stream?

PK: You were recently interviewed by the poet Ian Parks, and in that interview you quoted Jung, who said that whenever he goes to study an area of the human consciousness with science he finds that a poet has got there first. And thinking about the salmon, I thought: there's a lack of a certain type of curiosity that people have about nature. We're fascinated by how things work, and very good at finding it out, in some ways …

GH: Giving things names.

PK: Exactly: giving things names, categorising them, looking at how systems work to some degree – we're starting to do that with ecology. But there's very little poetic imagination applied to something like the salmon. So we might try and look for an evolutionary reason why the salmon might come back up the beck, but we won't think: maybe there just isn't one. Maybe the salmon is doing something as irrational and emotional as humans often do, and there isn't a reducible reason for it.

GH: They live in a different world, which is their world and not our world. They have their own, different consciousness – they clearly do. I watch them in the stream: I watch the young born, I watch the thick shoals of salmon parr in the beck in June and July, and they clearly have a consciousness that is not ours. There's not a lot to be gained in trying to understand scientifically what part of a salmon's brain lights up when it does this or that.

PK: But that seems to be the only question that we give ourselves permission to ask, in this culture. That's an acceptable way to explore what nature is, but other ways are nonsensical or Romantic.

GH: What's the salmon's god like? I think that's a legitimate question. It is an extraordinary life cycle, and it is completely beyond human comprehension. Blake said that if the doors of perception were cleansed everything would appear as it is – infinite. We're prisoners of our senses – imprisoned behind the five doors of perception. We can't see through any others.

PK: Do you see your poetry as a way of trying to look through other doors?

GH: Well, I haven't got any answers. The poetry just reflects my sense of what you might call the miraculous; especially the last year, around this small place. All my work previous to that had actually been rather different. I got into the toils of recording this valley and its history – I was about to say the materialistic history of this place but in fact that's not true. It's been about material history, yes, especially a rather savage, radical point of view, but that's only been part of it. It's also been about how to dramatise what's happened to the spiritual life of people here, through Methodism and the rest of it, down the centuries. All my previous work's been about that, but suddenly I'm writing about nature as I used to when I was a boy. In fact, I'm restoring a lot of the attitudes that first set me off writing.

PK: You talk, early on in *Bull Box*, of your 'first escape' aged 'five or six', and that seems to mean an escape into the countryside, into nature. And you write these lines:

> *When following oracles in the countryside*
> *I seemed to pass through a pane of glass*
> *and feel an inner rising.*

I understood that because I've had experiences like that myself. That's quite a Wordsworthian thing to put into a modern poem, isn't it?

GH: Yes, it's Wordsworthian, but the reason is that Wordsworth was the first person to write about these experiences in that way – or at least the most prominent writer to do so. Or perhaps the way of communicating it is Wordsworthian, but of course Shakespeare and Milton and others, they all had their moments of recalling this childhood sense of wonder about the world.

PK: I find that people I come into contact with who have strong feelings for nature as adults have pretty much always had experiences like that as children. And conversely, people who just don't get it have never had this kind of experience. I don't know if that's about personalities or upbringing or location or just luck, but I do find that this kind of thing is really impossible to explain to someone who hasn't *felt* it.

GH: I'm sure it's the case that most people who get passionate about environmental matters are aghast because the world that fed those feelings is being destroyed around them, all over the world. And they realise, after first of all being shocked by it – horrified by it – they go on to realise that it's going to make human life an impossibility. And they can see the extent to which it's motivated by greed and selfishness, and eventually come to see that it's a spiritual matter, not just a material matter.

PK: And that's the gulf, isn't it, that some people don't jump across and some people do?

GH: Our spiritual life is so dependent upon our sense of the natural world.

PK: But it seems to become harder all the time. Looking at your work over the years, there's a sense of how much has changed since you started writing, in terms of how much open space there is and how much connection to nature people have an opportunity to get.

GH: Yes, it's ironic isn't it? We've got better cars, better roads, aeroplanes ... and yet we have less access. It's retreated behind the screen of materialistic interest. I don't know what we should do. I think we should keep doing all we can to try and restrain this rapacious attitude towards nature. But there are, as you say, two kinds of people, and it's almost a spiritual war between them.

You could put it in all sorts of religious terms – you could talk about good and evil – but there's a strong sense of two kinds of person battling it out: one person approaching nature to get as much out of it as possible, whether it be crops or minerals or profit. And there's the other kind of person that is so deeply shocked by the lack of wish to preserve the sacred in nature – and this sense of the sacred becomes as important as profit to the other side. And these two attitudes are ancient. I mean, Blake's full of it. Read Blake and you see the whole warfare between the two sides, expressed in his language.

PK: In *Millstone Grit* [Hughes' 1975 Calderdale travelogue-cum-history-cum autobiography] there is a striking passage in which as a young man you are up on the Pennines and you run your hands across a stem of grass, and soot comes off it and covers your fingers. And you realise that the moors are not untouched by industry, and in many ways are actually ruins – places where forests used to be or extinct farming communities. It's a caution against Romanticism, I suppose, but it also seems to suggest that we are, as humans have always been, somewhere in a great cycle of the rise and fall of civilisations.

GH: Yes, absolutely. And it's all cleaned up now, of course. Spring is wonderful here when it comes, and the irony is that this place which has been so desecrated and covered in soot and industry and everything has, in a mere few decades, cleaned itself. Nature has cleaned itself. We've just stopped pouring soot all over it and it's cleaned itself.

PK: *Millstone Grit* gives a real sense of how dirty everything was. You're always describing rivers as 'greasy'...

GH: The interesting thing is that there's not really any farming round here; there are sheep in the fields but there's no really intensive farming, so the spring is wonderful in Calderdale. But if you go back to Cheshire or

Leicestershire or Lincolnshire, the whole landscape is devoid of spring flowers because of industrial farming. It's kind of ironic that this rebirth has taken place in an area which used to be so black and industrial.

PK: You grew up in Cheshire on a council estate, and you've said that there was no inherited culture there. And you arrived here, in this valley which at the time was dirty and rundown and decaying, and you have stayed here for forty years. What was it that made you stay?

GH: It had depth to it. The housing estate I grew up on hadn't been there long – it was new in the 1930s, when I was born, and in those days the council house was a new idea. They brought people in from all sorts of places and threw them together and they had no common culture at all. But this place, Calderdale, had a deep sense of the old, industrial, working-class solidarity. They all had a common way of life and a common history that they touched. That fascinated me. The first Chartists were here, in this valley. There weren't any of those around Altrincham!

PK: A sense of this deep culture, of trying to drill down into it, comes into most of your writing. I've been reading *The Hawthorn Goddess* ... [Hughes' 1984 novel set in eighteenth century Calderdale, which focuses on the persecution of a strange young woman]

GH: Yes, well that's a fable. It's an effort to do a mythic version of the old battle between nature and human culture. She's a wild spirit, Anne, she's not quite human.

PK: In that book you seem attracted to but also repulsed by this narrow, local culture which has the strength of solidarity but the weakness of rejecting outsiders. The good characters in that book are the ones that read and who want to see the wider world, while the ones who persecute Anne are those who never go anywhere, never ask any questions.

GH: The ones who persecute her are the ones who are interested in profit, those who live by exploiting. I was trying very deliberately there to personify the persecution of nature in the shape of this woman who is so strange, so uncomfortable, so at odds in the world of people. Which is how nature has been treated. The roses have thorns, and we wish they didn't have.

PK: There's a sense in which throughout most of history we have been afraid of nature ...

GH: Yes, terrified. It's very archetypal.

PK: And yet today we feel, probably wrongly, that we are in control of nature, that it is weak and precious and we have switched from being afraid of it to nurturing it, feeling that it needs our protection. It's almost as if we feel that the master-servant relationship has been reversed.

GH: We can treat nature as a toy when it's in our garden, but then when it does threaten us again, in the shape of something like climate change, we don't treat these things as natural disasters – we are somehow fearful on one level that this is our doing; it's our fault. It's our first thought, isn't it, 'what have we done to create this?' It's very biblical. We still fear it. We don't call it God any more, but we still fear it.

PK: One of the things we talked about in the Dark Mountain manifesto was nurturing the kind of writing which doesn't see humans as the centre of all things, and there is some writing in *Bull Box* which seems to take this perspective. The salmon in the beck make you feel that 'I am not the owner of my planet/even in imagination'; and later, in 'June', you write that 'creatures bless me with their disregard.' There's a sense that you almost relish being put in your place by nature.

GH: I relish being made aware that I am part of this; I'm not the owner of it. It's a wonderful feeling. I love feeling like just another creature, and I love it when other creatures regard me in the same light. I can remember getting up at dawn one spring, it must have been in May because the hedgerows were in flower, and walking around that district. And all the wild creatures were busy: a stag leapt over a hedge and went across the fields; all the birds were active in their particular way. And they all behaved as if they didn't expect a human to be around at that time in the morning, and it was marvellous. It was as if it was in their consciousness, 'what's this one doing around at this time? This is not his world.' It was quite uncanny.

PK: The late Australian ecologist Val Plumwood was attacked by a crocodile a few decades ago when she was out canoeing, and she wrote about how that experience changed her life – she said it gave her a real awareness that she was part of nature and not just an observer, that she could be the prey as well as the predator.

GH: I'm acutely aware that coming from this safe society I am quite a privileged observer of nature. Though even here, you can get lost on the mountains and feel very vulnerable. It can be very alarming. But I've never been attacked, except by farm dogs!

PK: But I suppose death is an attack by nature?

GH: It certainly is. Certainly is. It feels like an occupier: a Viking, some marauder inside my body. It roams around and will always find another place to rest. They tell me there is no point in more chemotherapy after this round. They can kill it in one place and it comes back in another.

PK: In *Millstone Grit* you quoted a local writer who used to live around here ...

GH: Oh, Billy Holt, yes!

PK: He sounded like an incredible character: He was a communist, a writer, a painter, a horseman, he met Nehru and H. G. Wells and he fought in the Spanish Civil War ... But anyway, you quote him as saying that the things which used to be the simplest pleasures were now the privileges of the rich. So you have to get to a certain level of income before you can eat lots of meat, wear fur, go hunting, own a boat ...

GH: It's all been closed down. We are sold aspiration instead. Earn enough to get on a plane and fly somewhere else to lie on a beach. Why? You don't need it. Go round the corner and lie in a field instead.

PK: Coming back to that sense of being small, being part of nature – I don't see much in contemporary poetry that takes that perspective. Do you?

GH: No, I don't, I think I'm a bit of a lone voice really now.

PK: I suppose the last prominent British poet who addressed similar concerns would be Ted Hughes. You do come at the same themes in many ways ...

GH: Well, I don't write like Ted Hughes. But yes, Ted did of course have this huge sense of nature – but his environmentalism was a bit like Prince Charles'. He was fighting for the River Torridge, for instance, but that was because he owned the fishing rights.

PK: You knew him, didn't you?

GH: Yes, I knew Ted. Of course, he came from Mytholmroyd, a few miles from here.

PK: What was he like as a person?

GH: What was he like? Well, he was not at all like the myth. He was very much the *bon viveur*. Liked food and drink. He was very talkative, but at the same time he wouldn't waste time talking to anyone who didn't interest him. He had no manners about that – he simply refused to talk to anyone who didn't interest him. He was very kind to other writers, though, remarkably so. He was a man who knew exactly what he wanted to do at any moment.

PK: So who created the myth? Was it him or his readers?

GH: I think it just gathered out of the poems, from the persona of the poems. They seemed to project this misanthropic man, and he wasn't at all like that. Because of *Crow*, and all those terrible post-Sylvia Plath poems ... I don't mean terribly *bad*, I mean terrible in their message about what life is. Well, how could you not have a grim view of life? And it wasn't just Sylvia who died, it was Assia as well. Awful. And it all fed the myth.

PK: You once told me that he had accepted the Laureateship because he had an almost primal sense of the importance of the monarchy – something quite ancient and mystical ...

GH: Oh yes, it was very atavistic. Yes, Ted was a great monarchist, long before he became Laureate. It was tribal. He was very conservative, Ted – spent all his time with businessmen and landowners and farmers. There's an interesting poem he wrote, though; it was never published in his lifetime, but it's about sitting up on the Bridestones, on the moors around here, and some gamekeeper coming and chasing him off, and it's a very defiant poem. He's saying, 'I've got every right to be here.' But it's unfinished, and it was never collected until he died. So he didn't always have that conservative attitude. But then he became a landowner ...

PK: To get back to contemporary writing, in the interview you did with Ian Parks you talked of 'the strangled feeling one gets overall from much of, in fact the most accomplished, contemporary British poetry'. What did you mean by that?

GH: It's as though it all takes place in a small circle of people, who are controlling all the publishing outlets, the publications, the events, and creating a consensus around the way poetry should be and should look, and what it should be about.

PK: Something else you said in that interview: 'Poetry has ... suffered near disastrously by taking over for itself the journalistic modes of thinking ... A whole strand of the most liked and widely known poetry of our day is in fact versified journalism.'

GH: It's true. Most poetry now – I don't want to name names – reads like opinion pieces from the Sunday papers cast into verse. Why? It's the poets looking for a public. Nobody reads poetry really, so they're looking for an answer: Make it like journalism, then people will read it. It doesn't work, of course. And it has got worse in my lifetime: There's been a collapse in poetry. My first poetry pamphlet sold a thousand copies – just a little pamphlet. It's unthinkable now.

PK: What happened?

GH: The publishers have stopped thinking it's worthwhile – most of the big publishers gave up on poetry, and the little publishers are overwhelmed with too many people wanting to be published. The grants have gone.

There are too many poets and not enough readers now. Perhaps the rise of the creative writing course is partly responsible. We've an oversupply of writers and not enough readers.

PK: To come back to this valley. The end of *Millstone Grit* is quite heart-breaking. You've taken this journey around this area, and you end up back at Intake Farm, where you lived and worked for a while, and you tell the story of Tommy Toat, an old tenant farmer who works the land his father worked, has no electricity in his house, and seems both at one with the land and at odds with the world outside it. And you write of how he is thrown off his farm in his old age when it's sold for housing, and how it breaks him, and you talk of all the 'unassessed and disregarded cultures' of the land, which are cast aside before we can understand them.

GH: Yes, it is about those connections being lost. It's really all gone now. I loved being at that place. I've been back since … It's awful now. It's strange … it's a very old seventeenth-century farmhouse, and they've plastered it over with fake half-timbering. It's a genuine, old, wonderful building, and they've covered it with this stuff that's a fake representation of the old times.

PK: It sounds like another death. Someone who has engaged a lot with Dark Mountain is Vinay Gupta, an engineer who creates systems designed to withstand crises, and he suggests that Western societies are simply unable to come to terms with death. In India, say, or Mexico, the reality of death is part of everyday life, but here it is hidden away and feared, and almost denied.

GH: Yes, that's very true. We live in a society that does think it can control everything, and it will not accept the existence of death because we can't control it. But I don't feel like that. I feel quite relaxed about it, really.

PK: That's not something that you might expect to hear from someone facing their own death.

GH: Well, you know, 'Rage, rage against the dying of the light', and all of that. That's what you're supposed to do, isn't it? Whereas I'm writing poems at the moment about just lying in fields. It's all I can do. I'm very happy just lying in a field – going to sleep, waking up and being surrounded by all this beauty. What more is there?

GLYN HUGHES

Three poems

Summing The Stones

He thought of his reaching for his soul
as like fumbling for the string
of his coat when a sharp March wind
ruddied him with anxiety.

He thought of his struggle for his soul
as climbing to a sea-bird's egg,
oval so that it rolls safe in its nest
of straws on a high sea-ledge.

His peering for his soul
was like muttering at an awkward sheep
For Gawd's sake do as thas told;
in truth this was to a wife long gone.

Or like scaring off crows that blind his lambs
in the moment they first see their mothers.
His moment then, driven by pity
to battle stiff feathers, is as a child's —

not for long, nor much. For the frightened who haven't yet lived,
the truck will come up the mile-long track —
he watches it slip and grind up the track —
to give him next to nowt for the defeated

then he back wifeless to the udder,
ten cows and a loved horse,
to the preacher and stiff schoolmaster.
He, like the master with Bible and sums,
living the coward's way, bold with victims.

*

Why should she stay among brambles and gorse,
in this cage so unlikely for a spirit of air?
For the soul owns no master
and an imprisoned genius wrecks its house.

*

At times there were for him these beams,
just as lights would dart upon the moor
or fling into the church
when the sun charged outside
whereas indoors in dark he would not dare
to more than mutter, *Lord*.

Yet the soul must live through its journey here,
even imprisoned in such as he
 with barns, with hoof prints sculpted in mud,
with cats as feral as rats.
                                        But not so,
for the kernel is sweet within, the shy bird
summoning stone. How he summed the stone.
He's done his farming sums.

Prognosis

I am told that my atoms assembled into a bomb
exploded in Space would outshine the sun.
But I am thinking of cremation, scattered on water.
The Atlantic wears even granite into atoms
and energy is freed from its prison of substance at last.

When my ashes flow on the stream maybe the salmon
will take a mouthful through the Atlantic,
my threads will wriggle even backwards in time
as happens, says quantum physics

                              and who will know but God,
and perhaps my descendant disturbed one night
by thoughts and dreams that seem like memories?

The Buttercup Fields

I was twelve when I cycled to my granny's
whom I did not know, only vaguely where she lived
twenty miles from my parents' house
from which mysteriously she was banished.
I do not wish to indict that misery:
the hard stuff crushing our house.
Yet I cycled to outreach the silence of home
where few came and no-one quite *talked*.
Though Mam dropped hints and Dad sometimes tried
recalling what bright hopes had seduced them to
the shadow of silence between them to the grave.

Cycled, staring through lanes banked with flowers;
at buttercups in field upon field in Cheshire's glow.
Nature was all, already. Love, I gave
to flowers unceasing unfolding, again and again
in rhythms never resting.

Reached Wells Street, Sandbach. Recalled
the number scrawled on a letter back home.
Knocked on a dark door. A dark interior opened.
A dark old Welsh woman with lit eyes
recognised me not seen for twelve years.
I don't recall much said.
But what had she done? Other than as we all do: lived
her life as she could see how to, until there came
life's calcinations, ever recurring; when will they end?

I never told my parents of my visit
nor met again this container of my past;
her whom I know far less of, than of buttercups.

After five years Dad went to her funeral, alone.
No consolation from us. When he came home
he slammed to his bedroom, shut the door and cried.

That epiphany of buttercups stays in my mind
from the day when I was swamped by timeless knowing
through – even as I see them today – the glowing,
yellow firmament stretching.

HIGH WATER MARK

by Dan Grace

THE TANGLE HEAP OF WIRES, INTESTINES
SPILT FROM A HIGH-TECH WRECK,
WE USE TO BIND EACH BRANCH BACK
TO 45°, WORK WITH THE RISING SAP.

ILLUSTRATIONS ~ LAURENCE LORD

PUNCHED-IN MONITORS AND T.V. SETS,
TYRES AND RUSTING CAR SHELLS
WE FILL AND PACK WITH SPADES OF EARTH
AND SPILL SEEDS ACROSS THE BARE SOIL.

METAL PULLED FROM CRUMBLING FAÇADES,
WORDS WE NO LONGER CARE TO READ,
WE HAMMER INTO SICKLES, HOES, TOOLS OF WORTH
THAT REST SOLID IN THE PALM.

AND WE LEAVE THE RIND OF MUD BENEATH
THE NAILS OF OUR FINGERS, INTERTWINED.
THE FLOTSAM IS ALL THAT SURVIVES,
NOW THE HIGH WATER MARK HAS PASSED.

CHRIS T-T

Empties

WILFRIED HOU JE BEK

Poetry First, Engineering Second

Uncivilised Writing & Primate Poetics

The Dark Mountain manifesto demands a new 'uncivilised writing'. To quote the crucial two paragraphs:

> Uncivilised writing is writing which attempts to stand outside the human bubble and see us as we are: highly evolved apes with an array of talents and abilities which we are unleashing without sufficient thought, control, compassion or intelligence. Apes who have constructed a sophisticated myth of their own importance with which to sustain their civilising project. Apes whose project has been to tame, to control, to subdue or to destroy – to civilise the forests, the deserts, the wild lands and the seas, to impose bonds on the minds of their own in order that they might feel nothing when they exploit or destroy their fellow creatures.
>
> Against the civilising project, which has become the progenitor of ecocide, Uncivilised writing offers not a non-human perspective – we remain human and, even now, are not quite ashamed – but a perspective which sees us as one strand of a web rather than as the first palanquin in a glorious procession. It offers an unblinking look at the forces among which we find ourselves.[1]

Oh, tautology! Writing is, of course, the very token of civilisation, the great measuring stick by which to separate the primitive from the civilised, the savage from the cultured. To argue for voluntary illiteracy in order to de-culture ourselves back to the stone age, as primitivist thinkers like John Zerzan have done, seems too drastic even to the latest wave of deep culture pessimists, but it is certainly true that for most of human history we did do fine without it. Illiteracy today equates with powerlessness: according to UNESCO, 20 per cent of the world's adult population is illiterate, virtually all of them live in the poorest parts of the world, and two thirds are women. The oldest known cave art is 30,000 years older than the oldest known writing and 25,000 years older than agriculture. Literature does not need writing, and oral traditions have been able to carry massive literary traditions across the centuries. The imagination, intelligence and wit contained in oral literature is undisputed, unarguably created by civilised minds, capable of rigid intelligence.

No language is primitive, and before stepping outside the human bubble we should first try to step outside our Western language bubble. Native speakers of English, spoiled by the ready availability of people who speak their language in the remotest corners of the world, are especially notorious for their linguistic tunnel vision. But stepping outside the comfortable conventions of the novel – Murasaki Shikibu is mother to us all – means facing up to a cultural sphere where all your linguistic, social and imaginative preconceptions are challenged. Consider the following story, translated from the Pirahã language by Steve Sheldon and given by Daniel Everett in his book *Don't Sleep, There are Snakes*:

> Xoii spoke. Xopisi is not here.
> Xoii then spoke. Xaogíoso is dead.
> Well, he was called.
> I called Xoii. The only one.
> I thus spoke to Xoii. Xaogíoso has died, Xaogíoso.
> Xoii did not go to see her on the floating dock.
> Xaogíoso is really dead.
> Well, I am really fearful.
> Xoii then spoke. Xitaíbígaí did not tell about it.
> He said she did not tell.
> Xaogíoso did not die!
> I then spoke. Xaogíoso has become dead.
> She is no longer here.
> Xoii did not go to see her on the floating dock.
> Xopísi, you are Xiasoaihí's husband.
> Xaogíoso is dead.
> Well, I called to Xoii. Go see her.
> Xaogíoso has become dead.
> She is no longer here.
> Xaogíoso dropped [gave birth to] her child.

I said to Xoii. Xoii gave her medicine. Xoii did not go to see her again.
Xoii then spoke. Hoagaixóxai said nothing, Hoagaixóxai.
Xaogíoso is very, very sick.
The medicine was not given to her.
He did not tell anyone, the younger one.
Xaogíoso, don't get bad.
He did not say anything.
You did nothing for the people.
All alone she went.[2]

According to UNESCO, more than half of the 6,700 languages spoken today
are in danger of disappearing within this century. Language is (part of)
culture, and the disappearance of a language means the death of a literature
and a distinct way of organising space, time and knowledge. The world would
be poorer without active use of languages in which: (1) it is impossible to have
a sentence inside a sentence (Pirahã); (2) trees are named for the sound the
autumn wind makes when it blows through the branches about an hour after
sunset when the wind always comes from a certain direction (Micmac); (3) it
is grammatically impossible to construct a valid sentence without explicitly
stating how you came to know the knowledge of your statement (Tuyuca).
The collapse of the ethnosphere – Wade Davis' term – is happening everywhere except in Europe, where we have taken cultural and linguistic mono-
cultures as the norm a long time ago. We are our own worst enemy.

'Engineers will be of more use to the future than poets,' someone quoted
somebody else, during the Dark Mountain debates on the *Guardian* website.
The worldview which equates engineering with progress, which assumes all
flaws – engineered or otherwise – can be engineered out of existence, is exactly the 'story' that should be analysed, criticized and retold. The !Kung will
never build anything like the new Heathrow terminal, say, but who is to say
that living a life of affluence in the Kalahari desert is not an equal achieve-
ment? Or to quote Jerome Rothenberg's central revelation of ethnopoetics:

> Measure everything by the Titan rocket & the transistor radio, & the
> world is full of primitive people. But once change the unit of value
> to the poem or the dance-event or the dream (all clearly artifactual
> situations) & it becomes apparent what all those people have been
> doing all those years with all that time on their hands.[3]

Poetry first and engineering second, or third, or fourth, or not at all.

The Dark Mountain manifesto makes an inexcusable howler when it refers to humans as 'highly evolved apes';[4] it is a biological orthodoxy with which only creationists will want to argue that all creatures are equally evolved. We humans are not on a higher plane of evolution than apes, or birds or bacteria. It is difficult, from our human perspective, not to think of ourselves as in some ways special. We do not know if animals share this opinion, but, as Gary Snyder's startling insight goes, animals 'admire us and love us', so maybe they do.[5]

But to turn to the central point raised by the manifesto, what are the possibilities of a literature which moves beyond the human bubble? All beasts signal, most beasts communicate and several beasts have language. The line between communication, which uses inflexible symbols of some kind, and language, which is flexible and can be refined and redefined at will, is a difficult one. Some will argue that the distinction is absolute and cognitively determined, that it is hallmarked by the availability of grammar, and that so far only humans have been shown to possess it. Others argue that communication/language is mapped along a continuum, that it is culturally determined, and that the communication of apes, parrots, whales, dolphins, coyotes and other animals has been shown to fulfil at least some criteria of language. Language does not imply spoken language, let us note; the medium is unimportant. Sign-languages are languages in their own right and possibly older than spoken language.

If non-humans have language, do they also have a literature? Let us not get mixed up in funny ha-ha about the chimpanzee with a typewriter hammering out the first Great Primate Novel. Let us instead begin with a definition of literature. Following Gary Snyder, I like to use the definition proposed by pre-Chomsky linguist Leonard Bloomfield who said in 1933 that 'Literature, whether presented in spoken form or, as is now our custom, in writing, consists of beautiful or otherwise notable utterances.'[6] Literature starts, in other words, with something that is worthy enough to be repeated by someone else. An unread novel or poem would therefore be outside of literature; a nice thought.

Can an ape learn a human language? Not on our terms. However, when apes find themselves in a pleasant environment surrounded by humans who are friendly and welcoming, they will make an effort to try to understand what a human is trying to say to them. And they will also, with patience and deliberation, try to make the human understand what they would like the human to know. The open secret of Great Ape Language Research is that ape language projects are only successful when they allow the crystallization of a pidgin language to happen between the languages of the different species involved, Language is what comes naturally from a reciprocal attempt to create mutual understanding.

The modern scientific history of ape language research goes back to home-raised chimp Gua in the 1930s. Gua was raised by Winthrop and Luelle Kellogg together with their nine-month-old son Donald. The project was abandoned when Gua failed to speak human but Donald did start to make chimp food grunts when he wanted his breakfast. This pattern has kept repeating itself. Language is not a one-way street, it does not flow from us to the ape like water always finding the lowest point. Consider the following quotation from Sue Savage-Rumbaugh:

> Just before we reached the Treehouse, I felt Kanzi's body began to stiffen, and I noticed that the hair on his legs, which was all I could see of him when he was astride my shoulders, was beginning to come erect. Kanzi made a soft 'Whuh' sound and gestured to the side of the trail. There, a short distance from my foot, was coiled a very large snake. I screamed and jumped back several feet, almost falling as Kanzi grabbed hold of my head to hang on. Kanzi's keen eyes had enabled him to give a last-minute warning that had just come in time. I returned Kanzi to Jeannine, found a very long, sturdy stick, and proceeded to prod the snake with the stick, Kanzi produced extremely loud 'Waaa' calls, as though to warn me that what I was about to do was dangerous. Each time I actually struck the snake with the stick, Kanzi felt it necessary to 'Waaa' yet again. Pretty soon Jeannine and I were 'Waaaing' ourselves. 'Waaa' seemed to be a pretty good word for 'snake', and when it was uttered with the gusto that Kanzi mustered, the ferocity of the sound itself was almost effective enough to scare the snake away. I soon became so accustomed to giving 'Waaa' barks to alert Kanzi whenever I saw a snake in the woods that I began to find myself 'Waaaing' even when I was walking home alone and came across a snake.[7]

Ape language research brings together a large variety of linguistic forms: human language, ape language, human body language, ape body language, artificial human language, and a ragbag of ad hoc codes and signals. In trying to find a common ground, the human tries to speak ape and the ape understands it; the ape tries to speak English and the human knows it. Nor can ape language, whatever it is, be seen as a uniform thing; apes of the same species born in the wild, and acculturated apes used to human ways, know different things and do things differently. Ape language can enter human language and the reverse has been shown to be possible on many occasions. The ape and human language bubbles can exchange items. (So, to make a lateral jump, it can be imagined that the Neanderthal and human bubbles mixed in the past and remnants of Neanderthalese may remain buried in human language.)

The language the ape develops in unison with humans is not a short cut to food or attention. Once great apes have learned some derivative form of human language, it becomes a natural part of their behaviour: They use it to comment on the things they see and do; they use it to tell about what they are going to do next and whether humans will like it or not; they use it to talk ape-to-ape; they use it to argue, and they are able to say the same thing in different ways. They also show awareness of the degree of language ability in others: Chimpanzee Washoe was expert in ridiculing students who signed sloppily by making his signs slowly and deliberately, as if talking extra loud to a foreigner. Swearing is another graphic example of unprompted linguistic creativity. Once Washoe had learned the ASL sign for faeces, 'dirty', he quickly made a point of adding it to all things he did not like: 'dirty monkey', 'dirty food', 'dirty Roger'.

Great apes, in short, have what it takes to be literati: They are intensely self-aware, capable of anger, empathy and compassion, playful as well as deceitful, rumbustious and self-aggrandizing. Bonobo Kanzi talks about his own behaviour as 'good' and 'bad' when he thinks no one is watching him. Apes are perfectly able to juggle mental concepts and invisible objects, while their deep sense for social hierarchy makes Jane Austen look like an insensitive brute. They have talents in which they surpass us, such as a superb short-term memory. (Perhaps they can manage to follow the maddening use of nick-names in Cao Xueqin's classic Chinese novel, *The Dream of the Red Chamber*.)

Most importantly, they have metaphysical imagination. Savage-Rumbaugh reports on the 'mythology' she has created for the pan/homo culture lab in Ohio. In this cosmogony, worthy of M. Night Shyamalan, the powers of the goodwill bunny and the evil forbidding gorilla constitute a precariously balanced system of otherworldly forces.

We would be able to understand a hypothetical great ape novel, but the ape will remake the language we think of as ours in her own image, and for most of us it would be like learning to read again. Or, to quote Giambattista Vico, 'Anyone who wishes to excel as a poet must unlearn all his native language, and return to the pristine beggary of words.'

We ourselves are apes, 'the third chimpanzee,' as Jared Diamond said. Language is a primate heritage, and in looking at the language of the other apes we are also looking at our own language from a distance. PrimatePoetics is not just appending a new chapter, a new language, a new mind, to existing literature, it completely upstages the way we have organised language and literature around our human selves. In the uncivilised order, human language will no longer be the immobile centre of language, but just another threshold of language, another example of language amidst the countless number of languages that dot the 15-million-year-long periphery of primate language. The challenge PrimatePoetics poses to 'uncivilised writing' is to incorporate these insights in new works of art.

Notes

1. Dougald Hine & Paul Kingsnorth, *Uncivilisation: The Dark Mountain Manifesto* (Dark Mountain, 2009) p.13.

2. Daniel Everett, *Don't Sleep, There Are Snakes: Life and Language in the Amazonian Jungle* (New York: Pantheon Books, 2008).

3. Jerome Rothenberg, *Technicians of the Sacred: a range of poetries from Africa, America, Asia, Europe & Oceania* (University of California Press, 1968).

4. D. Hine & P. Kingsnorth, *Uncivilisation*. See the beginning of this article, and note 1 above.

5. Gary Snyder, *Poetry and the Primitive, Notes on poetry as an Ecological Survival Technique in Earth House Hold* (New Directions, 1969).

6. Leonard Bloomfield, *Language* (New York: Henry Holt, 1933).

7. Sue Savage-Rumbaugh, Stuart G. Shanker, and Talbot J. Taylor, *Apes, Language and the Human Mind* (Oxford: Oxford University Press, 1998).

GERRY LOOSE

from 'Fault Line'

I

about right for these parts
mostly birch
some oak
my living room
where the white hind has
scented me
though I'm glassed in
standard class
on the halted train
through Glen Douglas
she follows my gaze
over her shoulder
to hillside bunkers
trots downwind
in the direction of
the sea's drifting
foam specks
Faslane

commentary:

while an owl
edits my sleep
an object

II

consider these lilies
what you talk about
when you talk aesthetics
& these sweet coils
woodbine razorwire

commentary:

my fixed point of the hills
grasping peerless sunlight

III

states of matter
halogen lights
safely do away
with night & day
abolish the moon
barn owl
snatches song
all twenty four hours now
a siren
rock to my hard place
these men talk
to their lapels

commentary:

meniscus
mergansers dive
see
the bridge
see the water
see the bow wave
turning

IV

the streets are lined
today I found a penny
yesterday a pound coin
it's on my shopping list
tea wine gold
that everyday hero
Midas
warned me

commentary:

inadvertently
making the sign
of the cross
on that train
no other
he offers me wine

V

more than one sun
in the sky now
the heron's auguries
no longer to be trusted
she too stands
on the street corner
hand to mouth
hand to ear
I still worry
about the apple trees

commentary:

dawn
here if
it's rosy fingered
it's brambles
or blood

VI

when his teacher's
lecture
was a flower
between thumb
& forefinger
Kasyapa smiled
I'm collecting
dead bees
from the meadows
above

commentary:

notice there
a hole
of quietness
knit
by birdsong
by plants' dormancy
by submarines' winches
15 of them
lifting galaxies

VII

the poor boys
of a religious order
are in town
for a drink
& a walk
their fathers
who are not priests
but workers
pushed buttons
with forefingers
detonated

commentary:

trees' ocean
swell

VIII

what is brought
in the mouths of
lilies of the valley
but spring
it's not that the
bunkers
reamed into the hill
don't wound it
they do
but that geology
is newer
than words in flower
fear piled on fear
how then is anything
possible

commentary:

true believers
village elders
iconic
mountain ptarmigan

IX

the artist
brought his own stones
to this stony field

commentary:

in the old east
functional economics
overtakes ancient aesthetics
form follows

X

another heroic struggle
among trees
beith luis fern
sail nin huath
oak & hazel
Sweeney
& the missiles

commentary:

giddy ripples

XI

evenings spent
shelling beans
early purple orchid
adding interest

commentary:

when here it must be greeted
when elsewhere celebrated
bruised sky & no sign
of last night's swan
snow on ice the length
of canal east to dawn
white then pink
where else the desert
we will become
that the brain is part
of the body
an intimate struggle
personal dolour

XII

elder
self sown on the
pier's timbers
I saw the Kilcreggan ferry go
run dunlin run
& warships
rounding the point
zulus skiffs & smacks
hulking the shoreline

commentary:

look at the breaking day
only the waves not ice
Beinn Bhuidhe white
again silk whistling seven swans
high over frozen waters
magpies clatter mourn
a fallen glacial rook fellow
corvid we burn our
carbon corpses
& the whole sun sinks
in the sea

ROB LEWIS

The Silence of Vanishing Things

1

The scientist holds a steel ball
over a thin pane of glass
then drops it ...

the audience flinches at the crash
yet remains
unconvinced.

He reaches down, slides out another
pane of clear fact
holds it out over empty air
raises the steel ball ...

2

A gem hunter takes his sapphires, malachite, moonstones and rubies
from town to town, pouring from creased leather pouches
onto dusty wooden tables, small nuggets that blaze
like the seeds of stars.

By midmorning a small crowd is pressed around his table,
all drawn in by the same mysterious gravity.
But then he comes to a town where no one notices his dazzling array.
Beside him a butcher hacks at a carcass hanging from a hook.
On the other side a shoe cobbler bends over a pair
of riding boots for a local lord. But the people
just walk by, not even slowing their strides.

What the old gemological savant doesn't realize,
is that years ago the town glass maker figured out
how to trick glass into resembling REAL RUBIES,
ACTUAL JEWELS. And the townspeople loved them.
They studded their tools, doorways, carriages with them,
until at last they were everywhere; and now the people
can't tell anymore – the real from the unreal,
the trinket from the jewel.

3

The whole family has arrived. Aunts and uncles from afar,
grandparents and grandkids. They are seated around
a long wooden dining table, playing a card game,
the kids excited, playing each card with theatrical flourish.
    Beneath all the chatter and giggles, a fire has started in the basement.
It climbs a stack of boxes, and then fans out across
the ship-lath ceiling. Not smoke, but the odour of smoke
seeps through the floorboards. The uncle is the first
to notice, then the grandparents who look at each other,
and then look at the mother, who looks at the father.
They all are looking at the father now, who's eyes are fixed
and lips pressed tight, as he repeats to himself:
the smoke is a lie, the fire is a hoax.

There's something wrong with the way we talk, or don't talk, about Earth. I
don't mean wrong in the moral sense, although that case could be made, but
wrong in the not-right sense, as in a bicycle without handlebars, or a staircase
ending in air. Our words and Reality no longer meet. The scale and depth of
ongoing destruction finds no corresponding expression in the scale and depth
of our language, which is coolly technical, bureaucratic and quantitative.
Scientists report round upon round of new data, which by now is crystal clear,
and adds up to facts that are shattering: 70 per cent of large ocean fish – gone;
the north and south poles, the remaining great apes, tigers, polar bears and up
to 1000 other species per day – going; floods, droughts, catastrophic storms,
burning forests – coming. Science has crashed a thousand panes of glass before

our eyes, yet we remain strangely unmoved. We are causing the greatest mass extinction since the demise of the dinosaurs, yet we seem to experience it only as fact, not as feeling; as a loss of biodiversity, not kindred life. The Vanishing swirls around us, but is somehow never brought to words, only numbers. As the planet burns, we count the trees and species, but we do not scream.

Have we become like the townspeople, awash in fakery, so inundated with the artificial that we have become inured of the real? No human generation has ever had to contend with the kind of 24-hour-a-day, digitised, sense-saturation that this one has. Is our vision so managed by the round-the-clock redundancy of screens – TV screens, computer screens, cell phone screens, electric billboards – that what is central, the very basis of life, appears distant, while what is most artificial fills the eyes and seems always of the moment?

Just as fields can be subdivided, paved and planted with neon signs, so can thoughts and beliefs. It's not done with bulldozers and cement mixers, but with words and stories, assumptions and myths. It's the industrialisation of the human mind, and it's been going on for a long time. But rather than growing out of this cycle of seduce-and-buy, we've merely taken it to new and ridiculous heights. Here's a poem-like thing I constructed using only lines of contemporary advertising:

> *Believe.*
> *It's everywhere you want to be.*
> *Anything is possible*
> *When you ride the light.*
> *Digitize the experience.*
> *The nature of things to come.*
> *Your world*
> *Delivered.*

The authors, or corporate sponsors, of this chilling little ditty are, in order, AT&T, Visa, Qwest, Subaru, Zenith, Cargill, and Visa. These are their words, and very carefully selected. They are meant to create a sense of ease, of going forward, of happy anticipation, but where they really lead is ecocide. For they raise a shimmering curtain of unreality, behind which the Real, the Earth of living things disappears. Limits and consequences fade away. All you need do is *"Believe."* Believe in what? That *"it's everywhere you want to be."*

Here is where we find the father at the family gathering, refusing to acknowledge that the house is on fire. The fire, of course, represents climate change, the house is Earth, and the father represents the corporate and governmental centres of power. But he could also be an actual father, one of millions around the world staunchly denying climate change, and unaware that in so doing he is failing his first fatherly charge – to look out for his family. He claims it's the data; he distrusts it. But it has nothing to do with data. It has everything to do with ideology, and with the preservation of belief; for to acknowledge climate change is to shatter the looking glass. The free market we so revere turns out to be not so free, dependant on denial and mired in a fundamental impossibility. *Earth has limits,* climate change says. But to a society bound to the myth of progress and growth, the very idea of limits is heresy, a moral hand-grenade. The ego cannot hear it. It would rather let the house burn down.

What is environmentalism's response to this cultural miasma? There is none, really. We are too deep in the data. Our technical, data-driven language doesn't speak to the father as *a father*. It presents only facts, and then offers more facts. Nor does it address the modern, media-barraged consumer, whose awareness may be so dulled by technology and advertising that he may no longer really 'see' Earth living and breathing around him; especially when that living, breathing Earth is continuously presented in the terminology of scientists and environmental experts.

This is not an indictment of environmentalists or scientists; everyone is doing the best they can in a nearly impossible situation. Indeed, you could say that today's oceanographers, climatologists, wildlife biologists, forest ecologists and so on, comprise a thin green line between human appetite and what remains of Earth. But their language should not be our language; for it is a quantitative language, set up to handle data and computer models, not moral dilemmas and cultural inertia. It speaks technically when we need to speak plainly. It orientates itself around facts when we need to orientate ourselves around feelings. It elucidates data when we need to elucidate meaning. And it altogether ignores the sacred, which we can no longer afford to do.

The thing is, we have tried numbers. We have generated so much data that people have become numb to it. But what if we leave the graphs and data sets for a while, and turn to the beliefs and mores that ultimately generate them? That is, what if we shift from the work of numbers to the work of language? Language is the workshop of consciousness, and if a shift in consciousness is what's needed, here is where our most powerful tools will be found.

*

The substance of creation cannot be separated from a word...
Do not force it to labour in some low phrase.
  – Gerard de Nerval (1854)

First, what of the language we've been using – the language of environmentalism. Why isn't it working? Why doesn't it move people anymore? And exactly why is it so technical? These are complex questions, but a key lies in the word itself – the verbal flagship of the whole movement – 'The Environment.'

We take this term for granted, and use it largely without thinking. But what does it really mean? Where did it come from? And how is it different from the word it replaced: 'Nature'? Merriam-Webster Online defines 'environment' as 'the circumstances, objects and conditions by which one is surrounded'; and 'the complex of physical, chemical and biotic factors that act upon an organism or an ecological community and ultimately determine its form and survival'. 'Nature' on the other hand is 'the inherent character or basic constitution of a person or thing' and 'a creative and controlling force in the universe.'

Note the difference in language. The environment: circumstances, objects and conditions. Nature: inherent character, essence. The environment: a complex of physical, chemical and biotic factors. Nature: a creative and controlling force in the universe. An obvious question arises. Why are we fighting on behalf of a complex of physical, chemical and biotic factors and not a creative and controlling force in the universe?

And why from the very beginning do we verbally devitalize (or denature) our subject? Carl Jung said, 'the only important thing is to follow nature'. Shakespeare wrote, 'one touch of nature and the whole world's kin'. Would they have said the same about 'the environment'? What other meanings and associations were lost when we traded 'Nature' for 'the environment'? And why did we do it in the first place?

The answer to that last question came to me quite accidentally one year in the form of a writing journal given by a friend. The journal had been bound using the old hardback covers of a 1950s high school science textbook. Inside were mostly blank pages with a few pages from the original textbook inserted here and there for humour and interest. There was a section entitled 'Better People in a Better World,' and of course 'The Importance of Industry.' The introduction crooned about such new terms as supersonic flight, sonar,

electron gun, neptunium, plutonium, atomic clock, motor jet, pulse jet, ram-
jet, turbo jet, DDT, JET, gramicidin ... and so on. Across the maroon cover
a cargo ship, an aeroplane and a lone seagull cruised beneath the title: 'Our
Environment: How We Use and Control It.'

You can see what was happening. The age of technology was afoot and
science had vast new powers to 'use and control' Nature. A new word was
needed for this new ambition, a spiritually neutral (or neutered) term, one
without the sacred overtones of a creative and controlling force in the
universe. This new term needed a clean, scientific edge. And it needed to be
suitably abstract and objectifying. There should be no emotional conflict about
using and controlling. As it turns out, around 1930 the emerging science of
psychology had adopted the term 'environment' (from the French 'environs')
to refer to an individual's exterior influences as opposed to their inner nature
and genetic predisposition. Later, the term proved ideal for the scientific age
of the 1950s; for it denoted a clean split between inner and outer, between fact
and mystery, between the human and the rest of creation. Now bolstered with
the imprimatur of science, 'environment' migrated, through the educational
system, out into public speech.

That the green movement later co-opted this word is a measure of success,
I suppose, but you have to wonder who co-opted what. We may have gained
a shiny new word, but with it came a technical orientation that has come
largely to define how environmentalism is not only spoken, but practised.
Around this word there has accumulated an entire vernacular of technical,
quasi-scientific verbiage. There has even been a book written about it: 'The
Language of Environment', by George Myerson and Yvonne Rydin. In it the
authors describe an 'environet' in which technical terms and phrases hover in
space and intersect. Today we would all recognise much of this terminology –
hazard mitigation, environmental impact, carbon capture, parts per million,
biodiversity, ecosystem, sustainable development.

The problem with this environet is that it hovers above the heads of most
people; people who may not be versed in the language of science, and may not
really want to be. For the listener, the earnest pleading of the science may be
more threatening than enlightening; or even incomprehensible and faintly
elitist. The sad result is that the most common thing between us – the natural world – has become lost to our common speech. We feel we need a specialised scientific vocabulary just to discuss it.

It's important to bear in mind that this mental category, 'the environment',
didn't always exist, and that we have not always viewed Earth through the

lens of science. Consider Ralph Waldo Emerson's seminal essay *Nature*, written in 1836. In it, Emerson speaks of nature not in scientific, quantitative terms – marine ecosystem, desert ecology, riparian zones, etc. – but in terms of *qualities,* such as Beauty, Idealism, Discipline, Spirit and even Language. Note that these are qualities we commonly place in the human sphere, thus Emerson's subtle but far reaching insight: it's Nature that makes us human.

Emerson then goes on to assert something equally daring. Nature he says 'stretches forth its arms to embrace us'. 'Only let our thoughts be of equal greatness'. Think about this awhile. Not only does Emerson grant nature consciousness, but it's a consciousness that inclines toward us. Earth is not simply something beautiful to look at, play around in or even preserve. It's something to be in *relationship* with; perhaps the most fundamental relationship of our lives. Equally remarkable, the path to that relationship, the return gesture, requires not the stereotypical notions of inner silence or humility, but 'thoughts of equal greatness'. Nature, says Emerson, not only makes us human, it calls us to greatness.

Of course, this is not how we usually think of things. 'Greatness' is a human quality: the stuff of generals and presidents, physicists and industrialists. But Emerson says, no – it is the stuff of Nature, and it is free to all. Emerson gives us something science can't, a path to know nature without any specialised education. He, as though anticipating the coming language of technical categorisation and political abstraction, pre-liberates Nature from the arms of the experts and returns it to common human embrace. Beauty, Idealism, Discipline, Spirit, Language. No degree required. And the education is ultimate.

What follows from this understanding is the question of what will happen to our own inner natures when outer nature has been wholly corrupted. What will it be like for us when the snowy peaks, whose gleaming crowns once called forth our inspiration and optimism, begin to melt and darken, growing sullen and looming with foreboding? What of Discipline when the poles are melting? The bleakness I describe here is not willful. That is the tragedy. The unimaginable is already upon us, and it can't be comprehended in only technical terms.

*

And, Mother of Nature, if a word with immense
energy is needed, the people remember yours.
— Friedrich Holderlin (1798)

So what if were to change our terms, let go of the predictions of graphs and models, and speak instead from the standpoint of the soul? What would that language look like? What would be the words and symbols, nouns and adjectives, metaphors and syllogisms? I wouldn't try to speculate on that, but my expectation is they will arise on their own, organically, from many places at once. But I don't expect any new, all encompassing meta-word to arrive that replaces 'the environment.' When I cast about in my mind for alternatives, plenty of good candidates appear: Nature, Creation, Life, the Land, Reality, the Universe. But they all have their limitations, and they all carry that quality inherent in words which tends to separate speaker from subject.

Perhaps the problem is not the names themselves, but our way of naming; the expectation that an abstract label can speak for anything, let alone a planet. And maybe modern language doesn't really care to speak for things anyway. The objective now is pure efficiency; to label and file and clear the way for 'use and control.'

As is so often the case, we can learn something here from indigenous peoples. Native languages tend to name things not with abstract labels, but with phrases, descriptions, small stories which place things in the mind's eye. To the Aleut, for example, Alaska is the 'place the sea breaks upon'. The Apache town which on our maps is called Cibecue is to the Navajo 'the valley with long red bluffs'. In the same manner, rather than 'the environment' we could say 'this house of life' or 'this place that feeds us'. Rather than saying 'species,' we could say 'our fellow creatures,' or 'our non-human neighbours'.

Of course, this feels awkward, and has been put here inelegantly at best. But perhaps we live in a time where awkward is right; where anything that slides down too easily should be suspect. If indeed we have forgotten where we are, if we have lost the sense of what feeds us and gives us life, then the first job of language is to remember, to help us speak our way back. It is no longer enough to simply convince with facts and logic, 'issue' by 'issue.' The need has grown deeper, and more difficult, than that. We need to recover lost consciousness; we need to reclaim nature as the sacred centre of human life.

When geometric diagrams and digits
Are no longer the keys to living things…
And people see in poems and fairy tales
The true history of the world…
         – Novalis (1800)

Environmentalism traditionally shies away from such territory. Words like 'sacred' and 'holy' are carefully avoided, lest they label the speaker as woolly-minded and 'unscientific.' True to our educations, we like to stick to the science and frame our arguments accordingly. But in so doing, we render ourselves voiceless at the very roots of the crisis. Transnational corporations are able to roam the world pillaging for profit because they exist upon a moral foundation that says 'it's fine, this is just the way it is.' The dominant religions long ago laid this foundation, and now the dominant cultural narratives echo it, maintaining a moral architecture that permits and rationalises the destruction of Earth. The question confronting us now is: How can we expect to mount a defence of the non-human without confronting these foundational beliefs? How do we intend to raise Earth's status in our cultures without first acknowledging its real, felt, sacredness?

Ultimately, in these times, to speak of Earth in only technical terms seems to me an evasion, or – worse – a kind of tiptoeing politeness. No one needs to challenge another's personal beliefs or morality, or their own for that matter. Certain truths can be avoided, such as the fact that we are all complicit in an economic system that is fundamentally cruel and which in order to function must render life as dead matter, raw material for endless product. At the same time, certain myths are left to stand, unchallenged, such as the belief that this planet somehow exists for *our* sake; or that a separate, detached God up there somewhere put Earth down here for us to proudly plunder.

One thing we can be sure of: Those determined to exploit what remains of our beleaguered home want nothing more than to keep the conversation just where it is, on a technical plane, confined to 'the environment.' There it remains a political abstraction, technical and distant, separate from our deeper lives and easily filed away by the mind. It's time we stop speaking into this trap. We can no longer be willing to sit in our environmental corner, proffering data and pleading for mitigation. Our subject demands more of the floor. Hell, it *is* the floor, and the building that contains it, and the house that contains the building. But it can't speak for itself. That's our job.

*

> *The natural world is a spiritual house,*
> *where the pillars, that are alive...*
> – Charles Baudelaire (1856)

Common wisdom sees human beings as the users of tools and the makers of things. But we are also the creators of words, stories, letters, constitutions, epistles, ballads, contracts, laws, declarations of war, manifestos, proclamations, poems. And it's these assemblages of words that determine not only what things we make, but toward what purposes we make them, and within what rules. It's not the user of tools assiduously denying the climate crisis; it's the user of words. And we are not a people at odds with 'the environment.' We are a people at odds with Life, with Reality, with the only planet we've got.

And yet, despite our blindness, the sun shines today the same as it ever has. Leaves unfurl, seeds crack open, the 'procreant urge of the world' goes on. Some things can't be turned off. And despite all we've done to it, Nature, or Creation, or Blessed House, or whatever we need to call it, still 'stretches forth its arm to embrace us...'

Only let our words...

MARIO PETRUCCI

Three poems for a Newborn Son

All Began With

your iris
eyes – sky
couching two

thin washers of
itself then lips
twin wands

of coral
bacterially
shoaled end

to end enjoin yet
shift to father's
incoming tide

as bodied
movement
makes fauna

of flesh pushing
each compass
point out at

once to
draw breeze
to nexus while

your pate as un-
known to you
as any polar

freezes under
with figment bone
& over: antler velvet

as subcutaneous
deltas & corp
-uscular

forests flop
with rainwater
till you – upright

stride into a world
you already are
small tree

How Heartwood Is

the old hand
light-wrinkled

guides younger
fingers together

– push one plump
pulse through sand

then water ah feel
that pressure each

small yield in resi-
stance as pleasure

rises to flood what
is coldly scanned

in time : that stone
shifts with planting

worlds whose past
-ured loam stands

bent with shadow
to show itself now

thumbed & shoved
through death into

whatever might be
dared to life though

as the subtle earth
is palmed back over

neither quite known
nor knows which is

seed to whom

Tulip i

as a boy
pressed into
loam the hole

spoon-dug over
wide too
deep

a bulb
hairlessly gently
lobed firm with pressings

-out into world pure
white grazed
jaundice

where light
had caught but
plumped all over

raw-healthed keened
by aromas soil
makes

of itself
as if exuded
by vegetable flesh

coolly perspiring after
sun in pursuit of
its seeming

form yet
held by some
consistent chord in

ground so down you
go so shallow
& grave

let damp
life seep in
mould to you

as you ascend
make you
green

DARREN ALLEN

This Autumn Everyone is Going to Fall in Love

My plan is this. Get lots of people together and rehearse for a day or two. Then, a day later, over the course of a couple of hours, in ones and twos and fours, we all go into a very large coffee shop (or similar public space) and do normal things there until the signal; a man plays to his girlfriend, through tinny mobile phone speakers, a classic love song. At this point (apparently unrelated) a couple in the queue start kissing, then a tearfully moving phone call begins at one of the tables, then two friends warmly agree, shaking hands ...

Then a few things happen at once: someone says, 'I know this is not the most romantic venue, but it's now or never ...' (inaudible muffles followed by quiet delight), someone else starts reading a newspaper story about the coming cataclysm with approval, another comes in and recognises a long-lost friend – they embrace – talk of the war. Two friends, talking about their plans for a friend's funeral, burst into warm laughter. The events – low-key, natural, subliminal – snowball; flowers are produced and tenderly laid, a very old woman is led totteringly to a seat where she spreads very large normal cards, two mourners – tear-stained – order lots of milk; more vague but catastrophic news is read from a laptop with approval, strangers in the queue start talking to each other 'you too?' 'yes, me too'; a couple of chin-dribblers wibble-wobble their way yawpingly, some small-scale magic from one of the tables (levitating cutlery?); the music gets louder – but still quiet. A man and wife knock their heads together, two more lovers reach a startlingly pleasant conclusion 'it is finally happening', someone unrolls a large poster that says 'History is Ending', a hearse passes outside, muffled music – the same song as the speakers, but live from outside. The rumour spreads, 'it is finally happening.' More fundamental behaviour, general relief, doors flung open, music floods in, a coffin enters followed by a carnival of flamboyantly attired orchestral brass, cartwheeling and sadly coroneting, a festival of the dead, children, mules and cripples; bannered with happy asteroids and cheerfully apocalyptic slogans. The place erupts in trombones and everyone, now half-choir, falls in enthusiasm, sad ecstasy and fellow-feeling; inanimate objects are cared for, many nodding in shared yes, layered descants and the world waltzing for a moment gives up to the friendly trumpets of infinite loss.

CHARLES HUGH SMITH

The Art of Survival, Taoism and the Warring States

When people start talking about the coming bad times and how best to survive them, I soon find myself shaking my head. It's not that I want to be difficult, but I can't help cutting against the grain when my experience runs counter to the standard received wisdom.

If you've followed discussions of peak oil and economic collapse across the internet, you probably know the kind of 'survivalist' wisdom I have in mind. In its full-blown version, it runs something like this: Stockpile a bunch of canned or dried food and other valuable accoutrements of civilised life (generators, tools, firearms) in a remote area, far from urban centres, and then wait out the bad times, all the while protecting your stash with an array of weaponry and technology.

Now while I have no problem with the goal, I must respectfully disagree with just about every assumption behind this strategy. In fact, if anyone asked me for advice on riding out the difficult years ahead, I would recommend almost exactly the opposite. Once again, this isn't because I enjoy being ornery, but because everything in this strategy runs counter to my own experience in rural, remote settings.

You see, when I was a young teen my family lived in the mountains. To the urban sophisticates who came up as tourists, we were 'hicks' (or worse), and to us they were 'flatlanders' (derisive snort).

Now the first thing you have to realise is that we know the flatlanders, but they don't know us. They come up to their cabin, and since we live here year round, we soon recognise their vehicles and know about how often they come up, what they look like, if they own a boat, how many are in their family, and just about everything else which can be learned by simple observation.

The second thing you have to consider is that we have a lot of time on our hands. There are plenty of kids who are too young to have a legal job, and many older teens with no jobs, which are scarce. After school and chores,

240

we're not taking piano lessons and all that urban busywork. And while there are plenty of pudgy kids spending all afternoon or summer in front of the TV or games console, not every kid is like that.

So we're out riding around. On a scooter or motorcycle if we have one, but if not then on bicycles, or we're hoofing it. Since we have time, and we're wandering all over this valley or mountain or plain, one way or another somebody is going to spot that trail of dust rising behind your pickup when you go to your remote hideaway. Or we'll run across the new road or driveway you cut, and wander up to see what's going on. Not when you're around, of course, but after you've gone back down to wherever you live. There's plenty of time; since you picked a remote spot, nobody's around.

You see, what you think of as remote, we think of as home. This is our valley, or mountain, or desert, all twenty miles of it, or what have you. We've hiked around all the peaks, because there's no reason not to and we have a lot of energy. Fences and gates are no big deal, (if you triple-padlock your gate, we'll just climb over it) and any dirt road, no matter how rough, is an open invitation to see what's up there. Remember, if you can drive to your hideaway, so can we. Even a small pickup truck can easily drive right through most gates (don't ask how, but I can assure you this is true). If nobody's around, we have all the time in the world to lift up or snip your barbed wire and sneak into your haven. Its remoteness makes it easy for us to poke around and explore without fear of being seen.

If you packed in everything on your back, and there was no road, then you'd have a very small hideaway – more a tent than a cabin. You'd think it was safely hidden, but we'd still find it sooner or later, because we wander all over this area; maybe hunting rabbits, or climbing rocks, or doing a little fishing if there are any creeks or lakes in the area. Or we'd spot the wisp of smoke rising from your fire one crisp morning, or hear your generator, and wonder who's up there.

When we were 13, my buddy J.E. and I tied sleeping bags and a few provisions on our bikes – mine was a crappy old three-speed, his a Schwinn ten-speed – and rode off into the next valley over bone-jarring dirt roads. We didn't have fancy bikes with shocks, and we certainly didn't have camp chairs, radios, big ice chests and all the other stuff people think is necessary to go camping; we had some matches, cans of beans and apple sauce and some smashed bread. (It didn't start out smashed, but the roads were rough.)

We camped where others had camped before us, not in a campground, but just off the road in a pretty little meadow with a ring of fire-blackened rocks and a flat spot among the pine needles. We didn't have a tent, or air mattress, or any of those luxuries; but we had the smashed bread and the beans, and we made a little fire and ate and then went to sleep under the stars glittering in the dark sky.

There were a few bears in the area, but we weren't afraid; we didn't need a gun to feel safe. We weren't dumb enough to sleep with our food; if some bear wandered by and wanted the smashed bread, he could take it without bothering us. The only animal which could bother us was the human kind, and since few people walk ten or more miles over rough ground in the heat and dust, we'd hear their truck or motorbike approaching long before they ever spotted us.

We explored old mines and anything else we spotted, and then we rode home, a long loop over rutted, dusty roads.

You get my point: however well-hidden your hideaway, the locals will find it. Any road, no matter how rough, might as well be lit with neon lights which read, 'Come on up and check this out!' If a teen doesn't spot it, then somebody else will: a county or utility employee out doing their job, a hunter, whoever.

It's not just us 'hicks' who understand this kind of thing. Consider the philosophy of Taoism, which developed during an extended era of turmoil known as the Warring States period of Chinese history. One of its main principles runs something like this: if you're tall and stout and strong, then you'll call attention to yourself. And because you're rigid – that is, what looks like strength at first glance – then when the wind rises, it snaps you right in half.

If you're thin and ordinary and flexible, like a willow reed, then you'll bend in the wind, and nobody will notice you. You'll survive while the 'strong' will be broken, either by unwanted attention or by being brittle.

If the chips are down, and push comes to shove, then what we're discussing is a sort of war, isn't it? And if we're talking about war, then we should think about the principles laid down in *The Art Of War* by Sun Tzu quite some time ago.

The flatlander protecting his valuable depot is on the defensive, and anyone seeking to take it away (by negotiation, threat or force) is on the offensive. The defence can select the site for proximity to water, clear fields of fire, or what have you, but one or two defenders have numerous disadvantages. Perhaps most importantly, they need to sleep. Secondly, just about anyone who's plinked cans with a rifle and who's done a little hunting can sneak up and put away an unwary human. Unless you remain in an underground bunker 24/7, at some point you'll be vulnerable. And that's really not much of a life – especially when your food supplies finally run out, which they eventually will. Or you run out of water, or your sewage system overflows, or some other situation requires you to emerge.

So let's line it all up. Isn't a flatlander who piles up a high-value stash in a remote area, with no neighbours within earshot or line of sight, kind of like a big, tall, brittle tree? All those chains and locks and barbed-wire fencing and bolted doors just shout out that the flatlander has something valuable inside that cabin, or bunker, or RV.

Let's say things have gotten bad, and the flatlander is burrowed into his cabin. Eventually some locals will come up to visit; in a truck if there's gas, on foot if there isn't. We won't be armed; we're not interested in taking the flatlander's life or goodies. We just want to know what kind of person he is. So maybe we'll ask to borrow his generator for a town dance, or tell him about the church food drive, or maybe ask if he's seen so-and-so around.

Now what's the flatlander going to do when several unarmed men approach? Gun them down? Once he's faced with regular unarmed guys, he can't very well conclude they're a threat and warn them off. But if he does, then we'll know he's just another selfish flatlander. He won't get any help later when he needs it; or it will be minimal and grudging. He just counted himself out.

Suppose some bad guys hear about the flatlander's hideaway and stash. Now, the human animal is a much better predator than it is an elusive prey. It is large and poorly-camouflaged, lacking the keen senses of smell and hearing of a goat or a wild turkey, and it's usually distracted and unaware of its surroundings. All you need to stalk any prey is patience and observation, so no matter how heavily armed the flatlander is, he'll become vulnerable at some point to a long-range shot. (Even body armour can't stop a headshot or a hit to the femoral artery in the thigh.) Maybe he stays indoors for six days, or even sixty. But at some point the windmill breaks or the dog needs walking or what have you, and he emerges – and then he's vulnerable.

So creating a high-value horde in a remote setting is looking like just about the worst possible strategy in the sense that the flatlander has provided a huge incentive to theft or robbery, and also provided a setting advantageous to the thief or hunter.

If someone were to ask this 'hick' for a less risky survival strategy, I would suggest he move into town and start showing a little generosity, rather than a lot of hoarding. If not in town, then on the edge of town, where you can be seen and heard.

I'd suggest attending church, if you've a mind to, even if your faith isn't as strong as others'. Or join the Lions Club, the Kiwanis, or Rotary International, if you can get an invitation. I'd volunteer to help with the pancake breakfast fundraiser, and buy a couple tickets to other fundraisers in town. I'd mow the old lady's lawn next door for free, and pony up a dollar if the elderly gentleman in line ahead of me at the grocery store finds himself a dollar light on his purchase.

If I had a parcel outside town that was suitable for an orchard or other crop, I'd plant it, and spend plenty of time in the local hardware store and farm supply, asking questions and spreading a little money around the local merchants. I'd invite my neighbours into my little plain house so they could see I don't own diddly-squat except some second-hand furniture and a crappy old TV. And I'd leave my door open so anyone could see for themselves I've got very little worth taking.

I'd have my tools, of course; but they're scattered around and old and battered by use; they're not shiny and new and expensive-looking, and they're not stored all nice and clean in a box some thief could lift. They're hung on old nails, or in the closet, and in the shed; a thief would have to spend a lot of time searching the entire place, and with my neighbours looking out for me, the thief is short of the most important advantage he has, time.

If somebody's desperate enough or dumb enough to steal my old handsaw, I'll buy another old one at a local swap meet. (Since I own three anyway, it's unlikely anyone would steal all three because they're not kept together.)

My valuable things, like the water filter, are kept hidden amidst all the low-value junk I keep around to send the message there's nothing here worth looking at. The safest things to own are those which are visibly low-value, surrounded by lots of other mostly worthless stuff.

I'd claim a spot in the community garden, or hire a neighbour to till up my back yard, and I'd plant chard and beans and whatever else my neighbours suggested grew well locally. I'd give away most of what I grew, or barter it, or maybe sell some at the farmer's market. It wouldn't matter how little I had to sell, or how much I sold; what mattered was meeting other like-minded souls and swapping tips and edibles.

If I didn't have a practical skill, I'd devote myself to learning one. If anyone asked me, I'd suggest saw-sharpening and beer-making. You're legally entitled to make quite a bit of beer for yourself, and a decent homebrew is always welcome by those who drink beer. It's tricky, and your first batches may blow up or go flat, but when you finally get a good batch you'll be popular and well-appreciated if you're of the mind to share.

Saw-sharpening just takes patience and a simple jig; you don't need to learn a lot, like a craftsman, but you'll have a skill you can swap with craftsmen and women. As a carpenter, I need sharp saws, and while I can do it myself, I find it tedious and would rather rebuild your front porch handrail or a chicken coop in exchange for the saw-sharpening.

Pickles are always welcome in winter, or when rations get boring; the Germans and Japanese of old lived on black bread or brown rice and pickled vegetables, with an occasional piece of dried meat or fish. Pickling is a useful and easy-to-learn craft. There are many others. If you're a techie, then volunteer to keep the network up at the local school; do it for free, and do a good job. Show you care.

Because the best protection isn't owning 30 guns; it's having 30 people who care about you. Since those 30 have other people who care about them, you actually have 300 people who are looking out for each other, including you. The second best protection isn't a big stash of stuff others want to steal, it's sharing what you have and owning little of value. That's being flexible, and common, the very opposite of creating a big fat highly-visible, high-value target and trying to defend it yourself in a remote setting.

I know this runs counter to just about everything that you'll see recommended on the survivalist web forums, but if you're a hick like me, then you know it rings true. The flatlanders are scared because they're alone and isolated; we're not scared. We've endured bad times before, and we don't need much to get by. We're not saints, but we will reciprocate to those who extend their good spirit and generosity to the community in which they live and in which they produce something of value.

ANTONIO DIAS

Something for Nothing

Some nights, when the surf angled in just right and the tide was high enough for the waves to break close in on the slope of the beach, the pounding waves sounded like distant artillery fire. When that happened, he awoke drenched in cold sweat, not knowing why.

He stayed out at the old lifesaving station anyway. He'd gone out there at first thinking he'd last a few weeks, and that had turned into months. Its bohemian 'owners' had gone back to the City for the winter, so no one bothered him much as the season had closed in.

He liked the clean, open emptiness it gave his days, at least when the sun was out. This was even more so late in the Fall like this when the low sun bounced off the hills of sand and the vibrant blue vault of sky ached in his head.

It was better than being in town. No-one bothered him out here. In town, he felt hedged-in. Everyone seemed to know his business. Out here, he did what he wanted, or nothing at all, spending whole days on the weathered, sandblasted stoop, shifting to stay in the warmth of the sun as it arced around, smoking and staring at the horizon. He found he'd longed for this for so long. Just to be. The mad rush of life stilled for once.

He'd lose himself, not in thought but in simple sensation. He found that a morning would melt away, an afternoon, the early dusk would close in around him and only as the air took a more pronounced chill did he realise he'd been sitting there all day. Other times, he'd walk. He'd find himself back at the station late, a waxing moon rising across the dunes, and have no idea where he'd gone. Sitting, walking, simply breathing the thin, cool air seemed to him at those times to be enough. More than enough, as if this were *sufficient* for life; to simply let it wash over him, quietly, without shocks or surprises.

It wasn't bright and sunny every day. More and more, days wouldn't dawn so much as groan into existence, the deepest darkness of an overcast night on the backshore slowly lifting so he could make out the window frame, then the horizon; not sharp and dancing far away like it did on a bright day but close in, barely perceptible. The grey of water met the grey of sky and melded into a unified cocoon, a blanket, as the dull soft sand below reflected its monotony, only broken by startlingly erotic clumps of dark beach-grass perched atop some hummock, a *mons* of dune.

The closeness of such days, even that vague call towards sex tugging at him even as he buried it, led him to irritation. He'd fuss and find that everything about the place, inside-and-out annoyed him. He was low on food. The lantern oilcan was empty. The books he had with him bored him. He was out of tobacco and papers, and matches. He'd find himself trudging off towards town, grudgingly welcoming its hassles as he began to meet people; its low buildings and houses shut off the far horizon. Tall, narrow strips of distance showed between, lost without detail in the glare of contrast with the dark walls that shut him in.

He would wander the town, wrap himself in a shell of frustration, ignore everyone he passed, daring anyone to try to break into his day. If he met up with someone he knew, he stared right past them and kept walking. He almost believed himself that he hadn't noticed, as old friends or passing acquaintances stopped and stared after him, shaking their heads.

At a lunch-counter, in a shop, he'd push his way through. Affecting annoyance at the bustle and contact of others, but wincing in mixed pleasure and pain at the accidental pressure of another body against him. By the end of the day, he'd have haphazardly attended to his errands and be back to the station before dark. His larder restocked, plenty to smoke and drink, and a new book from the library, or a paper, or magazine on his bedside table to tempt him with glimpses of a world beyond the sound of wind and rain and sea.

The last time he'd been to town, it hadn't been a particularly dreary day. A steady, sharp wind out of the Northwest blew across a cluttered sky as clouds shifted past. There was a different feeling about the town as he entered. People seemed preoccupied. Passing a storefront he noticed the headlines on a Boston paper, in oversized Gothic typeface hard to read, something about a submarine, trapped sailors, a collision. The most startling thing about it all, in a strange way, was seeing the name, PROVINCETOWN, in that tall type with all the rest. A byline in the *Boston Globe*:

'PROVINCETOWN'

The entire town appeared caught up in a story of stricken sailors. Walking along Front Street, Peter caught fragments of conversation as he strode along, one hand deep in his jacket pocket, the other balled in a fist, pumping. The scar on his thigh ached. On almost every step, the muscle around it pulled. It felt as if it would tear around the shard of shrapnel buried there. He half-welcomed the pain. Faithful at least, it never left him. It gave him a place to focus his anger. So much burned in him, it was good to have a place to put it all.

He smoked as he walked. A hand-rolled cigarette firmly held between his thumb and two fingers, like a pencil or a brush. His breath often caught in a wheeze. He coughed and kept on walking just a little too fast. He brought his cigarette up to his lips and took another sharp, deep drag, suppressing the urge to cough, holding the smoke an extra beat to prove to himself that he could.

*

The meeting at the Town Hall had been a farce.

He'd been drawn to the commotion as he headed up the street. It dawned on him why the streets had seemed so empty. A small crowd trailed from its main entrance down the steps and out towards the street. Some of its side-windows were open despite the cold, as if to let out the furore within. He could tell without making out the words that this crowd wasn't happy. Without thinking, he'd found himself entering.

Hit by the noise in the crush, he pushed his way through to a spot by a window. Passing from the doors swung open to the lobby, pushing in from under the overhanging balcony, he saw that the entire shallow-vaulted space was full. Everyone talking, a loud, angry buzz. On a narrow stage stood a podium. Flags ranged to one side and some military men stood in a line. He made out two men who caught his attention, a younger, tall officer, dressed, what, as a captain? He wasn't too sure how to read the ranks in the Navy, never had been. The other was short, older, obviously senior.

He pieced together the gist of what was going on. A submarine had been struck. 'Revenue-ers? Perfect!' he thought. 'They've got nothing better to do …' The Navy had arrived in force, tugs, a salvage ship. Some sailors were still alive on the submarine. Yet the rescue flotilla had returned to port after a first diver had made contact.

When was that? Yesterday? He wondered. He wasn't sure, it might have been a couple of days ago already. Christ! They've been down there how long? That fucking admiral, or whatever he is! He looked across at the older man standing at the lectern, who was was paternally explaining why the Navy couldn't do anything so long as it was so stormy. 'Condescending bastard!' Peter muttered. The old man looked like he was addressing some ladies lawn party, not a hall filled to the rafters with fishermen and their families, men who knew a lot more about storms than he ever would.

'Ahm afraid, we had to break off diving operations yesterday,' the senior officer intoned in a faint drawl. 'Until the weather improves, we won't be able to send anyone back down.' Peter stood at the side, leaning against the wall directly below one of the tall windows. The hall seethed as the officer spoke. Here and there, louder disturbances broke out. A stout, red-faced Portuguese stood up. His hands grasped his braces as if to keep himself contained, the skin on his knuckles was drawn tight and white against his red flannel shirt.

'We NET your submarine! We haul it to the beach! Is so close to shoah! O meu Deus!' His words, exploding from him, were answered by a roar of agreement.

The admiral took a half-step backwards, his hands clutching the podium for support. His gaze travelled around the hall, over the heads of all those standing at their seats on the main floor, and below the eyes of those in the balcony leaning over its edge as if the space couldn't contain them. The golden glow of polished wood and the living crowd that filled the hall set the space vibrating. It felt like a giant violin, the hall both the site of a performance and its instrument.

The admiral's face waxed a shade paler than his normal office-bound pallor. He turned to his side, looking at the officer in charge of dive operations. He gritted his teeth, and for a second, Peter saw all the bureaucrat's anger focused on that man.

*

'It's always the way!' He muttered aloud as he walked, remembering. He'd had to leave. He felt he'd explode otherwise. Walking down the street again, fury in his low voice palpable,

'It's always the fucking way!'.

Heads turned around him in alarm. He ignored them, caught up reliving events at the hall. He walked on, balling up this new anger and his frustration, adding them to his long list of examples of military fuck-ups he'd seen in the war.

'Generals fart and men die! It never changes!' He kicked at a wadded-paper sack in the street. 'What am I doing back here anyway?' he blurted turning his thoughts to his own problems. He could see those six sailors huddled below, not knowing – or knowing, but not ready to accept it.

*

Once, on the front, after a 24-hour barrage, he and his men had come out of a bunker in time to catch the last trickle of faint light bleed out of the western sky. None of them had believed they'd ever see the sky again. The sight of it hurt. Not its brightness – acetylene torches lighting that pit had been brighter; sharp, hard stabs of light without colour, hissing like serpents, accentuating the gloom with their barely contained violence. They'd been constantly assailed by premonitions of the instant when a direct hit would break in on them, tongues of flame and tons of earth engulfing them, incinerating and entombing them faster than they could imagine. Those lights had been a focus for their fears as they repeatedly imagined what their deaths would feel like.

That's what they'd expected would happen. Not to come out into the dying day alive. Or were they? What hurt them most was their numbness. They'd spent a night and a day building it up, wrapping themselves in its protection like so many bandages. Bandages not meant to protect a physical wound, but intended to protect them from hope, from even the last vestige, the last torn scrap of it. Fear and hope had begun to feel like the same thing to them after a while, mere irritations they felt across their skins and deep within their bodies. A jangle of raw nerves, it stopped mattering if it came from a moment of terror at the proximity of a near miss; or a moment of respite, an insinuating glimmer of hope that welled up when a lull or a wide-miss gave them a vague sense of gratitude that they'd been spared that time.

They'd been spared, but what about the poor bastards it had hit? Next time it might be our turn …

*

He knew too much about what it must be like down there. 'Give it up boys,' he said tenderly, as he lit another cigarette. He pinched out the dying match between his thumb and finger, enjoying the tiny blast of pain, an exploding bee-sting, as he wished them well, and dead.

ANTHONY LIOI

Trilobite

n. Any of the numerous extinct marine arthropods of the class Trilobita, of the Paleozoic era, having a segmented exoskeleton divided by grooves or furrows into three longitudinal lobes.
 – *The American Heritage Dictionary*

> You had no cell phones —
> the sea was sweet without
> satellite communication or
> the latest coffeehouse in Prague.
> In fact, given fossil photographs —
> shovel-headed centipedish spider-mite —
> you make the horseshoe crab
> who lately spawned at Brigantine
> appear the sleek Manhattanite.
>
> If, as I recall, you perished at the Permian frontier,
> could you clear something up: what's death-by-asteroid
> *feel* like? My species is conducting little tests.
> No asteroids – we're not Zeus yet,
> but cowfart, Oldsmobiles, and the mysteries of Wal-Mart
> pull a whack-job on the kingdoms of the living.
> Anyway, annihilation:
> Does it hurt?
> Is it a hoot?
> Do extinction-angels giggle as the last of you bite it?
> Is it being sealed in glass,
> Sleeping Beauty with no prince to kiss 'er?
> Or driving Jersey's Turnpike when everyone has EZ-Pass
> and you've got a quarter.

Maybe you should save your breath.
Just answer this:
Did you pardon the bullet that ended your age,
or sit at eternity's HDTV
longing for mammals to die in a blur
of scorched milk and burnt fur?

CATHERINE LUPTON

Wandering Around
With Words

So, civilitas, civilisation. Etymologically, the word contrasts with
barbarity: the civilian with the soldier, civil law with criminal law.
The problem with it, and thus our need to consider 'Uncivilisation,'
comes about when the term gets co-opted by various forms of
domination. That doesn't make civilisation bad. It only affirms the
badness of domination masquerading as civilisation. We should
remember that our civil rights and civic duties are also part of civilisation. So is the duty to civil disobedience in the name of uphold-
ing a more civil sense of what is civilised. *I don't think we need to
engage too much in the displacement activity (displacement from the
urgent imperatives of action) in fussing about how we use these words.
People who fuss overmuch about words rarely get much done. Let actions
speak louder.*
　　Alastair McIntosh, 'Popping the Gygian Question', in *Dark Mountain:
　　Issue 1* (Summer 2010). Emphasis added.

As a writer who is constitutionally incapable of not fussing (endlessly) about
words, I bristle whenever I'm told, as by those three sentences, to shut up and
just act. Now I can grasp what Alastair McIntosh is bothered by here, and
sympathise with his frustration. Pedantic sparring over the roots and meanings of words can often, in an insulated academic context, work as displacement; undermining and muddling the strength of motivation and belief that
action requires. But to silence all conversation and enquiry around words, to
set action up in opposition to words, even in an off-the-cuff remark, creates a
loss. It throws a heavy tarpaulin over a predicament and hopes it will go away.
If I were to go along with what this quotation asks of me, that would mean

253

silently accepting that 'barbarians' = 'soldiers' = 'criminals'. But predicaments like whether, or when, such an equation holds true, never go away. I'd like here to unwrap these bundled predicaments of words, turn them around to consider their different sides; redress them in fabrics, ribbons and twine to enhance their shapes and expressions. In order to honour them, to listen more closely to the stories they might have to tell.

Language is a process, constantly changing but at different rates, some fast enough for humans to notice, others not. There are words whose meanings alter drastically within the space of a generation: I still can't get used to 'sick' meaning 'fantastic' for people half my age; in the same way that my mother could never quite cope with 'gay' getting rerouted from jollity to homosexuality. Other words shift far more slowly, at the rate of hour hands, creating the illusion that they're not moving at all. 'Human', perhaps? Thus, fixing a meaning to a word as a prerequisite for action is a bit like standing in a forest and shouting at a beech tree to stop growing, so that you can do something about it.

The Earth, as we know too well, is rapidly losing diversity. Diversity of plant and animal species, of human lifeways, of languages. One of the basic understandings of modern ecology is that diversity is a requirement for healthy and robust ecosystems: the more different varieties of, say, potatoes, that you have, the more likely that at least some will prove resilient to new diseases and pests, or to changes in climate, ensuring both their own survival and that of the creatures who depend upon them for food and shelter.

There is a parallel loss of diversity in how we use everyday words. I'm not thinking so much of documented reductions in vocabulary; I'm trying to get at the growth of an encultured resistance to engaging with the layers of meaning and possibility within specific words, a defensive need for words to function as one-dimensional labels, and an outpouring of dysfunctional reactions (anger, hysteria, silencing, denial, polarity), when faced with circumstances in which words won't operate like that.

More precisely, certain words are getting yanked and distorted within our culture in two seemingly contrary directions at once. One good example is 'violence'. Ran Prieur has a great essay unpacking this word 'violence', in which he pinpoints one half of the problem: a tendency to use 'violence' as a catch-all propaganda term for a variety of acts and behaviours which, when scrutinised more closely, are not all accurately described by labelling them thus.[1] His survey considers 'vigour', 'control', 'cruelty', 'extermination', 'eating', 'toolmaking', 'toolbreaking', 'spectacle', 'nihilism', 'revenge' and 'balance'. Throwing the tarpaulin labelled 'violence' over all these actions and attitudes points to a loss of elasticity and diversity in thinking, and a spreading intolerance towards certain kinds of energetic and animal behaviour, especially on the part of humans: strong emotional reactions, standing up vigorously to an aggressor, or killing another creature in order to have something to eat.

The other half of the problem is exponential doublethink: instances in which the word violence would be absolutely appropriate, but where it has been swept out of mind and denied to feeling by contorted rebrandings like 'collateral damage', 'ethnic cleansing', 'enhanced interrogation'. As Derrick Jensen observes, violence is sustained most effectively where it is rationalised out of sight, and relabelled as perfectly reasonable behaviour.

Pinned between these encroaching walls, how it is possible not to keep questioning words? Or, to look at the predicament from another side, what happens if we act in the name of certain words without questioning them? They might, for a while, set hard enough to make a crust to stand upon, to rally around. 'Sustainable development', 'stop the war', 'uncivilisation'. But underneath, molten questions and challenges are moving all the time; sooner or later the pressure of what has been left unsaid and unexamined will break to the surface and demand attention. Part of the momentum of the Dark Mountain project for me is just such a breaking-through under pressure, to examine words and stories that have become sclerotic, out of touch, no longer flexible enough to cope with our probable futures.

But there are two aspects to this rallying and shattering around campaigning words, which need to be distinguished. A reality is that campaigns often fail simply because entrenched power interests ride roughshod over them, even when the words are well-chosen and there is widespread support for what they embody. The Blair government's decision to go ahead with the invasion of Iraq in 2003, in the teeth of massive public opposition, is one obvious example. In the aftermath of defeats, there's always the possibility of lashing out sideways, worrying away at the defeated words; when under the circumstances, campaigning words are the wrong trees to be shouting at. But on another side, the drive to campaign under headings honed down in the interests of clarity and simplicity – or, more precisely, honed in reaction to an encultured inability to engage productively and compassionately with complexity – is going to leave awkward questions and vital nuances unaddressed, and the campaign platform a hostage to seismic lurches in credibility.

It helps to find ways to question words without getting into adversarial arguments with them, for such arguments tend to replicate the original problem of trying to stick fast to a preferred meaning. Anthony McCann offers the beautiful suggestion that we might lift up words and look beneath them for the attitude of the person who wrote them; in like spirit, I try to pay attention to the qualities of energy and attitude which animate how a person uses words, to work out if I'm allowed to just sit and enjoy the sunshine with them, if we can begin a tentative conversation, if I'm being invited to help, if I'm going to be properly heard, if my listening skills are being tested, if all we can have is a tit-for-tat educated debate, if I'm being shouted at, if I'm just supposed to shut up and sign up to the master plan.[2] All of which can apply as much to reading a book by a long-dead author, as to sitting in a lecture theatre listening to a talk, as to the effort to be more mindful as to what qualities I'm projecting into what I say and write.

A number of critics of Dark Mountain have reached for the blade labelled 'just a load of poetry' to twist. Why is poetry pretty much a dirty word in some cultural circles? Poets get caricatured into oblivion, underfunded, shunned like a plague, pushed to the margins, divided into competing factions and ruled over. One response is that poetry works hardest to question words and their uses. You've probably played the game of saying a word over and over and over ('kettle' is my particular favourite, I have no idea why), until it stops meaning what it's supposed to mean, gets unmoored from the thing or idea it is supposed to stand in for. Poets do this as part of their vocation. They turn words around and around under magnifying lenses, run them through experimental mazes, subject them to extremes of heat and cold and pressure until they disintegrate and miraculously reform. They have long, rambling conversations with words, learning their stories with an inquisitive ear and eye. They learn to budget with words, getting to know which are cheap, which expensive. They tune into the synaesthesia of words. Beside what 'violence' *means* (and great poets never lose sight of this), what does it sound like, alone or tucked between other words? How does it look, sitting in twelve point Georgia font upon a page of 100 gram laid ivory paper? What are its rhythms, its accents, its velocity, its heft? How does it feel brushing against the skin of your inner forearm? If you made like a two-year-old and put everything in your mouth to test its worth, how would 'violence' taste, sticky with your saliva? What inklings does it bring? Who are its helmeted and crinolined ancestors?

Poetry is always facing outwards as a specialist branch of literature, while plotting in secret to spill all over the place and refuse to stay put. Once it gets a word within its treacly, salty embrace, that word becomes a baby again, full of promise, demanding to be endlessly fussed over, never behaving exactly as predicted.

No wonder we're scared of it.

NB: *This essay was kicked off swiftly and reactively, as essays can be, by one passage in 'Popping the Gygian Question'. Later, I came around to reading both Alastair McIntosh's sensitive review of* Dark Mountain: Issue 1, *which tracks a reciprocal shift in his understanding of 'uncivilisation', and his deeply inspiring book* Soil and Soul. *These made me not exactly want to head back contrite into a rewrite; but at least to acknowledge that my appreciation of his writing is no longer stranded where I fixed it after that first encounter.*

Notes

1. Ran Prieur, 'Violence Unraveled', November 11, 2002. http://ranprieur.com/essays/viunrav.html.
2. Anthony McCann, 'A gentle ferocity: a conversation with Derrick Jensen', *Dark Mountain: Issue 1* (Summer 2010).

ADRIENNE ODASSO

Mantra

Let me try to explain

that the wind on the water is the voice
in the trees, that the sun on the leaves

is an iron seared to blood, is the reason
for the pain through which I can't breathe.

Let me try to name

my beloved dead for you, spin the thread for you
like the girl locked in the tower that I am:

doomed to stay here, doomed to pray here
in wild, far-ranging voices not my own.

(*Let me try to say*

what I mean; let me repeat
what I have said. Fate

sings in my veins,
and there is hope

in this gold thread.)

JOEL MOORE

Resignation

Lying here in the dark beside your heavy breath
I can hear a decade of bad jobs
straining your tired body

its pronouncement certain in the whistling air
through a clenched jaw of tightly fastened teeth
toward this stagnant black cloud above

And I think about getting up to write
as the dog barks and runs from something I can't shoo away
in his dream at the foot of our bed

My comfort is stored away in a small grey metal box
under some books on a shelf in a broom closet
behind a thin brown door with a rusty knob
at the end of a long dim lit hallway
in the back alley of my mind

It's a thought about a feeling
scribbled on a coffee stained napkin that says,
"Remember,
even though the failed years pile up
to gradually weaken your furious grip
on the desires and hopes of youth
at least for now
there is warmth and soft belief
in her touch
that is true"

DOUGALD HINE

Remember the Future?

I am retracing my steps, trying to work out where I last saw it.

In the north of Moscow, there is a park called VDNKh. It was built in the 1930s, under Stalin, and then rebuilt in the 1950s as an Exhibition of the Achievements of the National Economy. An enormous site, full of gilded statues, fountains and pavilions dedicated to different industries and domains of Soviet cultural prowess.

I don't know in what year the exhibitions within those pavilions were last updated, but if you visit the Space pavilion, you will find a display on a dusty wall towards the back. It climbs from floor to ceiling, measuring decade by decade the achievements of the Soviet space programme. You start in the 1950s with Sputnik, then images of the Soyuz rockets, and it counts up as far as 1990, and there is the Buran shuttle flying off past the year 2000, into the 21st century. By the time I made my visit, the rest of the pavilion had been put to use as a garden centre.

I am fascinated by the way that history humbles us, the unknowability of the future. It seems like a good thread to follow.

It doesn't take a history-changing failure on the scale of the Soviet collapse to leave such Ozymandian *aides-memoires*. After the first Dark Mountain festival in Llangollen, I went to stay with friends in South Yorkshire. One afternoon, we climbed a fence into the grounds of a place called the Earth Centre. You can find it between Rotherham and Doncaster: get off the train at a town called Conisbrough and you walk straight down from the eastbound platform to the gates of the centre, but those gates are locked. So we walked instead around the perimeter to find the quietest and least observed place to climb over, and spent an hour or so wandering around inside.

The Earth Centre was built with Millennium Lottery funding to be a kind of Eden Project of the North. It was planned as a tourist destination and an education centre about sustainable development. It had the largest solar array of its kind in Europe, when it was built; and its gardens are wonderful now, overgrown into a vision of post-apocalyptic abundance, because the Earth Centre itself turned out not to be sustainable, in some fairly mundane ways. Unable to attract the projected visitor numbers, it closed for the last time in 2004.

I can't think about Conisbrough without also remembering the artist Rachel Horne who comes from the town, who was born during the Miner's Strike and whose dad was a miner. Her work and her life are bound up with the experience of a community for whom the future disappeared. She grew up in a time and a place where the purpose of that small town had gone, because the pit had closed. As she took me around the town, on my first visit, one of the saddest moments came when she pointed out a set of new houses by the railway line. 'That's where my dad's allotment was.' The allotments were owned by the Coal Board, and so when the pit closed, not only did the men lose their jobs, but also their ability to grow their own food.

Horne grew up in a school that was in special measures. Her teachers would say to her, 'you're smart, keep your head down, get out of here as fast as you can'. She did: when she was sixteen, she left for Doncaster to study for A-levels, and then to London to art school. She was two years into art school when she turned around and went back. The work she was doing only made sense if she could ground it in the place where she had grown up, to work with the people she knew, and make work with them. So she put her degree on hold and came home to work on the first of a series of projects which have inspired me hugely, a project called *Out of Darkness, Light*, in which she brought her community together to honour the memory of the four hundred men and boys who had died in the history of the Cadeby Main colliery. Led by a deep instinct for what needed to be done, she had found a way back to one of the ancient and enduring functions of art, to honour the dead and, in so doing, give meaning to the living.

When we talk about 'collapse', there is a temptation to imagine a mythological event which lies somewhere out there in the future and which will change everything: The End Of The World As We Know It. But worlds are ending all the time; bodies of knowledge and ways of knowing are passing into memory, and beyond that into the depths of forgetting. For many people in many places, collapse is lived experience, something they have passed through and with which they go on living. What Horne's work underlines, for me, is the entanglement between the hard, material realities of economic collapse and the subtler devastation wrought by the collapse of meaning. This double collapse is there in the stories of the South Yorkshire coalfields, as in those of the former Soviet Union.

Yet perhaps there has already been something closer to a universal collapse of meaning, a failure whose consequences are so profound that we have hardly begun to reckon with them. In some sense, 'the future' itself has broken.

Looking back to the 1950s and 60s, I am struck by how, even in a time when people were living under the real threat of Mutually Assured Destruction, the future still occupied such a powerful place within the cultural imagination. It was present in a technological sense – the Jetsons visions of the future which we associate with 1950s America – and in a political sense, a belief in the possibility of a revolution that would change everything and usher in a fairer society. Or, on a quieter scale, in the creation of communities oriented around a utopian vision of making a better world.

Somewhere along the way, the future seems to have disappeared, without very much comment. It doesn't occupy the place in mainstream culture which it did forty or fifty years ago. You can look for pivots, moments at which it began to go. The fall of the Soviet Union might be one, in a sense. 'The End of History' was one of the famous aggrandising labels attached to those events, but perhaps 'The End of the Future' would be closer to the truth?[1] Or are we dealing with another consequence of the political and cultural hopes which hinged on the events of 1968?[2]

Perhaps it is simpler than that. If we no longer have daydreams about retiring to Mars, is it not least because fewer and fewer people are confident that retirement is still going to be there as a social phenomenon in most of our countries, by the time we reach that age? When students take to the streets of Paris or London today, it is no longer to bring about a better world, but to defend what they can of the world their parents took for granted.

So if the future is broken, how do we go about mending it? How do we re-member it, gather the pieces and put them back together? Like all griefs, the journey cannot be completed without a letting-go.

Where traces of the future remain in our mainstream culture, it is as a source of anxiety, something to be distracted from. When we, as environmentalists, talk about the future, it is often in language such as 'We have fifty months to save the planet.' One reason I am suspicious of this way of framing our situation is that it is so clearly haunted by a desire for certainty, and for knowing, and (by implication) the control which knowledge promises. Whereas the hardest thing about the future is that it is unknown, that history does humble us, that people often fail to anticipate the events which end up shaping their lives, on a domestic or a global scale. This isn't an argument for ignoring what we can see about the seriousness of the situation we are in, but it is an invitation to seek a humbler relationship with the future, and to be aware of the points at which our language acts as a defence against our uncertainties. It seems to me that such a historical humility may help us navigate the difficult years ahead, and perhaps begin the process of recovering from the cultural bereavement which our societies have gone through in recent decades.

When I get up from my writing and go to the balcony of this small flat, I can see on the horizon to the north the strange landmark of the Atomium, a remnant of the World Fair held here in Brussels over half a century ago. Such structures exist in an eery superimposition, relics of a future which didn't happen. Nothing dates faster than yesterday's idea of tomorrow. It is remote in a way which the most mysterious and illegible prehistoric remains are not, because they were once part of the lives of people more or less like ourselves. And while it is possible that your parents or grandparents were among the hundreds of thousands who, in the summer of 1958, queued to visit the abandoned future which graces this city's skyline, they could do so only as tourists. Those huge atomic globes have never been anyone's sanctuary or home.

The future to which such monuments are erected has little to do with the direction history is likely to take. It represents, rather, an attempt by those who hold power in the present to project themselves, to announce their inevitability in the face of the arbitrariness of history. It is a doomed colonial move, as foolish as those rulers who from time to time have sent their armies against the sea. However confidently they set their faces to the horizon, their feet rest uneasily on the ground. History will make fools of them, too, sooner or later, arriving from an unexpected direction.

Paul Celan knew this, when he wrote:

> Into the rivers north of the future
> I cast out the net, that you
> hesitantly burden with stone-engraved shadows.

One direction from which I have begun to find help in remembering the future is the practice of improvisation.

To understand this, it may help to start with words, to pull words to pieces in order to put them back together. 'To provide' is to have foresight. The word improvisation is very close to the word 'improvident', and to be improvident is not to have looked ahead and made provision. 'To improvise' turns that around, into something positive, because improvisation is the skill of acting without knowing what is coming next, of being comfortable with the unknown, with uncertainty, with unpredictability.

I have come to see improvisation as the deep skill and attitude which we need for the times that we're already in and heading further into. Part of the truth of how climate change, for example, will play out at the level where we actually live our lives is through increased unpredictability. Less able to rely on processes and systems which we have taken for granted, we are confronted by our lack of control. This will throw us acute practical challenges, but also – as in the coalfield communities of Rachel Horne's life and work – the challenge of holding our sense of meaning together in times of drastic change.

When you consider the history of improvisation, you encounter something like a paradox. Because it is arguably the basic human skill, the thing that we are good at. It is what we have been doing for tens of thousands of years, over meals and around camp fires, in the marketplace, the tea house or the pub. Every conversation you have is an improvisation: words are coming out of your mouth which you didn't plan or script or anticipate. And yet we are accustomed to thinking of improvisation as a specialist skill, a kind of social tightrope-walking; this magic of being able to perform, to draw meaning from thin air, to make people laugh or make them think without having had it all written out beforehand.

Our fear of improvisation is, at least in part, a result of what industrial societies have been like and what they have done to us. I want to offer the distinction between 'improvisation' and 'orchestration' as two different principles by which people come together and do things. In these terms, we could talk about the industrial era as having been peculiarly dominated by orchestration.

Orchestration is the mode of organisation in which great amounts of effort are synchronised, coordinated and harnessed to the control of a single will. At the simplest physical level, picture the large orchestras of the nineteenth century: the coordinated movements of a first violin section are not so different to the coordinated movements of workers in a factory. The position of the conductor standing on the podium is not so different to the position of the politicians, democratic or otherwise, of the industrial era, addressing unprecedented numbers of people through new technologies which make it possible for one voice to be amplified far beyond its true reach.

The same shift away from improvisation can be seen in the basic activities of buying and selling. Think of the marketplace, a space in which economic activity is tangled up with all kinds of other sociable activities, a place for telling stories, hearing songs, catching up on news, eating, drinking, meeting members of the opposite sex (or members of the same sex). The social practices of buying and selling in the marketplace are themselves full of sociable performance. Haggling is not only a means of coming to a price, it is a playful encounter, a moment of improvisation. From there, swing to the opposite extreme, the huge department-store windows of the later nineteenth century, their shock-and-awe spectacle before which all one can do is stand silent, mouth open; just as, for the first time, it had become the convention that an audience would sit in silence in the theatre, a silence which would have been unimaginable to Shakespeare.

The story of the industrial era can be told as the story of a time in which orchestration paid off, allowing us to produce more stuff and to solve real problems. Of course, there were always challenges to be made, and around the edges we find the other stories of those who challenged the dehumanisation, the liquidation of social and cultural fabric, the counterproductivity and the ecological destruction. (Set these against the changes in life expectancy and infant mortality over the same generations, and perhaps the only human response is a refusal to draw up accounts; an assertion of the incommensurability of reality, of the need to 'hold everything dear'.)

What we can say is that, increasingly, even within our industrial societies and the places to which they have brought us, the pay-offs of orchestration are breaking down. Systems become more complex and unstable; it becomes less effective to project the will of one person or of a central decision-making process through huge numbers of others. Under such circumstances, improvisation – the old skill edged out by the awesome machinery of Progress – may be returning from the margins.

There is another thread here, concerning time – time and desire – which could help us draw together this story of orchestration and improvisation with the question of the broken future.

Since I began talking and writing about the failure of the future, I have noticed two kinds of response, which might broadly be identified as a post-modern and a retro-modern attitude. The first shrugs ironically, 'Worry about it later!' A hyperreal refuge-taking in the present, in a consumer reality where styles of every time and period are mashed together with no reference to the history or the culture which produced them, in one seemingly endless now. Against this, there emerges a second, more alarmed attitude, which manifests as a kind of nostalgic modernism; a desire to reinstate the future as a thing which can inspire us, which can be a vessel for our hopes.

However desperately, sincerely or cynically they are held, it seems to me that neither of these attitudes will do. They are not up to the situation in which we find ourselves. So where else do we turn? One route to another attitude may be to say that the role of the future which characterised the modern era was never satisfactory. There was something already wrong with it. Yes, it has broken down – and the fact that people just don't like to think about the future is part of what makes it difficult for us to motivate and inspire others to do the things we know need doing, if we're to limit the damage we are going to live through. But the answer is not a return to the heroic striving towards the future which structured the ideologies of industrial modernity. Because that was already twisted, a tearing out of shape of time, that could only end badly.

Another story we could tell about the age of industrial modernity, of capitalism and the changing culture in which it flourished, is the story of the loss of timeliness. Max Weber saw the origins of this economic culture in the Protestant work ethic, a new emphasis on hard work and frugality as proof of salvation.[3] Historians have questioned his account, but in broader terms, the journey to the world as we know it has been marked by shifts away from the sensuous and the specific, towards the abstract and exchangeable; and one of the axes along which this has taken place is our relationship to time. Not least, the shift from a world of seasonal festivals to a world of Sabbath observance marked a new detachment from the living, sensuous cycles surrounding us. (The replacement of the festive calendar with the weekly cycle also happened to offer the factory owner a more consistent return on his capital.) With this detachment from rhythm and season, there was also a loss of that sense which surfaces in the Book of Ecclesiastes, that there is a time for everything:

> a time to embrace and a time to refrain from embracing,
> a time to search and a time to give up,
> a time to keep and a time to throw away,

a time to tear and a time to mend,
a time to be silent and a time to speak,
a time to love and a time to hate,
a time for war and a time for peace.[4]

This contextual, rhythmic sense of our place in the world gives way to a preference for abstract, absolute principles. The universalism which was always strong in monotheistic traditions is now let fully off the leash of lived experience, engendering new kinds of rigidity and intolerance (though also the progressive universalism which will drive, for example, the movement to abolish slavery).

Following the line of this story, we could see the history of capitalism as a history of the contortion of the relationship between time and desire. In its earlier form, to be a good economic citizen is to work hard today for a deferred reward; the repressive morality we associate with the Victorian era is then a cultural manifestation of this perpetually-deferred gratification. To push this further, perhaps the cultural upheavals of the second half of the twentieth century represent a similar knock-on effect of the lurch from producer to consumer capitalism? In the countries of the post-industrial West, to be a good economic citizen is now to spend on your credit card today and worry how you'll pay for it later. Despite the glimpses of freedom as we pivoted from one contortion to the other, desire remains harnessed to the engine of ever-expanding GDP; only, we have switched from the gear of deferred gratification to that of instant gratification.

The cultural experiment of debt-fuelled consumption appears to be already entering its endgame. When its costs are finally counted, perhaps the loss of the future which we have been retracing will be listed among them?

Whatever stories we tell, each of them is only one route across a landscape. Some routes are wiser than others, and some are older than memory. As we turn for home, let us find our way by an old story.

Of all the figures in Greek myth, few seemed more at home in the era of industrial modernity than Prometheus. The ingenious Titan who stole fire from the gods stood as an icon of the technological leap into the future. Once again, words themselves are full of clues. Prometheus means 'forethought'. He has a brother, whose name is Epimetheus, meaning 'afterthought', or hindsight. The figure of the fool, stumbling backwards, not knowing where he is going. His foolishness is confirmed when he insists, despite the

warnings of Prometheus, on accepting Pandora as a gift from the gods, and
with her the famous jar. And so, the story goes, came all the evils into the
world. It is a deeply misogynist story; but we are not at the bottom of it.
Dwelling on the name, Pandora, 'The All-Giver', there is the suggestion of an
older path, a deeper level at which Pandora is not simply another slandered
Eve, but an embodiment of nature's abundance and our belonging within its
generous embrace.[v]

The name of Epimetheus may long ago have been eclipsed by that of his
forward-looking brother, but there is one great, unnamed, high modern icon
made in his image; the figure conjured up in the ninth of Walter Benjamin's
theses on the philosophy of history:

> A Klee drawing named 'Angelus Novus' shows an angel looking
> as though he is about to move away from something he is fixedly
> contemplating. His eyes are staring, his mouth is open, his wings
> are spread. This is how one pictures the angel of history. His face is
> turned toward the past. Where we perceive a chain of events, he
> sees one single catastrophe that keeps piling ruin upon ruin and
> hurls it in front of his feet. The angel would like to stay, awaken
> the dead, and make whole what has been smashed. But a storm is
> blowing from Paradise; it has got caught in his wings with such vi-
> olence that the angel can no longer close them. The storm irresistibly
> propels him into the future to which his back is turned, while the
> pile of debris before him grows skyward. This storm is what we call
> progress.[6]

Written in the shadow of the Second World War, this is the tragic obverse of
modernity's idolisation of the future; to look backwards is always to have
hindsight, and hindsight is forever useless.

But perhaps there is more to hindsight than Benjamin's dark vision allows.
Those who practice improvisation talk about the importance of looking backwards. Keith Johnstone, one of the founders of modern theatrical improvisation, writes powerfully about improvisation as an attitude to life, a mode of
navigating reality. In one passage, he describes the kind of wise foolishness
which it takes to improvise a story, in strikingly Epimethean terms:

> The improviser has to be like a man walking backwards. He sees
> where he has been, but he pays no attention to the future. His story

can take him anywhere, but he must still 'balance' it, and give it shape, by remembering incidents that have been shelved and reincorporating them. Very often an audience will applaud when earlier material is brought back into the story. They couldn't tell you why they applaud, but the reincorporation does give them pleasure.[7]

There is a deep satisfaction at the moment when something from earlier in the story is woven back in, for the listener and for the storyteller. In that moment, another dimension emerges, beyond the arbitrariness of linear time, and we sense the embrace of the cyclical. There is the feeling of pattern and meaning, of things coming together. The ritual has worked.

If Johnstone's account of the craft of improvisation echoes with the footsteps of Epimetheus, in Ivan Illich's *Descanchooling Society* he is invoked by name.[8] In the closing chapter of his great critique of the counterproductivity of our education systems, Illich looks towards 'The Dawn of Epimethean Man'. The Promethean spirit of *homo faber* has taken us to the moon, but that was the easy part; the challenge is to find our way home, to find each other again across the aching distances our technologies have created.

Illich reminds his readers of the sequel to the myth. Epimetheus stays with Pandora, and their daughter Pyrrha goes on to marry Deucalion, the son of Prometheus. When an angered Zeus sends an earth-drowning deluge, it is Deucalion and Pyrrha who build an ark and survive to repeople the land. Writing in 1970, Illich could find resonance in this idea of a union of the Promethean and Epimethean attitudes, carrying humanity through a time of ecological disaster. Forty years on, perhaps the symmetry simply seems too neat to hold such weight.

And yet, in practical terms, I think that there may be some fragments of truth here. What gets us through the times ahead may well be those moments when we look backwards and find something from earlier in the story that we can pull through, that becomes useful again. Our leaders are very fond of talking about 'innovation', the point at which some new device enters social reality; we don't seem to have an equivalent word for when things that are old-fashioned, obsolete and redundant come into their own in the hour of need. (I think of the knights in shining armour sleeping under the hill in the Legend of Alderley, as told by Alan Garner's grandfather, and in so many other folk stories.)[9] I think we may need such a word, because as the systems we grew up depending on become less reliable, we will find ourselves drawing on things that worked in other times and places.

There is another clue here as to why official projections of the future date so quickly. If you want to imagine what the future is going to be like, it is a mistake to assume that it will be populated by the products, tools and systems which look most 'futuristic', or those most marvellously optimised for present circumstances. These are the things which have been tested against the narrowest range of possible times and places. The supermarket, for example, has been with us for two generations. On the other hand, the sociable, improvisational marketplace has endured through an extraordinary range of times and places. Almost anywhere that human beings have lived in significant numbers, there have been meeting points where people come together to trade, to share news, to exchange goods, to make decisions. Just now, it may survive as a luxury phenomenon, a place to buy hand-crafted cheeses and organic vegetables. Yet the cheaper prices in Tesco this year do not cancel out the suspicion that the marketplace will continue to exist in any number of quite imaginable futures, where today's globe-spanning systems become too expensive and unreliable to sustain the supermarket business model.

Whether we like it or not, we must live with the unknowability of the future, its capacity to humble us and take us by surprise, our inability to control it. This need not be a source of despair, nor is the choice simply between the hyperreal distractions of postmodernity and an effort to reignite the process of Progress. There is inspiration to be found in our own foolishness, stumbling backwards, muddling through, relearning the craft of making it up as we go along; cooking from the ingredients to hand, rather than starting with a recipe. If the collapse of meaning is as much of a threat as the material realities of economic and ecological collapse, not least because it debilitates us when we need all our resilience to handle those realities, then the art of finding meaning in the weaving together of past and future is not a luxury. Meanwhile, the spirit of Epimetheus should inspire us to treat the past not as an object of romantic fantasy, but nor as a dustbin of discarded prototypes. Learning how people have made life work in other times and places is one way of readying ourselves for the unknown territory north of the future, in which all our expectations may be confounded.

After all the evils of the world, one thing is left at the bottom of Pandora's jar: hope. As Illich comments, hope is not the same as expectation. It is not optimism, or a plan. It's not knowing what's going to happen. But it is an attitude which enables you to keep taking one step after another into the unknown.

Johnstone never makes explicit reference to Epimetheus, but at the very end of his handbook on improvisation, he recounts three short dreams, the kind that 'announce themselves as *messages*'. The last of these seems particularly familiar, like a name that is on the tip of everyone's tongue:

> There is a box that we are forbidden to open. It contains a great serpent and once opened this monster will stream out forever. I lift the lid, and for a moment it seems as if the serpent will destroy us; but then it dissipates into thin air, and there, at the bottom of the box, is the real treasure.[10]

Notes

1. After writing this, I found that the phrase had indeed been used as the title of an article in the penultimate issue of *Marxism Today*. Its author argued that the collapse of communism represented 'the end of the future – as a new place which might be visited'. Goran Therborn, 'The End of the Future', *Marxism Today*, November 1991, p.24.
2. For a discussion of the failure of the 1960s moment, see Dougald Hine, 'Death and the Mountain: John Berger's enduring sense of hope' in *Dark Mountain: Issue 1* (2010).
3. Max Weber, *The Protestant Ethic and the Spirit of Capitalism* (1905; English translation first published in 1930).
4. Ecclesiastes 3:5–8.
5. Could this echoing ambiguity, the way the name belies the official story, explain James Cameron's decision to call the rainforest moon of his sci-fi epic *Avatar* (2009) after Pandora?
6. Walter Benjamin, 'On the Concept of History' (1940).
7. Keith Johnstone, *Impro: Improvisation and the Theatre* (London: Methuen, 1981), p. 116.
8. Ivan Illich, *Deschooling Society* (1971).
9. Alan Garner, *The Weirdstone of Brisingamen* (1960).
10. K. Johnstone, *Impro* (1981), *op cit* p.208.

Mountaineers

David Abram lives with his family in the foothills of the southern Rockies. Nomadic by nature, he also travels and teaches on several continents. He is the author of *The Spell of the Sensuous* (1997) and *Becoming Animal: An Earthly Cosmology* (2010), and the co-founder of the Alliance for Wild Ethics – *wildethics.org*. The video of his conversation with Dougald Hine is available on the Dark Mountain website – *is.gd/davidabram*.

Darren Allen is a vaguely-gesturing, velvet-trousered, orbiting soap-bubble, a straight-talking, nuclear-minted vintage, a tight-harmony, wabi-sabi heart-trumpet and a gun-toting whiskey-drinking fiefdom of a man, who speaks Latin and eats rocks for breakfast. Darren publishes a blog called *Gentle Apocalypse* which is about how to feel warmly okay with atomic terror. Darren lives in a castle with his animals.

Luanne Armstrong lives on her organic heritage family farm on Kootenay Lake, in British Columbia, Canada. She writes nonfiction, novels, poetry and children's literature, and teaches Creative Writing for the University of British Columbia.

Melanie Challenger is the author of *On Extinction: How we became estranged from nature*, forthcoming from Granta Books.

Antonio Dias is an artist, designer and writer living in southern New England. Raised on a beach overlooking Provincetown on Cape Cod, he has built on early experiences there and in down-east Maine for his two novels in manuscript, *Shoal Hope* and *Something for Nothing*. He has recently returned to painting, and continues to keep his hand in designing wooden boats while writing essays for his blog *horizonsofsignificance.wordpress.com* and posting poetry at *antoniodiaspoetry.wordpress.com*.

Andrea Dulberger is originally from urban New Jersey, but has lived in Cambridge, Massachussets, for about thirteen years, after studying 'philosophy and literature' as an undergraduate in western Mass. She worked at a summer camp in the woods for five summers in her twenties, but it was a more recent combination of volunteering at a natural history museum and reading authors like Loren Eisely and Aldo Leopold that flipped a switch in her mind regarding the human vision of nature and time.

Warren Draper makes pictures out of words, pixels, paint and plants. He walks the forgotten places of South Yorkshire with seeds in his pocket and mud on his mind. He can be found via *warrendraper.wordpress.com*.

The General Assembly are a band from Melbourne, Australia. Their first EP, 'Dark Mountain Music' was released in September 2010.

Dan Grace lives, writes and works in Sheffield. His poetry has been published in *Dark Mountain: Issue 1, Symmetry Pebbles, Decanto*, and *The Heron's Nest*. He blogs about public libraries and their role in building community resilience at *resilientlibrary.tumblr.com*.

Pat Gregory has lived in Cardiff for 27 years and is a member of the core group of the Cardiff Transition Project. Her printmaking draws on themes from fairytale, myth and issues around personal and social transformation.

Jay Griffiths is the author of *Wild: An Elemental Journey*, which was shortlisted for the Orwell Prize and was winner of the Orion Book Award. She is also the author of *Pip Pip: A Sideways Look At Time*, which won the Barnes and Noble Discover award for the best first-time writer in the USA. Her novel *A Love Letter From A Stray Moon*, from which the extract here is taken, is published by Text Publishing in Australia. *www.jaygriffiths.com*

Vinay Gupta is an innovator in disaster response and poverty alleviation. He has worked, with varying degrees of compatibility and success, with entities as diverse as the Pentagon, the Red Cross, and the Burning Man community. He is best known as the inventor of the hexayurt shelter system, and simple critical infrastructure maps. *twitter.com/leashless*

William Haas lives in Portland, Oregon, USA. 'Coal Sarcophagus' is one in a cycle of triptychs titled *Oil, & Other Catastrophes*. Others can be found in *Dark Mountain: Issue 1, Spittoon*, and *The Tusculum Review*.

Dougald Hine is co-founder of the Dark Mountain Project. He starts organisations as a way to avoid finishing books. He currently has one foot in London and the other in Brussels. *dougald.co.uk*

Wilfried Hou Je Bek is a blogger from Utrecht and the g/local Amazon with a passion for psychogeography, ethnopoetics and urban reinhabitation. His work can be found at *cryptoforest.blogspot.com*. For more information on PrimatePoetics see: *http://fightthegooglejugend.com/primatepoetics/primatepoetics.html*

Glyn Hughes has published an autobiography, novels, poetry, and broadcast radio plays and features. He was awarded the Guardian Fiction Prize (1982) and the David Higham Prize (1982) for his first novel, *Where I Used To Play On The Green*, has been shortlisted for the Whitbread Prize, considered for The Booker and has won national prizes for his poetry collections. *A Year in the Bull Box* is published by Arc Publications. *glynhughes.co.uk*

Nick Hunt writes fiction in an attempt to grasp the cultural and psychological implications of climate change and the mass extinction of species and languages. He is also a freelance journalist. Read more of his work at *nickhuntscrutiny.wordpress.com*.

Thomas Keyes lives, works and eats the Black Isle with his partner Boe and trio of assorted children. Graffiti writer turned gardening forager and scavenging artist, he aims to eat richly, has to live cheaply, and enjoys a good bonfire when it all works out, or a good ale either way.

Paul Kingsnorth is co-founder of the Dark Mountain Project. His new collection of poetry, *Kidland*, is published by Salmon. *paulkingsnorth.net*

Naomi Klein is an award-winning journalist, syndicated columnist and author of the international bestsellers, *The Shock Doctrine: The Rise of Disaster Capitalism* (2007) and *No Logo: Taking Aim at the Brand Bullies* (2000). She writes a regular column for *The Nation* and the *Guardian* and is a contributing editor at *Harper's* magazine. In 2004, she wrote and co-produced, with director Avi Lewis, *The Take,* an award-winning feature documentary about Argentina's cooperatively-run, occupied factories. She is at work on a new book and film about how climate change can be a catalyst for economic transformation. Her contribution to *Dark Mountain 2* is adapted from a TED Talk delivered in December 2010 in Washington DC. *naomiklein.org*

Rob Lewis is a natural materials painter and plasterer living in the northern Puget Sound city of Bellingham, Washington, USA. His poems and essays respond to the Earth, in its beauty and its pain, as well as humans enmeshed in their stories and illusions.

Anthony Lioi is native to the green and poisoned land of New Jersey, USA. He has published poetry in *Environmental Philosophy* and *Watershed*, as well as critical essays on ecological literature and culture. He teaches English at the Juilliard School in New York City. When the revolution comes, he will be rooting for the swamp dragons.

Gerry Loose lives on a boat close to the Royal Navy's nuclear submarine weapons base at Faslane in Gare Loch, on the Highland *fault line* in Scotland. He is currently writing about the flora, fauna, language, geology, human ecology and politics of that area. He is the author of several books of poetry, including *that person himself* (Shearsman 2009). He is also an artist whose medium is plants and plantings.

Laurence Lord (aka Monkeyzbox) is a fine artist and freelance graphic designer from the outskirts of North East London. He spent 2006 to 2009 working and traveling in Brazil and other parts of Latin America. He now paints pictures and designs websites whilst considering his next move. *laurencelord.co.uk*

Catherine Lupton is a recovering academic, wanderer and wonderer, who currently writes and makes photographs in Berlin. Her blog is *catlupton.posterous.com*.

Simon Lys is a playwright whose work includes *tipping point, Blessed be the Immaculates* and *Bel, the Girl who would Dance*. He is a co-founder of gaia theatre collective. He has also written for television, as well as a number of short stories and a novel, *Black Dog Running*. He lives in a community in south east England with his partner and their son. *simonlys.org*

Joel Moore is a writer from rural Tennessee who has been living in New York City since 2000. He writes prose, poems and songs.

Benjamin Morris is a native of Mississippi, a poet, fiction writer, playwright and essayist. His work has appeared in publications across the US and the UK, and recently received a fellowship from the Mississippi Arts Commission. He is a researcher for the Open University, an editor at Forest Publications, and an administrator at the Uptown Messenger in New Orleans, Louisiana, where he lives. *benjaminalanmorris.com*

Adrienne Odasso's poetry has appeared in a variety of strange and wonderful publications, including *Sybil's Garage, Mythic Delirium, Jabberwocky, Cabinet des Fées, Dreams & Nightmares, Goblin Fruit,* and *Illumen*. Her print chapbooks, *Devil's Road Down* and *Wanderlust*, are available from Maverick Duck Press. Her first full collection, *Lost Books*, was released by Flipped Eye Publishing in 2010. *ajodasso.livejournal.com*

Mat Osmond is an artist, writer and illustrator. He lives with his wife and three children in Falmouth, Cornwall, where he lectures on the MA Illustration: Authorial Practice course, at University College Falmouth. *Drawing on Water* is an image and text sequence which originated in the experience of swimming through phosphorescence in the Helford Passage estuary. It was published as a 10-page concertina book by Atlantic Press in 2007.

Jonathan Penney is an illustrator determined to take back the power of the image from theforces of evil. *jonathan-penney.co.uk*

Mario Petrucci, a natural sciences graduate with a PhD in optoelectronics, is an award-winning poet, writer, educator and broadcaster. The three poems in this book are taken from a sequence of 111 poems, due to be published as a collection entitled *crib*. *mariopetrucci.com*

Albert Pierce Bales was raised in San Francisco as a feral youth in the late sixties and lived on the west coast of the US for far too long. He has spent his moment of history evading the yoke of literature by working as a logger, a pressman, a social service researcher, a hack journalist, a mortgage loan officer and electrician. He is now in search of the angry truth as a stimulant to killing the ennui of the digital age.

Venkatesh Rao is a blogger at *ribbonfarm.com,* and the author of the book *Tempo: timing, tactics and strategy in narrative-driven decision-making.*

John Rember is the author of two short story collections, *Coyote in the Mountains* and *Cheerleaders from Gomorrah,* and a memoir, *Traplines.* His latest book is *MFA in a Box.* His weekly blog on writing can be viewed at *mfainabox.com.*

Susan Richardson is a Wales-based poet, performer and educator, and a Fellow of the International League of Conservation Writers. Her second collection of poetry, *Where the Air is Rarefied*, a collaboration with printmaker Pat Gregory, from which 'Tip of the Icetongue' is extracted, has just been published. *susanrichardsonwriter.co.uk*

Charles Hugh Smith is a novelist and economic commentator. He has been observing social and political events in the United States for the past forty years. *oftwominds.com*

Rima Staines is a painter, clockmaker, accordion player and tale teller who travelled for a year and a day in a wooden house on wheels to the edge of Dartmoor, where she shares happy days in an old cottage on a hill with a poet and a hound, finding beauty in otherness. *intothehermitage.blogspot.com*

Em Strang is currently studying an MPhil in ecopoetry at Glasgow University's Dumfries campus. Winner of the 2010 Kirkpatrick Dobie Prize For Poetry, she has published poems in the *Glasgow Herald* as well as in a number of poetry journals including *Markings, Poetry Scotland, Causeway, Southlight* and *Swamp*. She was born in England and has lived in Scotland for the past 15 years, latterly in Dumfries and Galloway.

Matt Szabo lives with his family in Derbyshire, England. He has been involved in environmentalism on various fronts for twenty years and now finds himself wondering what's going to happen next. He usually works as a gardener and teacher, but occasionally moonlights in the energy sector and the world of environmental theory. He can be contacted at *mattszabo@yahoo.com*.

Chris T-T is a writer and musician living in Brighton. Since 1999 he has released seven LPs and, among other things, he currently writes a weekly column on the arts for *The Morning Star*. *christt.com*

Robert Keegan Walker was born in Oldham, Greater Manchester in 1985. He studied English Literature and Film at The University of Hull, graduating in 2008 and is currently living and working in Manchester. He wrote *The Record Keeper's Visit to Spurn Point* during 2010, working on it slowly and daily. This is his first published poem.

Stephen Wheeler is a writer, bodyworker and freelance cultural analyst. He is currently nomadic, but can most usually be found in London and South England. He exists online at *steelweaver.tumblr.com*.

Heathcote Williams is the author of *Whale Nation, Sacred Elephant, Falling for a Dolphin* and *Autogeddon*. He has recently been working on a touring show with the comedian Roy Hutchins. It's called *Zanzibar Cats*.

Wolfbird is an old, ill, bad-tempered Welsh person who finds access to bliss and serenity contained in each moment, via Soto Zen, and shelters behind a pseudonym in the belief that any degree of obscurity is a valuable blessing and to be cherished.

Roll of honour

The publication of Dark Mountain #2 has been made possible by financial and non-financial support from a large community around the world. The following Dark Mountaineers provided financial support beyond the call of duty. We are very grateful for their generosity, and for that of others who chose not to be named here.

Chris Frost
Robin & Ann Hine
Julia Macintosh
JoAnn Sal Moretti
Dave Rawlence
Mike Riddell
Eleanor Saitta
James Twiss

IN MEMORIAM

As this book was going to press, we learned of the sad death of poet
and novelist Glyn Hughes, at the age of 76, from cancer.

Glyn had been a friend of the Dark Mountain Project from the start,
and his writing appeared in both of our books. The three poems and the
conversation which appear in this volume are a moving testimony to
his stoical and thoughtful reaction to the approach of death.

In that conversation, Glyn described his lifetime's work as
'a protest on behalf of nature.' To be remembered as such a protester is,
we hope, an epitaph he would have appreciated.

†